YOUR FAMILY BUSINESS
A SUCCESS GUIDE FOR GROWTH AND SURVIVAL

YOUR FAMILY BUSINESS

A SUCCESS GUIDE FOR GROWTH AND SURVIVAL

BENJAMIN BENSON
with
EDWIN T. CREGO
and
RONALD H. DRUCKER

Dow Jones-Irwin
Homewood, IL 60430

658
B474
Cop.2

© RICHARD D. IRWIN, INC., 1990
Dow Jones-Irwin is a trademark of Dow Jones & Company, Inc.

This publication is designed to provide accurate and
authoritative information in regard to the subject matter
covered. It is sold with the understanding that the
publisher is not engaged in rendering legal, accounting, or
other professional service. If legal advice or other expert
assistance is required, the services of a competent
professional person should be sought.

*From a Declaration of Principles jointly adopted by a Committee
of the American Bar Association and a Committee of Publishers.*

Sponsoring editor: Jim Childs
Project editor: Susan Trentacosti
Production manager: Bette K. Ittersagen
Jacket designer: Renee Klyczek Nordstrom
Compositor: Eastern Graphics Typographers
Typeface: 11/13 Times Roman
Printer: Arcata Graphics/Kingsport

Library of Congress Cataloging-in-Publication Data

Benson, Benjamin.
    Your family business : a success guide for growth and survival /
Benjamin Benson, Edwin T. Crego, Ronald H. Drucker
        p.   cm.
    ISBN 1-55623-217-9   ISBN 1-55623-365-5 (Special edition)
    1. Family corporations—Management.   I. Crego, Edwin T.
II. Title.
    HD62.25.B46   1990
    658—dc20   89-17100
                                                      CIP

Printed in the United States of America

2 3 4 5 6 7 8 9 0 K 6 5 4 3 2 1 0

PREFACE

Behold how good and how pleasant it is for brothers and sisters to dwell together in unity.

The Book of Psalms

Am I my brother's keeper?

Genesis

Why me?

Owner of family business

Your family business can provide an opportunity for you, your children, and future generations to achieve independence, work fulfillment, financial security, and possibly wealth. *However*, as owner/CEO, you face two major challenges:

- The mixture of money, love, power, and jealousy, which occurs in family businesses, can be a witch's brew that destroys both your business and your family. This is the stuff that causes wars.
- Doing business today is increasingly complex, and competitors with greater resources are just waiting to beat your brains in. If your business is to survive, you must manage it effectively.

Your role as leader of the business can be lonely, and your decisions can have a profound effect on your own economic security and that of your family and employees.

You'll learn in this book how successful owner/CEOs deal with both the challenges and pitfalls, and you'll also learn about the mistakes that lead to the downfall of both the family and the business. As one owner put it, "Any damn fool can learn through his own mistakes. I'd rather learn through the other guy's."

This book includes practical approaches to help you answer questions such as:

- How can I best provide for continuity of the business into the next generation?
- How can I prevent or limit conflict in the family about the business?
- With the margin for error decreasing in today's environment, how can I manage my business more effectively?
- How can my business attract, motivate, and retain quality employees when they cannot own equity in the business?
- How can I plan my finances to assure myself a secure retirement?
- How can I plan my estate to protect my spouse, be fair to all of my children, and limit estate taxes?

FAMILY BUSINESS IN THE UNITED STATES

Family businesses are the backbone of the American economy, owning or controlling over 90 percent of its more than 15 million businesses. Most are small and midsized, but they range throughout the business spectrum. Even among the Fortune 500, over one third are family controlled. They include the innovators, movers, and shakers who have created most of the economic expansion of the 1980s, and they bode to be the driving force for growth in the 1990s. Tom Peters, coauthor of *In Search of Excellence*, says, "I know that the future does not belong to the companies I grew up with, the elephants that used to rule the world and that I used to serve. These wild and woolly times call for a new species of competitor—fast, agile, thriving on change. Welcome, . . . to the Age of the Gazelle."[1]

JOY, PAIN, AND LIFE EXPECTANCY

Family pride, tradition, and unity of purpose are strengths that enable many family businesses to outperform their counterparts, sometimes over several generations. This often entails personal sacrifice, with family members committing their lives to making their business dream come true. Many forego reasonable salaries for extended times so that

---

[1]Tom Peter, "Doubting Thomas," *Inc.*, April 1989.

the business can grow. The Weyerhaeuser family, owners of the giant lumber company, endured losses for 40 years before the company became profitable. Others routinely risk everything they own in the world by personally guaranteeing the business's bank loans.

Unfortunately, most family businesses don't last beyond the first generation, and many of the survivors become living proof of the old maxim: The first generation founds the business. The second generation builds it. And the third generation ruins it.

The statistics bear grim evidence to the difficulty of the task: It is estimated that less than three of ten family businesses last through the second generation, and only slightly more than one in ten through the third.

While some observers contend that this cycle is inevitable, we firmly believe that if you gain a greater understanding of the pitfalls and make the right moves *in time*, you can greatly improve your chances of success.

PLANNING IS THE KEY

A successful blend of family and business is difficult in the best of circumstances, complicated further because the very entrepreneurial qualities that may have helped create and build the business often work against its survival.

Both family and business situations cry out for planning and for thoughtful, clearly enunciated policies. Many owners/CEOs, however, tend to be "seat of the pants" managers, accustomed to informality and more comfortable in day-to-day operations than in planning for the future.

In the business, they often make themselves indispensable by failing to build competent organizations. In the family, they often discourage open dialogue and avoid making tough but necessary decisions that might upset the equilibrium of the family. The absence of open conflict can create a false sense of well-being for the owner while, beneath the surface, tensions may be building. When they retire or die, however, the results of their failure to plan properly for the future frequently haunt their successors.

So, after a lifetime of sacrifice and hard work, instead of a valuable asset, many owners/CEOs unintentionally leave legacies of silently ticking time bombs to the families that they love and to their loyal employees.

A PLAN OF ACTION

Family and business are inextricably intertwined, yet there are few books that consider both perspectives. The goal of this book is to help you gain a better understanding of the challenges that confront family businesses and to present strategies to help you preserve your business from generation to generation. Above all, our goal is to provide you with practical ideas that will help both your family and your business to be among the survivors.

There are no absolute "right" answers that fit everyone. In our experience, however, successful families tend to share certain characteristics as do unsuccessful families. In this book, we examine both.

This book is based on our conviction that the keys to success and survival lie in:

- *Understanding* the complex relationships that go with the territory.
- *Effective management* that directs the course of both family and business.
- *Planning* for the future of both family and business.

While practically every chapter involves both family and business to some extent, emphasis in the first three chapters is on the *family*, in the middle chapters on the *firm*, and in the concluding chapters on the *future*.

This book is primarily directed to established businesses with more than 20 or 30 employees; however, we believe that there is much in it for owners, family members, employees, and advisors of family businesses of all sizes.

We define a family business as one that is owned or controlled by one or more family members who are actively involved in the management of the business. These range from the corner dry cleaner to such well-known businesses as Marriott and Hyatt Hotels, Mars Candy, Johnson's Wax, Budweiser and Coors breweries, Ford Motor

Co., Estée Lauder cosmetics, Campbell Soup, and Gallo Brothers Vineyards.

OUR PERSPECTIVE

This book is not a theoretical treatise. It is the result of our many years of experience in consulting with family businesses of all sizes, augmented by the experiences shared by families at our seminars over the past several years and by the findings of other authorities in the field.

It is directed toward families who are committed to success, who are willing to confront the obstacles and make the changes that may be necessary. When we refer to a "successful family," we mean a unified family with a successful business that is a source of satisfaction and fulfillment.

Many anecdotes and quotes in the book are about real or composite situations that have been disguised to protect the privacy of the families who have so freely shared their experiences. Examples and stories that have been altered use only first names or no names at all. Last names are used only when the stories have appeared in the media. Although many of these relate to prominent companies, we believe that they apply to family businesses of all sizes.

We hope that female readers will not be offended by the use of male-gender words, particularly as they relate to the owner. While ownership of established family businesses is now overwhelmingly vested in men, the rate of growth of women-owned businesses is twice the rate as that among men, and daughters are increasingly taking over companies that in prior years would have been off limits to women. Use of male-gender words is for editorial convenience only, and "he" or "him" should be taken to include "she" or "her," unless otherwise indicated.

Reference to the "owner" or "CEO" refers to the usual situation of the "boss" who manages the business and controls the voting stock. Although family businesses may be organized as proprietorships or partnerships, most established companies are corporations and we have assumed that form of ownership.

We hope that our book will be helpful to educators, students, and professionals who advise family businesses, such as lawyers, accountants, financial advisors, insurance agents, and family therapists. Most of all, we hope our book will be shared within the family, that it will stimulate discussion, and that it will make a difference to the families in business who are on center stage, living the drama.

Benjamin Benson
Edwin T. Crego
Ronald H. Drucker

ACKNOWLEDGMENTS

Our clients and the participants at our seminars over the years were our principal sources of inspiration. Their willingness to share their experiences, problems, and successes have enabled us to gain insights that would not have been otherwise possible.

The discipline of consulting family businesses is relatively new, and the work of others in the field has been valuable. We are particularly grateful to Dr. Léon A. Danco of the Center for Family Business in Cleveland, the pioneer in this field, for his wisdom and support, and to Dr. John L. Ward of Loyola University of Chicago, a respected leader in the profession. Both have written important books on the topic.

In recent years, the body of knowledge has been expanded by information from family therapists, psychologists, sociologists, and organizational behavior and development consultants. With the increased focus on the importance of family business to our economy, several universities have conducted research and added programs on the topic. The Family Firm Institute, an organization comprised principally of advisors to family businesses was formed, and it started a new journal, *Family Business Review*, with Ivan Lansberg of Yale University as Editor-in-Chief. The research and insights of these professionals have helped us to gain a better understanding of the behavioral aspects of family business.

The support of Laventhol & Horwath (L&H), the national accounting/business consulting firm, was extremely important and we thank George L. Bernstein, executive partner, and Kenneth I. Solomon, chairman of national council, for their encouragement and commitment to this project. L&H initiated two research studies that provided valuable information about the attitudes of family business owners: "The

Challenges to Entrepreneurs" (the L&H entrepreneurial study) was conducted in 1985. An additional study was conducted in conjunction with the American Management Association in 1987 (the L&H/AMA family business study). Professionals at L&H also made important contributions. These include Barbara Shomaker (Chicago), Peter Schiffrin (Philadelphia), and Ernie Doud (Los Angeles).

Our thanks to Jim Childs, Senior Editor at Dow Jones-Irwin, for his guidance, and to Sharon Nelton, special correspondent of *Nation's Business,* Natalie Gelbert, and Minita Levenson for their help in editing the final manuscript.

And last, but by no means least, to Lucille T. Benson for her patience, support, and encouragement when it was needed most.

B. B

E. T. C.

R. H. D.

CONTENTS

control of the business. Creating the right estate plan. The place of life insurance. Estate planning strategies. An estate planning quiz.

CHAPTER 1

■■■■

WALKING THE HIGH-WIRE

Life is not a spectacle or a feast; it is a predicament.

George Santayana

The dynamics of family and business differ, and a delicate balancing act is required of performers with little training for the task. There are no safety nets.

Consider the case of Steve (68) who, starting as a young man with borrowed money, built what is now a highly successful trucking company. He is now tired and not in the best of health, so he would like to retire.

His son, Adam (34) bypassed college and joined the business 12 years ago. Although he doesn't have strong leadership qualities, Adam is a hard worker and has always assumed that he would take over when Steve retired.

However, Steve's daughter, Molly (31) joined the business a year ago after earning an M.B.A. and working for a national trucking company. Molly, who is more capable than her brother, has made it very clear that her goal is to succeed Steve as CEO.

Sparks are flying between father and son. In view of his seniority, Adam resents his sister's "instant" standing as operations manager and her salary, which is comparable to his. It also appears to Adam that Steve favors Molly as his successor, and Adam could never accept his kid sister as his boss.

What are Adam's alternatives? Should he resign himself to the status quo? Should he continue to fight it out? Should he accept the inevitable and get another job? He's never worked anywhere else, and he's not sure what his value would be in the outside world. It almost certainly would entail a substantial reduction of income and his wife wouldn't be thrilled about giving up their lovely home and comfortable lifestyle.

Steve's wife, Amy, is caught in the middle. The friction between her husband and son affects their family life. As a result, family gatherings, which used to be wonderful, are tense and less frequent. Adam's wife has grown increasingly resentful of the treatment her husband has received at the hands of her father-in-law, and Amy's once friendly relationship with her has deteriorated. As a result, Amy hardly ever gets to see the grandchildren who are the light of her life. She thinks of the business as more of a curse than a blessing.

What are some of Steve's alternatives?

• He could placate Adam by naming him as successor, but the business would suffer, and Steve is depending on it for his financial security in retirement. Molly, who is clearly more capable, would probably quit.
• He could bite the bullet and announce that Molly will be his successor. This would surely be the crowning blow that would split the family.
• He could try to solve the problem by selling the business; however, this would probably please neither of his children because both seek careers in the business.
• He could stay on and hope that the situation resolves itself. (This is the position that most of the Steves of the family business world tend to choose. Rather than helping to resolve the situation, it usually exacerbates it.)

Once the situation has reached this stage, it's rarely possible to arrive at a win-win resolution for all of the participants. Your best chances lie in gaining a greater understanding of the dynamics of family business and in taking the necessary steps to prevent situations such as this from developing.

STRENGTHS AND WEAKNESSES OF FAMILY BUSINESSES

A survey by *Venture* magazine (July 1988) inquired about the greatest strengths of family businesses. The respondents indicated that the most important was loyalty, which, combined with the pride that most family members feel toward the business, provides an important competitive advantage. One family member put it this way: "That's our name on the door. Our customers are buying a trust that's been earned over 85 years. They like to deal with someone in the family because when our product goes out they know that it will be right. I have a responsibility to honor that trust."

Samuel I. Newhouse started as an office boy and built a multibillion-dollar media empire that is now run by his sons. He started by borrowing money to buy a newspaper and then hiring his brothers and sisters to run it. His philosophy about growth was expressed when he said, "I will not let growth go beyond the point where attention to detail cannot be paid by key members of the family."[1]

While it would appear that the nepotism associated with family business would weaken it in a competitive environment, this is generally more than overcome by the commitment of family members who have a serious stake in the action. It has been amply demonstrated throughout the business spectrum that family businesses tend to outperform their competitors.

Family businesses also have weaknesses. There is often a conflict between family and business priorities and without the accountability that applies to most nonfamily businesses, many function in an informal and undisciplined manner. And because they often insulate themselves from ideas from outside, they also have a tendency to miss market trends and react tardily to technological advancements.

FAMILY THEMES

Persistent family themes get played out in family businesses, involving the legacies of past family patriarchs, leaders, or scoundrels who in turn, succeeded or failed, won or lost, were honest or dishonest, and were loved or hated.

According to Boston-based organizational consultant Dr. Sandor Blum, some of the historical themes include:

- *Loyalty versus Abandonment*
  Who has stayed loyal and contributed to the family system ver-

sus who has departed from, betrayed, or rebelled against family values?

- *Dependency versus Autonomy*
  Who within the family system has remained psychologically dependent on the family's love, values, and rules for gaining approval versus those who have found values outside the family upon which they base their self-regard?
- *Morality versus Immorality*
  In many family businesses, family ethics are a central theme. One generation tries to "screw the customer." Another tries to repair the damage. One abuses employees. Another tries to restore their confidence.
- *Justice versus Injustice*
  Family justice is a pervasive underlying theme of family life. What is fair? Who is entitled to more (or less)? Who has suffered the most or the least and how shall these different manifestations of family life be rewarded or punished?

A MATTER OF PRIORITIES

In every family business there is a threshold question of priorities between family and business. When the interests of the family have the highest priority, decisions in the business are based primarily on how they affect the family. The business may become a haven for incompetent and overpaid family members; sensitivities of family members may influence important business decisions, and the informality of family life is apt to prevail in the business.

In these circumstances, the business is there to serve the family's immediate needs, and if policies cause harm to the business, it may be of little concern to family members unless it jeopardizes their benefits. In one extreme situation, a business became so overburdened with family members that profitability declined and the business had to be sold. It was said that the new owner had to wake up the family members in order to fire them.

In the other extreme, when the interests of the business are paramount, the business may take on the attributes of a public company, as though the family didn't exist. The business may be managed by outsiders, and it may be more difficult for a family member to get a job in the business than an unrelated job applicant. In many ways, it's like a family investment rather than a family business.

Many families, however, find a balanced approach where the best long-term interests of both the family and business may be served. The family recognizes that, if the business is to succeed, it must be managed according to sound business principles and that a successful business is in the best long-term interests of the family.

Family members share in the shaping of policies governing their relationship to the business, and family participation in the business is encouraged; however, the performance of each family member is evaluated by business standards, and the business is not allowed to become a home for the indigent or a family sand-box. Ideally, the family approaches the business as a unified group, and family members are committed to make any sacrifices necessary to preserve the business from which all blessings flow. The individual needs of family members, however, are not disregarded, and ways are found, either through the business or outside of it, to fulfill them. This approach will be discussed in Chapter 3.

THE CONFLICT BETWEEN FAMILY AND BUSINESS VALUES

According to psychologists, family and business can each be viewed as systems that define people by their relationships with others in the same environment, rather than as individuals.

The family system is emotionally based, with emphasis on loyalty and the care and nurturing of family members, while the business system is task-based, with emphasis on performance and results rather than on the emotional considerations of family life. Is it any wonder that when these two basically incompatible systems overlap, as they do in a family business, there is conflict? See figure on page 6.

This is not to suggest that business life is unemotional, just that it is different from family life. In business, themes of status, "turf," and prestige outweigh familial themes of approval, love, and parental blessings.

In a "normal" situation, the overlap is within reasonable limits and thus manageable.

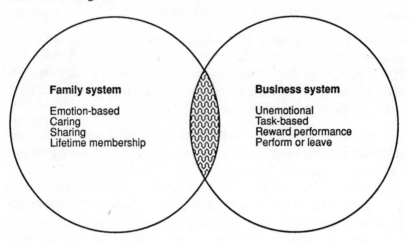

When the overlap is excessive conflict can be destructive.

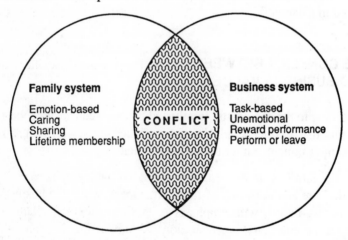

FAMILY VALUES IN THE BUSINESS

The excessive carry-over of family values to the business is a leading contributor to both business failure and family dissension. For example:

- Children may be welcomed into the business, regardless of their ability to contribute to it. If a job to suit them doesn't exist, it is often created—and it may include lifetime job security, regardless of performance, and the business becomes a family playground.
- Nepotism, the advancement of relatives on the basis of family considerations rather than on merit, can be destructive when carried to excess. It can inhibit the company's ability to develop able nonfamily managers, put the company under the burden of carrying incompetent family members, and may put the company at a competitive disadvantage. Owners may find themselves being forced to choose between keeping a relative on the payroll or breaking up a relationship in the family.
- Business decisions may be made on the basis of family politics rather than on the best interests of the company. For example, a marginally qualified family member may be put in charge of an important operation in order to justify his title.
- The business may be burdened with more family members than it needs or can support, resulting in conflict over roles in the business and over shrinking pieces of the financial pie.
- Family members are often paid far in excess of their value to the business. Sometimes the reverse is true, and they may be undercompensated "because they have an obligation to help out." This tends to drive competent family members to seek employment elsewhere and to burden the business with the drones.[2]
- Childhood sibling rivalry can blossom into full-bloomed internecine warfare in the business. Only now, instead of childhood squabbling over toys, the battling can affect the livelihoods of the participants and of innocent bystanders. This will be discussed further in Chapter 3.
- Children may be compensated according to need rather than performance: Laurie and Sue both work at the family's sporting goods store, with comparable responsibilities and salaries. When Sue married, she received a substantial increase in pay because "she needed it to buy a house." This attitude equates the reward system of a business to an extension of a childhood allowance.
- The family tenet that children be treated equally is often carried over into the business, resulting in equal rewards to children regardless of their commitment or ability. In one substantial business, a son is responsible for a division with annual sales of $300 million while another runs a division with sales of $60,000. The owner/mother is protective of the weaker son and insists on total equality in status and

compensation. Predictably, the high performer is dissatisfied, and there is conflict in the family. While the mother is able to hold family and business together during her lifetime, this is an explosion just waiting to happen when she dies. *Equal* and *equitable* may not be synonymous.

• Many owners follow the equality route in their estate plans, leaving their children with equal shares in the business regardless of their contribution to it. Harvey is the only one of five children to opt for a career in the family's construction business, and he worked hard to learn the business so that he could take it over when the time came. When his father died and left the business equally to all of the children, Harvey found himself outvoted by his siblings who neither understood the business nor had the same interest in it. He was unable financially to buy out his siblings and was forced to choose between selling the business or continuing as a minority stockholder, unable to control the destiny of the business. This issue is discussed further in Chapter 11.

• Family relationships, influenced by the birth order of children, may have a profound effect on business decisions. According to psychologist Dr. Kevin Leman, children tend to exhibit the following tendencies:[3]

> First child: "Perfectionist, reliable, conscientious, list maker, well-organized, critical, serious, scholarly."
>
> Middle child: "Mediator, fewest pictures in the family photo album, avoids conflict, independent, extreme loyalty to peer group, many friends, a maverick."
>
> The baby: "Manipulative, charming, blames others, shows off, people person, good salesperson, precocious, engaging."

THE EFFECT OF THE BUSINESS ON THE FAMILY

The building of the business is often an all-consuming task for the owner, and family life often suffers as a result. In some families, conflict about business policies is so intense, and there is so much togetherness during business hours that normal family life becomes impossible and relationships, that might otherwise have been close, are sacrificed on the altar of business.

A son says, "The warm togetherness that we used to have at Thanksgiving and Christmas is long gone. If I spent the holidays with my family, all we would talk about would be the business, and it would probably end up in an argument." A husband, whose wife works in the business, complains: "I love my wife and am pleased that she's excited about the business, but at home, when I'd like to put the business day behind me, that's all that she wants to talk about."

Jack Tramiel, who was the driving force behind the explosive growth of Commodore Computer and then, with his three sons, brought Atari Computer back from the ashes, said: "I taught them business from day one. Business isn't taught at Harvard. It's taught at home."[4]

Another owner, overly concerned about unduly influencing his children to enter the business, didn't allow any discussion about the business at home. As a result the family viewed it as "dad's business," and didn't identify with it. When the kids grew up and sought careers in other fields, he couldn't understand why.

THE NEED FOR BOUNDARIES

Conflict resulting from the overlap of family and business systems cannot be avoided; however, it can be contained, minimized, and managed by families who are able to establish appropriate boundaries between family and business.

Many families are never free from the business because it completely dominates every aspect of their lives, and the business is run as though it's an extension of the family. Successful families, however, tend to set boundaries between the two so that they can enjoy both the benefits of the business and the joy of a normal family life. These boundaries are clear, consistent, and practical, with enough flexibility to provide for the unforeseen.

In these circumstances, business decisions are based on the best interests of the company; family members earn promotions on merit, are evaluated on the same basis as employees, and are compensated according to market levels, rather than their positions in the family. Although not immune from family conflicts, they find constructive ways to resolve them, and family politics are not allowed to spill over into the business. The objectivity of these policies prevents or reduces jealousy and friction since everyone knows the ground rules and may have even participated in formulating them. Ways to accomplish this are discussed in Chapter 3.

Tom Ryan, a third generation member of a family construction and real estate development company, tells about being in business with his father. "Dad has treated me as a son and not as a business partner. . . . If I had a wish, it would be to have a better relationship where I could talk to him about things without our business problems interfering in every conversation. Part of the reason I work as hard as I do is to provide an opportunity for my children. Yet, I'm not so sure that if I passed the company on to my kids at the expense of a normal father-son or father-daughter relationship, I would be doing them or myself justice. If I couldn't maintain a good relationship with my children, I don't think I'd *want* to pass this company on to them."[5]

One CEO went so far as to have two hats made, one read "DAD" and the other "BOSS," which he changed as circumstances dictated. If more family members in business could make this distinction, it's certain that the dismal family business mortality statistics would nosedive.

While business discussion often takes place at home in successful families, it's not allowed to totally dominate their family lives, nor is the living room used as a daily extension of the company conference room.

Bob, who owns a substantial lumber company, has a healthy perspective on the separation of family and business. His daughter, after working for an advertising agency, expressed interest in joining his business. "I'm delighted to receive your application for employment," Bob said. "If it's accepted and you come to work here, remember that you are an employee with a special responsibility, and you'll be given every opportunity to prove yourself. However, when you come home at night, remember that I'm your dad." At this family's home, business experiences are often discussed at the dinner table, but problem-solving and differences are kept at the shop. The family owns a vacation cabin on a lake where they frequently spend weekends and vacations. There is an unwritten rule that business is never discussed at the cabin, and the family can enjoy their time together without the intrusion of business tensions.

There are families who are culturally unable to establish appropriate boundaries between family and business, and others who choose to ignore them. While these may appear to be successful in the short term, the chances of long-term success for these families are generally remote because of the inevitable conflicts that go with the territory.

Balancing the priorities often results in unpopular decisions. Commenting on this, one owner told the story of an old man, a boy, and a burro, traveling through Mexico. They entered a town with the boy leading the burro and the old man riding, only for the old man to run into the criticism of the townspeople. "How can you, an adult, ride while you let the child walk?" So they switched places and went to the next town. There the boy received the criticism of the townspeople. "How can you, a strong, young boy, ride while the old man walks?" Not knowing what to do, they decided that they both would ride and proceeded until they reached a rope bridge over a canyon. Under the combined weight, the bridge collapsed and, although the old man and boy survived, the burro was killed. "The moral to the story," the owner said, "is that when you try to please everybody, you lose your ass!"

THE LIFE CYCLE

The life cycle of a family business includes several stages, each posing different challenges. Chapter 4 will trace the business cycles of a growing business. Here are some generational implications:

First Generation

Starting the Business
Based on a need for independence and a desire to control his own destiny, the entrepreneur probably quit a well-paying job to pursue his dream of a business of his own. He risks everything and dedicates his life to the enterprise, often at the expense of his family. The principle objective is survival, and his total commitment, capacity for work, intuition, and business ability are forces that help the business to become safely established. He is *the boss* and is in control of every facet of the business.

Growth
If the business passes the survival stage, the nature of the challenge changes, and if the growth potential is to be reached, the one-man band

must become an orchestra conductor. Qualified people must be hired; controls and systems installed, and planning for the growth and continuity of the business commenced. Some founders are able to make this adjustment and to develop the management skills that allow their creation to reach its next level of potential. One owner said, "I may not be able to play all of the instruments, but I know when one of them is out of tune."

Many, however, continue in the survival mode, unwilling to share authority and responsibility, and limiting the growth of the business by their need to be all-controlling. Apple Computer is a graphic example. Steven Jobs, the brilliant cofounder/entrepreneur, was the driving force that made his company one of the outstanding success stories of our era. When it came to managing the next phase, however, he foundered, and only the hiring of John Scully, a professional manager, saved the company. Under Scully, the company reached new heights and Jobs left to start a new business.

The Plot Thickens

As the business (and the owner) mature, new problems emerge. The owner's mortality becomes an issue, often complicated by his reluctance to face the realities of age and death and by the fact that his management style has made him indispensable. His children enter the business, posing a new set of problems: What should be expected of them? How should they be paid? How should a future leader be selected from among them? Who should inherit the stock in the business? How will the employment of children affect loyal and productive employees? These decisions are complicated by the owner's dual roles as both parent and employer, and his reluctance to hand over the reins of the business that is such an important part of his life. Chapters 8, 9, and 11 will discuss these issues in depth.

Frequently the kids, with fire in their bellies and tuned into the rapidly changing environment, push for growth and change. The owner, uncomfortable with change and having taken his risks in the early years, is averse to anything that may threaten either his own financial security, or that of the business. As John Steinbeck said, "It is the nature of a man as he grows older to protest change, particularly change for the better."

Many owners intuitively develop healthy policies for family involvement in the business. Too often, however, when confronted with emotional questions that don't lend themselves to analytical answers, the owner avoids them. From his position of power, he puts down any unrest among the kids and retreats to his comfort zone, putting out the daily fires of business and hoping that somehow everything will come out all right.

Generally it doesn't, and most family businesses are "one trick ponies" that don't last beyond the shadows of their founders. The life of an established business is estimated at 24 years, which is approximately the business life expectancy of the founder from its inception.

Second Generation

In the first generation, there was no question about who was boss. Now a new leader must earn the respect and confidence of other family members who may feel that the role should have been theirs and of employees who may feel that nobody can fill the founder's shoes.

The ownership of the family's most valuable asset now becomes an issue. Whereas the founder had the power that went with owning all of the company stock, his successor may find that he has many co-owners and may even hold a minority interest in the company. This can be further complicated by the differing objectives of those who wish to build the business and those who would wish to partake more fully in its fruits, either to support a more elegant lifestyle or to pursue other interests.

Successors have many circumstances in their favor. They are the beneficiaries of an established business; they are probably better educated than the founder, with a better grasp of the management skills needed by the business at this stage. Many successors bring new talent and vitality to the business, fueling its success far beyond where the founder could have led it. However, others, brought up in an environment of financial security and lacking the commitment of the founder, institute the decline of the enterprise, often accompanied by disruption in the family.

Sometimes members of the second generation are, in reality, the real architects of the growth of the business. A small retail store is

built into a substantial chain; a machine shop becomes a large manufacturer—all because a child of the owner gained his initial exposure
in the parent's modest beginnings, saw the opportunity, and created a
vibrant new business.

Third Generation and Beyond

As the cast of characters increases, the difficulty of preserving the enterprise becomes almost exponentially increased, as most families become unable to solve the complex emotional and business problems
posed by multiple family ownership. In the second generation, for example, there may be a natural leader, or two siblings may be able to
develop a leadership accommodation between them.

However, when the stock in the company is inherited by the next
generation, it may be owned by several cousins, some of whom may
have neither aptitude for, nor interest in, the business. Each may have
different objectives, and perhaps some suffer from the maladies that
accompany wealth.

Many children in this generation, finding themselves on third
base, think that they have hit a triple. A company's right to exist must
be continually proven in the marketplace, and the ability of successors
to coast on the accomplishments of their predecessors is limited. Unless a natural leader emerges or one family unit buys out the others,
salvation generally lies in the centralization of control in responsible
hands through a voting trust or similar vehicle. This will be discussed
in Chapter 11.

Many larger businesses often engage professional managers at
this point. Those that survive under family management usually have
family cultures that are almost religiously dedicated to the perpetuation
of the business and that don't allow interpersonal differences to affect
business decisions.

Sometimes a circuitous route is used. In one situation, the founder
of a successful food distribution company left it to his four sons when
he died, with his oldest son as successor. Their inability to get along
threatened the company, but it was resolved when the successor gave
each of his brothers enough inventory and financial support to start
their own businesses. The successor's son now runs the business with
his son, daughter, and son-in-law, all of whom enjoy a harmonious re-

lationship. The chances of successful continuity appear to be bright, but if the second generation's problems had not been solved, the business would never have lasted.

The Estate Tax Impact

Each succeeding generation is affected by potentially crippling estate taxes which can exceed half the value of the business. The impact can be minimized through proper planning, which will be discussed in Chapter 11. However, many owners are reluctant to face their mortality, so they spend little time planning for it. The business, which usually comprises the bulk of the owner's estate, is generally not liquid, and estate taxes can create a serious cash drain unless there has been proper planning.

The Effect of Family and Business Cultures

The answer to why some families succeed and others fail is often found in their cultures—the shared values and assumptions that govern the behavior of both family and business. In a family business, the cultures are inextricably intertwined.

Family Culture

Family culture is influenced by several factors: the number of people in the family, their ages, divorces, and their problem-solving methods. Lee Iacocca describes how his family's culture influenced him: "I learned about the strength you can get from a close family life. I learned to keep going, even in bad times. I learned not to despair, even when my world was falling apart. I learned that there are no free lunches. And I learned about the value of hard work."

In his book, *Cultural Change in Family Firms*,[6] W. Gibb Dyer, Jr., explored three common cultural patterns in families, each representing different ways of handling authority, achieving goals, making decisions, and managing conflict:

In the *patriarchal/matriarchal family*, a family leader, usually a parent, establishes family goals and is the final authority in resolving disputes. The leader makes all of the important decisions, with the others expected to follow obediently.

With little or no confidence in the family's ability to handle information or responsibility, the leader is often secretive, rarely taking others (even his spouse) into his confidence. The family is unlikely to be aware of important issues relating to the business, such as the owner's plans for management succession or what will happen to his stock in the company when he dies—and they wouldn't dare ask.

This patriarchal pattern is particularly common to Latin-American, Asiatic, and European families, where the head of the family often dominates family life.

This design generally carries over into the business where the family leader is also the boss. Children are expected to be obedient, and employees are often treated paternally.

The *collaborative family* operates more democratically, with broad participation in family decision making. The goals and problems are shared by the head of the family with the spouse and children, who have the opportunity to provide input and to influence the outcome. There is a high level of trust, with priority given to family solidarity. Family members are aware of their dependency on each other, and emphasis is on cooperation among them.

In this open environment, the owner's dreams and problems are freely shared. Important issues are discussed openly, and the input of family members is valued. This leads, of course, to greater understanding of the business by the family and a more unified business approach.

In the *conflicted family*, it's everyone for himself. Every family member has his own goals and values. There is a low degree of mutual trust, and family members tend to constantly protect their interests. This is a breeding ground for conflict, and the environment doesn't encourage constructive resolution of differences. As a result, these families often are alienated, with conflicts being settled in the court room rather than the living room.

A third generation family member of a conflicted family reflects: "There was litigation between the founders of the business, and it happened again in the second generation. Now I'm suing my brother. It must be something in our genes." The answer, of course, is not to be found in genetics but in the culture of the family. The real wonder, in this case, is how the business lasted until the third generation. Conflicted families usually self-destruct long before then.

Business Culture

Every business has a culture, which in its simplest terms may be described as "the way things get done around here." In some businesses, if you asked the owner about the purpose of the business, he would respond, "to make a buck." Employees might answer, "to earn a week's pay."

Different businesses may be highly successful even though they have different cultural patterns. However, there is generally one common denominator among the winners: their values tend to be clearly articulated, and they encourage their people to work together in a common purpose, emphasizing pride, commitment, collaboration, and teamwork. This is not to suggest that profit isn't important. To the contrary, it is the fuel that drives the business vehicle, and no business can survive for long if it is not profitable. In successful businesses, however, profit is the result of doing everything else right and not an end in itself.

A survey of 80 substantial businesses was conducted to identify the factors that make for consistently outstanding company performance. The results were as follows:

- Of all the companies surveyed, only about one third had clearly articulated beliefs.
- Of this third, a surprising two thirds had qualitative beliefs, such as "IBM means service." The other third had financially oriented goals that were widely understood.
- *Of the 18 companies with qualitative beliefs, all were uniformly outstanding performers;* we could find no correlations of any relevance among the other companies—some did okay, some poorly; most had their ups and downs. *We characterized the consistently high performers as strong culture companies.*[7]

Surveys place Herman Miller, Inc., the office furniture manufacturer, high on the list of America's best managed and most admired companies. The founder, D. J. DePree, established profit-sharing and incentive-compensation programs for employees long before they became fashionable, and employees are fiercely committed to the company's objectives. The son of the founder, who now runs the company and is dedicated to sustaining the culture established by his father, defines its mission as "attempting to share values, ideals, goals, respect for each person, the process of our work together."[8]

The people at the Tandem Corporation, a highly successful computer company, share the commitment that is encompassed in the slogan, "Get the job done no matter what it takes." In another company, however, where the emphasis is on the work ethic, top executives say, "If you don't come to the office on Saturday, don't bother to show up on Sunday."

W. Gibb Dyer's book, *Cultural Change in Family Firms,* also explores cultural patterns in businesses:

In the "paternalistic" culture, the owner tends to extend the patterns of a patriarchal family. With a low level of trust in the ability of others to perform up to his standards, he limits the amount of information that is dispensed, makes all of the decisions, and gives employees little discretion in the performance of their tasks. In one extreme example, employees, after a trial period, are welcomed into "the family." There is a strict dress code, and rigid rules for behavior. This is accompanied, however, by lifetime job security and help for employees with financial needs due to family emergencies.

The "laissez-faire" culture is similar to the paternalistic pattern except that there is a higher level of trust, resulting in more latitude for employees in the performance of their work. The firm's ultimate mission and goals are defined by the founder and the family, but employees have wide latitude in achieving them. Thus, while the founder and family determine the ends, the employees are given the power to determine many of the means. In the paternalistic firm, however, the employer specifies both the ends and the means.

The "participative" culture, which is relatively rare in the American scene, is based on a high degree of trust, and decision making is group-oriented, with minimum recognition of the power and influence of the owner and family.

The "professional" culture often dominates when professionals take over the management of the business. It is based primarily on individual motivation and achievement, using methods associated with nonfamily businesses.

The Founder's Imprint

Founders are the original architects of their company's business culture, and their influence, (for better or worse), often lasts as long as the businesses are in existence. Not that the founders sit down and consciously decide what the culture will be. Rather, they decide what will be important, stress it, reinforce it, build it into the reward system, and get other people in the organization to buy into it.

For example, the founder of the food company, H. J. Heinz Company, established a tradition of using only the highest quality ingredients, and it became the standard for succeeding generations. In some companies, the culture is based on exploitation of its people and low ethical standards in dealing with customers and suppliers.

The Next Generations

The challenge to successive generations is to preserve the positive elements and to change the negative factors. This is often difficult because successors must often overcome the "we've always done it that way before" syndrome.

Because of the overlap between family and business cultures, it's often difficult for successors to institute change unless they control the company or enjoy the support of the family. After his death, the founder is often deified by the family, and successors who want to institute changes are usually met with horrified responses of, "Who are you to change Dad's policies?" This may result in "sacred cow" segments of the business that should be divested, but are retained because they were instituted by the founder or are the playground of present family members. Sometimes the cost consciousness of the owner prohibits necessary capital expenditures or the establishment of fair compensation levels for employees.

Steven K. Fox, the second-generation owner of Amot Controls Co. of Richmond, California, a successful industrial controls company, found that although the company was cash-rich, the business "would have died a slow death" if the company continued following the concepts established by the founder. The company had grown overly dependent on one segment of its business; key patents had expired; relationships among union employees "were marked by mistrust and hostility," and the company was locked into an overly conservative policy that restricted its growth by prohibiting the assumption of debt.

Fox embarked on a program to change the culture of the firm: product lines were broadened; the company's relationship with employees became more open and participative; a professional manager was hired; and strategic planning was commenced. After implementing the changes, the owner said that the company is now "really charging ahead" and on the way to being a company where people "can recognize change when it's coming, enjoy it, and see it as a chance to grow."[9]

The "Bottom Line"

If you're a typical owner of a family business, you may be thinking, "This is all very interesting, but what's the bottom line? Where are the answers?"

There are no quick fixes in this complex environment. Your best chances of success lie in increasing your awareness and planning for the future while you still have time. That's what the rest of this book is about.

SUMMARY

• The commitment of family members to the business is a source of strength that often allows them to outperform competitors with greater resources and to overcome the disadvantages of nepotism.

• The owners of a family business establish the priorities that determine how the family's relationship with the business will function. Sometimes the family's interests are paramount, and sometimes the business's interests. However, some families find an appropriate balance.

• Family and business values are basically different, and conflict between the two is inevitable. Successful families find a way to limit the overlap, to insulate their family and business lives, and to protect against the conflict that results when one set of values overwhelms the other.

• Family businesses go through reasonably predictable life cycles, with the probability of their survival decreasing as the number of owners proliferates.

• Families and business each have their own unique cultures that influence how they interact. Both internal and external environments change over time, and the outcome for both family and business may be determined by how family members react to these changes.

NOTES

1. Walter Guzzardi, "U.S. Business Hall of Fame, *Fortune*, March 13, 1989, p. 135.
2. Ivan S. Landsberg, "Managing Human Resources in Family Firms: the Problem of Institutional Overlap," *Organizational Dynamics*, Summer 1983, p. 42.
3. Dr. Kevin Leman, *The Birth Order Book* (New York: Dell Publishing Co., 1985), p. 14.
4. Mark Ivey, "Father Knows Best—Just Ask the Tramiel Boys," *Business Week*, December 15, 1986, p. 65.
5. Ann K. Ryan, "All in the Family," *Minnesota Business Journal*, December 1983.
6. W. Gibb Dyer Jr., *Cultural Change in Family Firms* (San Francisco: Jossey-Bass, 1986), pp. 35–36.
7. Terrence E. Deal and Allan A. Kennedy, *Corporate Cultures* (Reading, Mass.: Addison-Wesley Publishing, 1982), p. 7.
8. Kenneth Labich, "Hot Company, Warm Culture," *Fortune*, February 27, 1989, p. 74.
9. Sharon Nelton, "Cultural Changes in a Family Firm," *Nation's Business*, January 1989, pp. 62–63.

CHAPTER 2

INTRODUCING THE PLAYERS

If these characters are not liked, I shall be astonished; and if they are, my astonishment will not be less.

Jean de la Bruyere (*The Characters*)

The family business drama is a combination of Greek tragedy, Macbeth, Pygmalion, and the Perils of Pauline. The players each have differing perspectives.

Sometimes the family business drama involves only two players, and sometimes it resembles a "cast of hundreds." Whatever the size, each family member has his own objectives, problems and concerns. In trying to solve the family business puzzle it is important to understand each unique perspective.

THE MALE OWNER

According to the L&H entrepreneurial survey, the owner is most apt to be a white, married male with two children and a college graduate between the ages of 50 and 59. The L&H/AMA family business survey indicates that 53 percent are founders, 33 percent in the second generation, 9 percent in the third generation, and 1 percent beyond the third generation.

In his capacity as leader of the business and patriarch of the family, the owner is the central character in the family business production. Balancing these heavy, and often conflicting, responsibilities is complex and difficult, and while he may be capable in the business world, he has no training and perhaps limited aptitude for the task. The stakes are high; the preservation of the business and the harmony of the owner's family, as well as its financial security, may depend on his ability to succeed.

Many owners share one common characteristic; they are entrepreneurs. Psychologists tell us that these movers and shakers tend to be alike in many ways. They have a strong need to surpass their fathers. They're apt to be charismatic with high levels of confidence, possessing leadership skills, vision, and the ability to inspire others. In the early years, they're optimistic risk-takers with little fear of failure.

They're intelligent with a great capacity for work and a total commitment to their dreams. Billionaire Donald Trump, perhaps the quintessential entrepreneur, owns several magnificent homes, the world's spiffiest private yacht, and a fleet of private planes, yet he rarely takes a vacation. "I like to do business," he says. "Work is the pleasure of my life."[1]

In addition to the qualities that enable him to build the business, the owner often has a dark side. He is frequently autocratic with a need to be all-controlling in both family and business. This inhibits the development of strong subordinates and often results in a one-man show with the owner involved in every decision, ranging from major capital expenditures to the purchase of paper clips.

The owner is apt to be an intuitive manager with a bias against planning and formality. His informal style and management by "winging it" may be effective as long as he can get his arms around the entire business; however, they become limiting when the business grows to the point where organization and planning are needed. All too often, he commits his life to the building of his creation, yet ensures its demise by failing to build an organization with collective purpose that can survive after he's no longer around to pull all of the strings.

If owners hope to keep the business in the family, their major challenges are to identify, train, and install successors, which will be discussed in Chapter 8, and to provide for the new ownership of the business in the next generation, which will be covered in Chapter 11.

The owner is generally a complex character who can't easily be put into any mold. For example, Stephen M. Mindich, founder of a successful Boston newspaper weekly, is viewed by his friends as "philanthropic, artistic, public-spirited, wonderfully feisty, frank, passionate, and a hard-nosed businessman." Others, principally former employees, view him as "cheap, greedy, vulgar, egocentric, anti-union, frank, passionate, and a hard-nosed businessman." Said Mindich, "I think there's resentment for anyone who starts with nothing and works really hard. I try to treat people fairly. People work here voluntarily. They come and go. There are no indentured servants."[2]

THE OWNER'S TRADITIONAL WIFE

Traditionally, the wife of the owner stayed home and raised the kids while he dedicated his life to building the business. (In today's environment, however, she's a disappearing species.) Although the business had a profound influence on her life, all too often, the traditional wife knew little about it. Perhaps the owner was trying to protect her, or maybe he thought that she wouldn't understand it.

If the owner died unexpectedly, his widow often found herself unprepared for the responsibility of a business that had lost one of its most valuable assets, its leader. (For more on this, see "How to Make Your Widow Hate You" in Chapter 11.)

Sometimes, by necessity, she steps into the business and assumes control. Rosemary Garbett of Houston, Texas, was a 40-year-old housewife with four teenagers when her husband was accidently killed. When she learned that a sale would only bring half of the book value of Los Tios Mexican Restaurants, she decided to run the business herself. "When I took over," she recalls, "I was scared and had no confidence at all in my ability to do anything." She proceeded to grow the original three debt-ridden restaurants into 10 profitable units, employing 375 people.[3] The story is often not this uplifting, and it ends with an unprepared wife, bewildered by the enormity of the task, selling the business at the best price that she can get.

If the children are already involved, many different outcomes are possible. Matina Phillips DeSimone, after her five children ousted her as chairman of the family corporation, said, "For 15 years, *Boston Magazine* has selected the best and worst of everything. In 1988, my children were the worst."

The principal priority of most wives and mothers is the preservation of the family, and often, when there is conflict between dad and the kids in the business, she is the mediator and buffer that prevents civil war in the family. Sometimes, however, her husband's failure to keep her informed, coupled with a lack of business sophistication, can result in the owner's wife pressuring him to run the business according to her perception of justice. This could include hiring incompetent family members, overpaying them, and encouraging unsound inheritance practices. These "acts of love and caring" can unwittingly sow the seeds for the eventual destruction of both family and business.

Lloyd founded and built what is now a leading advertising agency in a midwestern city. His two sons, Zachary and Owen, both work in the agency, with Zachary in the financial end and Owen in the creative end. Lloyd's daughter, Lucy, is married to a struggling artist. Lloyd is nearing retirement and realizes that he must appoint a new leader to replace him. Owen has no business sense at all and often advocates "far out" policies that would be harmful to the business. Zachary is a capable manager, and Lloyd is convinced that he would be a competent successor.

Lloyd's wife refuses to allow her husband to name Zachary as his successor, saying, "It would blow our family apart. Let them settle it among themselves when the time comes." Lloyd is not willing to make the decision without his wife's support, so it's deferred to the future, at which time his wife's prophesy will almost certainly be fulfilled.

Wives often influence owners, particularly in family-related matters. In the L&H/AMA family business survey, owners were asked, "What, if any, influence does your spouse have on business decisions? The responses were as follows: a great deal, 22 percent; a fair amount, 20 percent; only a little, 23 percent; and none/other/and not applicable, 35 percent.

Whether or not a spouse influences the owner's business decisions, it makes sense for him to share both his dreams and problems, not only because of the benefits of sharing and the encouragement that might result, but because she might some day be forced to assume his responsibilities.

WHEN THERE'S A SECOND WIFE

In today's high-divorce climate, the owner's spouse is often a second wife. With the newcomer usually younger than their mother and possibly not much older than themselves, the children often are resentful.

Picture the scene as the owner introduces his new spouse to his children who work in the business. "Here's my new wife, kids. You better be good to her because she'll end up owning the company, and you better get along well with her children because they're coming into the business." If that sounds far-fetched, consider the case of Carroll Rosenbloom, former owner of the Los Angeles Rams professional football team. After his death by drowning at age 71, it was widely assumed that his son, Steve (33) who had worked with the team since age 12, would take over. Surprise! Rosenbloom left the bulk of his estate, estimated at over $100 million, to his wife and Steve's stepmother, Georgia, along with 70-percent ownership of the Rams. With this came the bombshell that Georgia was to oversee the operation of the football team. Predictably, Steve and Georgia had a disagreement soon afterward, and he was fired.

An owner's divorce, in addition to the stress it causes in the family, adds a new and potentially destructive factor in family-business relationships even if it doesn't go to the extreme of the previous example. Owners in this situation can alleviate many problems resulting from divorce by thinking through all of the business-associated implications and discussing the situation openly with their existing and new families. An independent board of directors, which is discussed in Chapter 7, can be of great help in these circumstances.

THE FEMALE OWNER

Despite their great progress in recent years, female employees are still second-class citizens in the corporate world, earning considerably less than their male counterparts. Many women have found a level playing field by starting their own businesses, which they are now doing at almost twice the rate of men.[4] According to the House Small Business Committee, the increase in the number of companies owned and managed by women is "the most significant economic development of recent years." The report also states that "women-owned businesses have become a central factor in the American economy and will become even more crucial in the years ahead."[5]

Women tend to start businesses for the same reasons as men, principally self-satisfaction (49 percent) and desire for freedom and independence (30 percent). Only 9 percent cited profit as a motive.[6] It's clear that the satisfaction of many women owners springs from their desire to advance beyond the limitations they experienced as employees in a male-dominated business environment. Many women-owned entrepreneurial businesses eventually become family businesses.

Because women's lives (and needs) are different from men's, they are often sensitive to opportunities that men have missed. An outstanding example is Elisabeth Claiborne Ortenberg who, with her husband and partner, recognized the apparel needs of career women and built Liz Claiborne Inc. into a billion-dollar enterprise.

HUSBAND-WIFE TEAMS

Traditionally, if the owner's wife worked in the business, she was the bookkeeper because he couldn't afford to hire anyone else. Even if the business progressed, her role frequently didn't expand into the managerial level, and in many cases she continued to do the same work as in the early days, or maybe she dropped out when the kids started coming.

No more. There are husband-wife teams at every level of the business spectrum, ranging from mom-and-pop shops to Ellen and Melvin Gordon, who run Tootsie Roll Industries, a New York Stock Exchange company. And women are not only filling lower-end jobs; sometimes they're the founders with their husbands either as co-CEOs or, in a reversal of traditional roles, at lower level positions.

There are many approaches to the question of who should be boss. Just as in many marriages where one is better at handling the money and paying the bills, either the husband or wife may be clearly more qualified to be the leader, and husbands are now less inclined toward hang-ups that prevent them from assuming a subservient role in the business if their wives are better qualified. A team approach without a boss can also work as long as both share the same business philosophies and can reach consensus on important issues.

The key is for spouses to separate their business and family roles so that criticism or conflict about business decisions don't become personal. According to Linda M. Schatz, who works with her husband in their management consulting firm in Alexandria, Virginia, "We resolve our differences by looking at the consequences to the *organization* not to our individual egos."[7]

Natalie Robinson-Garfield, a psychotherapist in New York who has counseled several husband-wife teams, says that these couples sometimes suffer marital stress more readily than those who don't work together. "Difficulties may arise simply from spending too much time together. Other problems include responsibility for child care, ego clashes, and the lack of 'neutral turf' to escape to when tensions build." She believes that a husband and wife business "is a hotbed for competition, jealousy, rivalry, and blame."[8]

Sharon Nelton, whose book *In Love and in Business* is based on extensive interviews with married couples in business, identifies the following "stress producers":

- "We have different management styles and work habits."
- "We worry or disagree about money."
- "We can't separate our business life from our personal life."
- "It hurts when my spouse criticizes me."
- "We disagree on business decisions or goals."
- "We don't have enough time."
- "We work too hard, and we're tired all the time."
- "We are together too much."
- "My spouse won't listen to me."
- "I have two jobs—being a business partner and running a household."

Nelton also identifies the common threads in successful husband-wife teams.

- Marriage and children come first.
- The spouses demonstrate enormous respect for each other.
- There is a high degree of close communication.
- The partners complement each other's talents and attitudes, and they carve up the turf accordingly.

- The parents are supportive of each other.
- There are strong family ties.
- They compete with the world outside, not with each other.
- They like to laugh.
- They put their egos in check.[9]

One couple has its own way of separating home life and business. When the husband leaves for work in the morning, he kisses his wife good-bye and heads off to breakfast at a local restaurant. When she arrives at work, she greets the employees and says hello to her husband as though she were seeing him for the first time.

The late Jan Erteszek, co-founder of the Olga Company, a lingerie firm in Van Nuys, California, liked to talk about business at home. However, he said, "Olga would fine me 25 cents for every word that I would utter about business after business hours. On Sunday, it was double. She made a small fortune on that invention."[10]

If divorce should ensue, the split-up often applies to the business as well. Barbara Burrell, who built an advertising agency with her husband, realized that everyone, her husband included, expected her to leave the company after their separation, but she decided to work out a business relationship that would remain in effect. "It was awkward. . . . We spent a lot of time avoiding each other. And it was highly embarrassing for him to introduce me. A client would ask, 'How are you two related?' and he would have to say 'This is my ex-wife.' " Nevertheless Burrell believes that divorced couples can remain business partners if "maturity and good sense prevail." Psychotherapist Robinson-Garfield, however, says that "it's just about impossible for a couple to work together after a divorce."[11]

SONS

The most common family combination in business is father-son, with sons almost triple the number of daughters who are actively involved, according to the L&H/AMA family business survey. While many fathers and sons enjoy loving and harmonious relationships both at home and at business, psychologists tell us that father-son relationships have a unique potential for trouble, and conflict between fathers and sons is one of the principal sources of trouble in family businesses. This is more fully discussed in Chapter 3, and father-son relationships, as they relate to management succession, are explored in Chapters 8 and 9.

DAUGHTERS

Although you don't see many businesses named "John Jones & Daughter," with the advancement of women in business, daughters are increasingly being considered as successors. In the L&H/AMA family business survey, owners were asked how they would feel about having a daughter taking over as a successor. Seven percent said more positively; 52 percent said just the same; 13 percent said less positively; and 28 percent said don't know/not applicable.

While the pendulum is swinging toward equal treatment of daughters as potential successors, this is generally only true when there are no sons or when a daughter is the oldest child. According to Louis B. Barnes, Professor of Organizational Behavior at Harvard Business School, in the family, "daughters and younger sons tend to rank lower than older and eldest sons."[12] Although it sometimes happens, it is unusual for a daughter to beat out an older brother for the top job.

Social scientist Paul C. Rosenblatt suggests that "the key to understanding the second-class treatment of daughters may be the fathers' perception that daughters are likely to leave the family for another. The possibility that a daughter will marry, take another name, and then be perceived as switching loyalty to another man and his family may well be the real reason daughters are ignored."[13]

A new term has recently entered the business lexicon, the so-called "Mommy track" that allows women new ways to balance career goals and mothering. While many women don't seek changes in their business careers because of motherhood, others prefer to cut back or modify their business lives temporarily during their childrens' growing-up years. This is made possible by the adoption of flexible hours, scaling down to part-time employment, or working at home and communicating by telephone and computer modem.

Katie Glockner, who works for Quaker Oats, opted to cut back on her pace when her son was born. "I was nursing the baby, and babies don't want to wait until the 6 P.M. meeting is over. I didn't feel comfortable giving up so much of the care. You can fall in love with those little people."[14] While her employer allowed her to cut back to a three day week, not every boss is as agreeable.

In a family business the owner is apt to be more receptive because he values the additional commitment that his daughter brings to the business and, after all, those are his grandchildren she is raising.

However many owners share the perception of some of their counterparts in the corporate world that women cannot be depended on for the long pull. One owner, despite his daughter's outstanding performance, was reluctant to advance her to an important managerial role. "What I think she really wants," he said, "is a house with a white picket fence, kids, and a Bloomingdale's charge card. While this would please me as a parent, it would leave the business without a key manager, and I'm not willing to spend years training her, only to see her leave."

Daughter/successors bring different dimensions to the role than their male counterparts, and owners should realize that women are not men with skirts but that they're different by temperament . . . not necessarily stronger or weaker, but different. Marilyn Loden, author of *Feminine Leadership—How to Succeed without Being One of the Boys*, explains: "I see feminine leadership as different from male-oriented management but equally effective. It favors cooperation over competition. Feminine leaders prefer to work in team structures where power and influence are shared more across the group, as opposed to a hierarchy where power is concentrated at the top. Feminine leaders rely heavily on intuition as well as rational thinking in solving problems. They focus more on long-term goals which are good for the entire organization, as opposed to short-term. And they generally prefer a 'win-win' approach to conflict resolution instead of the 'win-lose' approach favored by many male CEOs."[15]

The conflict between Arnold Daniels of Praendex Inc. and his two sons resulted in their leaving the business. "I was looking for somebody who would do exactly what I do, the way I do it," said Daniels, "and they were both too independent and too bright to be an echo of me." Arnie, Jr., put it this way: "It was a no-win situation. . . . I could find aggravation anywhere. Who needed it?" The solution? Although he had coaxed both sons back to the business, when he reached his 65th birthday, Daniels chose his daughter, Dinah, then 40, to be his successor. Dinah had previously worked in the company as a secretary during the summer while she was in high school and had been fired by her father. She went on to become public relations director of some world-class orchestras. Giving her the helm was "an act of desperation."

Dinah suggested that the company double its office size, adding expensive new conference space. "If one of the boys had suggested that, there wouldn't have been a prayer," said Daniels, "but when Dinah tells me I'm wrong or I don't know enough, I can consider it rationally. When the boys try to tell me the same thing, I react as if it were a personal attack."[16] Although she had no previous experience in the business, within 15 months Dinah professionalized the company's marketing program, launched a successful direct-mail campaign, and improved the company's relationships with its licensees. She explained, "We share a certain temperament . . . I'm the most logical and least emotional of his children. I have a conciliatory manner. And my father is much less difficult than some of the other men I've worked for."[17]

One of the principal difficulties of many daughters in family businesses is to overcome being "Daddy's little girl." It's difficult for a daughter to assume major responsibilities and to gain the respect of employees when the owner treats her as though she were still playing with dolls.

SONS-IN-LAW

Sons-in-law come in different shapes, sizes, and models. He may be a ne'er do well, who marries the boss's daughter for the financial benefits and security of working in the business. Or, he may be a committed and highly motivated family member who makes an important contribution to the business. Even though not involved in the business, a son-in-law may exert considerable influence in his role as his wife's principal advisor and confidant.

In the business, sons-in-law are often in the difficult position of being viewed as outsiders by family members regardless of their performance. A melodramatic illustration of this occurs in Mario Puzo's *The Godfather*. The trusted "consigliore" (Robert Duvall in the film) is intimately involved with the Godfather's activities. Yet sometimes he is excluded when the Godfather (portrayed by Marlon Brando) confers with his sons about "private" business matters.[18]

Sometimes an owner can enjoy a better relationship with a son-in-law than with a son because of the absence of father-son conflict. One owner tells of firing his son who was then the president of the company. When asked why, he explained, "He went into *my* office, sat in *my* chair, and put his feet on *my* desk . . . and the door was open so that the employees could see it." When asked who replaced his son, he proudly beamed, "My son-in-law. He's terrific."

The possibility of divorce must be considered. What if a son-in-law is the successor or if he has a key management role, and a divorce with the owner's daughter ensues? There are few instances where this doesn't affect the business relationship, and divorce generally includes both business and marital relationships. However, talent and commitment are rare commodities in business, and many owners with able sons-in-law generally find that the risk of divorce is well worth taking. Others take the same approach as the Rothschild family, which has had an iron-clad rule for several generations against allowing sons-in-law to work in the business.

DAUGHTERS-IN-LAW

A daughter-in-law is less likely than a son-in-law to work in the business; however, as with her male counterpart, she must often cope with being considered an outsider and with the realization that she married her husband, a business, and her husband's family.

Not uncommonly, a son in conflict with his father or other family members shares his travail with his wife, who may have limited knowledge about business in general. She may be a calming and supporting influence, or hearing only his side of the story, she may become resentful of her husband's tormentor, the owner, not to mention other family members who might live in more expensive homes or drive fancier automobiles.

Sometimes, daughters-in-law fuel conflagrations that might have otherwise been contained. One owner said, "Major decisions in this company are affected by the pillow talk in my son's house, and my daughter-in-law's attitude is one of our company's leading problems."

Sometimes daughters-in-law find themselves in the middle when there is a struggle in the family, being blamed for her husband's attitudes or shortcomings, or she may find herself in the role of peacemaker between her husband and the owner. Tragically, there are even times when the grandchildren are used as pawns in this battle.

As will be discussed in Chapter 3, a forum for frank and open discussion at a family council can be valuable in helping to make daughters-in-law feel that they are members of the family. The open forum that it provides can make it possible for the full story to be aired, and the free and open discussion that it encourages can be valuable in preventing debilitating conflict.

EMPLOYEES

A news item reads, "Top manager quitting job at Fidelity." The story tells about a 45-year-old executive who resigned from the multibillion dollar financial institution, saying, "The company has been and will be an excellent company, and I'm proud of my contributions, but essentially you just run out of room in a family-owned company."

Sometimes key employees are not satisfied unless they own a "piece of the action." As stock ownership is generally kept in the family, this often results in an impasse that is only resolved by the resignations of the employees, who sometimes start competing enterprises. One way of solving the problem is through the use of "phantom stock," which will be discussed in Chapter 6.

In our experience, most employees in family businesses don't expect to own shares in it. They want to be treated with respect, earn fair compensation, and have the opportunity to fulfill their career aspirations. Many employees enjoy the informality of working in family businesses as well as the personal relationship with the boss that is unobtainable in big, public corporations. However, they often have concerns about family involvement. One employee said, "I enjoy my job and have great regard for the boss. Sometimes, however, we employees get caught up in family tensions, and we are the pawns." Another said, "I don't see the boss planning for management succession, and I'm concerned that his kids won't be able to run the business. If they're forced to sell the business eventually, where will it leave me?"

The autocratic management style of an owner can inhibit the development of competent managers. As a result, the work force often consists of employees whose principal attribute is loyalty rather than ability. This can be part of another questionable legacy to the successor who may be faced with the distasteful and difficult task of cleaning up the old man's deadwood and replacing them with high performers.

Sometimes the role of a key trusted employee is ingeniously institutionalized by the family. A loyal and talented senior manager becomes a mentor to the next generation and may run the company if the owner dies before a member of the next generation is ready to take over. This loyal custodian usually has a good relationship with the family and may be feared, admired, and respected, despite the fact that his role is temporary.

SIBLINGS, PARTNERS, AND COUSINS AS CO-OWNERS

Most family businesses consist of a single family unit involving parents and children. As if this isn't complicated enough, it becomes even more difficult when more than one family unit becomes involved. For example, an owner bequeaths the business to his two offspring. If they each have two children who inherit their parent's stock, the single owner in the first generation is replaced by two in the second generation and four in the third. While the second consists of siblings, the third generation consists of both siblings and cousins.

Some experts believe that, despite sibling rivalry, siblings have a better chance of making it as partners than people who don't grow up together. "There is trust, affection, and knowing how the other thinks," says Karolus Smedja, a Chicago consultant to troubled partnerships. "There is a history of knowing how to negotiate differences —strategies to use to convince each other, prod each other, and get the best from each other. Strangers have no such history, no such glue to make them stick with the partnership when faced with serious disputes."[19]

Many businesses are started by unrelated partners. Sometimes they have a harmonious relationship and sometimes not, but the business relationship keeps them together. One ex-partner, after the business was sold, said, "We built a fine business together, but how I hated the son of a bitch. Being in business with him was like having a 28-year root canal." While business success often keeps these partnerships together during the lives of the founders, the question of the next generation must be faced.

Concerned about the perils of family involvement, the founders of a prominent scientific research company had an agreement from the beginning that their business would be a meritocracy and that no family members, including children, would ever be allowed to work in the business.

Multifamily ownership requires such a unique combination of people, attitudes, and skills, and the odds are so high against success that some consultants categorically advise that rather than attempting to continue the business under multiple-family ownership, the business should be divided or sold.

As will be described in Chapter 10, some families avoid interfamily conflict through the use of buy-sell agreements, providing for the buy-out of the stock of the first owner to die. There are few perfect answers in this situation. While a buy-out may solve the question of where the power will lie in the next generation and alleviate the conflict associated with having multiple family owners, it will affect the position of the children of the deceased, who may suddenly find themselves as employees (or ex-employees), rather than as co-owners and active members of management.

Some families solve the co-ownership problem by hiring professional managers to run the business; however, if voting control of the stock is spread around the family, there is still the risk of the differing needs of family members leading to disagreements or warfare. Practically the only way to avoid almost certain chaos in these circumstances is through centralized control of the voting stock, as will be discussed in Chapter 11.

Unless there is a deeply ingrained culture regarding the sanctity of the business, the problems of multiple-family ownership intensify, and few escape from the ultimate penalty of too many cooks in the kitchen.

SUMMARY

There is often a unique blend of players in the family business game.

• The owner, if he's a typical entrepreneur, is a complex individual. If the business is to survive, he must build an organization and set the groundwork for management and stock ownership succession to the next generation.

• The owner's "traditional" wife took care of the kids while the owner was building the business, and is often the buffer between them and her husband when they eventually work in the business. It's in the best interests of both that she be informed about the workings of the business.

• When the owner has a second wife, there are many additional issues, including the future ownership of the stock in the company and the possible involvement in the business of his new spouse and her children. These problems can be alleviated or prevented by open communication by the owner with both his original and new families and by the establishment of ground rules that are understood by all.

• Women are now starting businesses at twice the rate of their male counterparts. Many start their businesses out of frustration from failing to achieve equality in businesses dominated by men. Their different perspectives frequently allow them to identify new market niches.

• Husband-wife teams face a difficult challenge in blending marriage and business. Those that can insulate their career and home lives have a greater chance of success in both.

• Sons are still the predominant choice as successors to the owner. Conflict between father and son can spill over from the family into the business, often with destructive results.

• Daughters are gaining acceptance as successors. They bring different qualities than men to the role, and women are more apt than men to work toward consensus rather than confrontation.

• Sons-in-law may either be fortune-seekers or valuable, committed members of the family and business. They must often cope with the onus of being considered outsiders by the family and with the specter of possible divorce.

• Daughters-in-law, who often feel as though they are outsiders, can either be valuable sources of support or creators of dissension. A family council may help to make the relationship more constructive for everyone involved.

• Employees may either run out of opportunity and leave, or they may find that the business provides fulfilling careers. They are affected by conflict in the family and by the family's ability to achieve successful management succession.

• Multiple-family ownership exponentially complicates the inherent problems of family businesses. The solution often lies in either buy-out or other means of centralizing stock ownership.

NOTES

1. Otto Friedrich, "Flash Symbol of an Acquisitive Age," reported by Jeanne McDowell, *Time*, January 16, 1989, p. 54.
2. Carol Stocker, "One Tough Publisher Takes On One Tough Columnist," *Boston Globe*, April 7, 1989, pp. 32–35.
3. Sharon Nelton, "When Widows Take Charge," *Nation's Business*, December 1988, p. 41.
4. Dyan Machan, "Taking Charge," *Forbes*, March 6, 1989, pp. 154–156.
5. Janice Castro, "She Calls All the Shots," *Time*, July 4, 1988, pp. 54–57.
6. Richard Cuba, David Decenzo, and Andrea Anish, "Management Practices of Successful Female Business Owners," *American Journal of Small Business*, October–December 1983, pp. 40–46.
7. Sharon Nelton, "In Love and in Business," *Nation's Business*, November 1986.
8. Judith Burnes, "Breaking Up Is Hard to Do," *Savvy* (August 1983).
9. Sharon Nelton, *In Love and in Business* (New York: John Wiley & Sons, 1986), pp. 25–27, 54–62.
10. Sharon Nelton, "For Richer, for Poorer," *Nation's Business*, September 1985.
11. Judith Burnes, "Breaking Up Is Hard to Do," *Savvy*, August 1983.
12. Louis B. Barnes, "Incongruent Hierarchies: Daughters and Younger Sons as Company CEOs," *Family Business Review*, Spring 1988, pp. 9–10.
13. Paul C. Rosenblatt, "Family Inc.," *Psychology Today*, July 1985.
14. Elizabeth Ehrlich, "The Mommy Track," *Business Week*, March 20, 1989, pp. 126–34.
15. Marilyn Loden, "Feminine Leadership—How to Succeed without Being One of the Boys," speech at Notre Dame College, Baltimore, Maryland, on March 13, 1986.
16. Curtis Hartman, "Why Daughters Are Better," *Inc.*, August 1987, pp. 41–46.
17. Ibid.
18. Research Institute of America, "Personal Report for the Executive," October 15, 1985.
19. Phyllis Feurstein, "Brothers as Business Partners," *Talking to the Boss*, March 1989, pp. 6–7.

CHAPTER 3

MY FAMILY, RIGHT OR WRONG

Happy families are all alike; every unhappy family is unhappy in
its own way.

Leo Tolstoy

*If they are to prevail, families must learn to deal with common conflicts.
Through family strategic planning, a family can take control of its destiny and
establish a unified family approach to the business.*

It happens all the time. An entrepreneur starts a new business and suc-
ceeds beyond his wildest dreams. But rather than adding to the quality
of family life, the business serves as a catalyst for its destruction.
Sometimes, however, the business is a unifying force that brings the
family closer together. Much depends on the strength of the family.

In this chapter, we'll examine the common characteristics of
strong families and some of the principal causes of conflict that tend to
afflict family businesses. Then we'll explain how you can develop a
cohesive family approach to the business through family strategic
planning.

THE STRONG FAMILY

To get along in business, you must first get along at home, and lasting
businesses are usually owned by strong families. An extensive research study by Nick Stinnett and John DeFrain led to the conclusion
that these families tend to share the following common qualities:[1]

Commitment
Members value the unity of the family, share the same goals and values, and are concerned about each other's welfare. While family mem-

bers are encouraged to pursue their individual goals, the commitment to family would preclude pursuits that threatened the best interests of the family. This attitude, combined with a high level of trust, enables the team-building that is important in the business and tends to prevent the conflict that results from the pursuit of individual agendas. A member of a family insurance agency expressed this view: "We're trying to grow here, to expand so the children eventually will have more. We don't try to glorify ourselves personally; everyone pulls together."

Appreciation and Communication

Everyone has a need to be appreciated. Members of strong families have the ability to recognize each other's positive qualities and to share open and frequent communication. They find it easy to compliment each other—something other families would consider maudlin. This results in the building of self-esteem and an environment that is mutually supportive. These attributes not only strengthen family life but are valuable when carried over into the business.

Time Together

Strong families not only enjoy *quality* time but also spend *quantity* time together, not allowing outside pressures to pull them into going separate ways yet not stifling their individual identities. This might include one-on-one time with other family members or group activities such as meals together, family attendance at religious services, and regular family gatherings. The building of family tradition and group unity, which results from being together, is extremely valuable in helping a family withstand the conflicts of life together in business.

Spiritual Wellness

Strong families share a unifying force that encompasses integrity, honesty, loyalty, and high ethical values. Many gain strength through a belief in a higher power that can influence their lives; however, whether spirituality is expressed through participation in organized religion or through a moral code, it's an important influence on family life, and it's the foundation for the ethical standards of the business.

Coping with Crises and Stress

Every family is periodically confronted with periods of crisis and stress, and some collapse under the weight. Strong families tend to keep the problems in perspective and to cope by focusing on the positive elements and by pulling together, seeking outside help when it's needed. Their ability to communicate freely, their humor, and strong base of spiritual wellness are important assets in dealing with crises and in enabling them to resolve conflict among themselves. This foundation can be valuable when applied to the inevitable problems that arise from family participation in the business.

THE FATHER-SON RELATIONSHIP

Although daughters are becoming more prominent in the family business scene, the principal parent-child relationship in business still revolves around fathers and sons. Psychological factors in this complex relationship (but absent in father-daughter relationships) can cause devastating conflict, affecting both the family and the business

A study of 200 father-son business teams revealed that the stages of their lives had a profound influence on father-son relationships. The study indicated that sons between the ages of 17 and 25 seek their own identity and strive for independence from their parents. The years between 27 and 33 are spent in developing their careers, and a role model is sought, (often the father). They then tend to seek both independence and recognition, and are apt to be risk-takers, in the desire to build their own monuments.

Meanwhile, fathers are going through their own phases. From 40 to 50 years of age, they tend to grow their businesses and expand their personal power bases. In their 50s, they tend to mellow a bit; the competitive urge lessens, and they often make the transition from "doer" to "teacher." After age 60, they become more conservative and tend to want to hold on to what they have built, both financially and in terms of their position of power.[2]

Another study indicates that the "quality of the work relationship between a father and a son will change as each moves from one developmental period to the next and hence from one life stage intersect to another." When the father is in his 40s and the son is between 17 and 22, "the work relationship is relatively problematic.   When the father is in his 50s and the son is between 23 and 33, the work relationship is relatively harmonious. . . . When the father is in his 60s and the son is between 34 and 40, the work relationship is relatively problematic."[3]

Psychologists tell us that rebellion against the parent is a normal phase of a child's development. When the parent is also the boss and the source of economic sustenance to an adult child, this phase may be repressed. In one instance, a son who could not express his anger against his father (boss) acted out his anger against his wife, who in turn was jealous of her father-in-law. The marriage ended in divorce.

According to psychiatrist/organizational authority Harry Levinson, father-son rivalry is a unique problem. "The father wants the sons to serve him and to allow him to remain the head of the business as long as he possibly can. . . . In my experience, only very few fathers have stepped aside before they were compelled to do so. The father often communicates to the sons that he is building the business for them, that it is going to be theirs, and that they should not be demanding of either appropriate salary or appropriate power because they are going to get it all anyway in due time. Nor should they leave the father and the business because it is self-evident that he has been good to them and is going to give them so much. Thus they are manipulated into an ambivalent position of wanting to become their own persons with mature, adult independence on the one hand, and the wish to take of what they are being offered on the other. If they leave, seemingly they will be ungrateful. If they threaten to depose the father or demand to share his power, then they will indeed destroy him. If they don't do as he says, then they are disloyal and unappreciative sons."[4]

Levinson views this conflict as so pervasive that he offers this advice: "In general, the wisest course of any business, family or non-family, is to move to professional management as quickly as possible."[5]

A move to outside management would, of course, eliminate one of the major incentives of owners—to work in their businesses and control their destinies. Other psychologists take more optimistic viewpoints about resolving intergenerational conflicts. Wilfred E. Calmas says, "It is true that chronic problems are not resolved quickly or easily; but if there is a commitment for resolution, then resolution can be accomplished over a period of time via the consultative method" (i.e., obtaining the help of the right consultant).[6]

Deborah L. Slobodnick, a Boston-based family business consultant, feels that in many cases intergenerational conflict may be resolved by the passage of time, usually when the heir is in his mid-30s. She indicates that the heir must first attain the following prerequisites:

• The heir has established a new family beyond his/her family of origin which serves as the primary emotional support system.
• The heir feels competent in his/her professional life and has established outside-of-work interests.
• The heir has given up the romantic ideals of youth regarding relationships, parents' omnipotence, and the like.
• The heir has resolved his/her own sexual identity.
• The heir has "forgiven the parents" for not being perfect people. The easiest means to that end is for the heir to have become a parent, too.
• The heir is ready to feel a genuine compassion for his/her parents as individuals with real needs, fears, and dreams.[7]

Business differences between father and son often manifest themselves in the following ways:

• The father is most comfortable in an atmosphere of ambiguity which allows him to "call the shots" as situations occur, rather than being bound by clearly defined rules; the son wants and needs clear direction.
• The father is often most comfortable deferring decision making to the last possible moment; the son wants decisiveness.
• The father wants to exercise total control; the son wants freedom and independence to assume responsibility on his own.
• The father, having taken his risks in the early years, becomes aversive to new risks that might threaten his financial security. The son often has the entrepreneurial urge to conquer the world.

A son tells the story of his relationship with his father, who was the senior partner of a substantial law firm. "I loved my father, and it was always my ambition to become a lawyer and join his practice. It was one of his and my happiest days when I passed the bar and joined his firm. It was horrible. He was a member of the old school when practicing law was a genteel profession, and it was somehow beneath his dignity to ask a client to pay his bill or to recognize that there is a business side to practicing law. I couldn't get through to him that today's environment requires more businesslike practices. After five years, I couldn't take it any more and left to start my own firm. He accused me of jumping ship just as he was getting older and needed me, and for several years my beloved father didn't speak to me. We reconciled before he died, but it was the worst experience of my life—worse than a divorce."

Having seen many loving and successful father-son relationships in business, we take a more optimistic view than some that have been expressed. We believe that severe situations should be confronted at the earliest opportunity and resolution sought, possibly with third-party intervention. In the event that this is unsuccessful, the son is usually better off to leave and seek other opportunities. Sometimes, with the passage of time, the son is able to return, and a harmonious relationship is developed.

Unfortunately, we also see many situations where the battle goes on, causing misery to all until something gives. In one situation, a son made this sad statement: "Fortunately, my father died one year after I joined the firm."[8]

A grandson tells of his family's experience in this excerpt from "Elegy for My Grandfather":

> You hulked huge in your chair
> While highways reeled your salesmen off like film
> What a show you ran, director, chairman,
> Swiveling Ptolemy. Out of pride
> You hoarded business secrets like a warehouse,
> Wouldn't trust your son, called president
> For seven years of mocking letterheads,
> To learn your face, much less your trade.
> You'd forced him to resign in '21
> When, out of college, coach and teacher, not
> An underling, he joined the firm.
> You put him on the road,
> Framed him for sport and hunger, kept the wheel
> Yourself.
> By all that's holy in America
> What spectacle, what scope, what unmatched gall.
> I'm glad you're dead. My father's freedom sings
> Like a high wind over broken shells.
> He combs his strand under the parching year.[9]

SIBLING RIVALRY

When his father died and Alexander the Great ascended the throne, he ordered all real or imagined rivals put to death. Although many siblings in family businesses would like to adopt a similar approach, modern society frowns upon it, so they find different ways.

The Horvitz brothers of Cleveland, Ohio, were heirs to the real estate, newspaper, and cable television empire of their father, the tough, hard-drinking founder. All in their 60s, Harry, Leonard, and William Horvitz had been fighting for 10 years about who would control the business that they had inherited. Their battles became so fierce that their headquarters were sometimes known as "the bunker."

One of their arguments centered around the salary of Harry's son, Peter, who was an employee of one of the family's newspapers. Harry, seeing no other way to make his point, kicked Leonard in the groin. Leonard responded by punching his brother in the eye. When the brothers were asked about their situation, Leonard said: "What we inherited is a curse." Peter commented: "Decisions were based on how the brothers felt when they were 12." Harry made the saddest comment in one of the family newspapers: "Do I love my brothers? Probably not. I didn't have anything to do with their birth. That was my mother and father. My relationship to my brothers is an accident of birth."[10] The business ultimately had to be sold.

Instead of childhood arguing about toys, siblings now contest for bigger stakes—power, status, and money. It's little wonder that quarrels among siblings result in family business tragedies that are lose-lose situations for everyone. Prominent family business consultant Léon A. Danco observed that perhaps the only way to succeed in this area is to be "the competent only son of an only son."[11]

Experts tell us that sibling jealousy is rooted in the deep desire of children for the exclusive love of their parents. Underlying this is the child's concern that if the parent shows love and attention to a sibling, maybe the sibling is worth more, and the child is worth less.[12] The feelings may be intensified by the parents' insistence that the siblings be "good friends" even though they don't like each other. An older brother, dominant as a child by virtue of age and size, is resented by his siblings. A sister is jealous of her sister's perceived beauty or is forced to be "the good one" to compensate for her sister's bad behavior.[13]

Sibling rivalry is normal. The issue is whether it's allowed to dictate the behavior of siblings and become a destructive force that threatens the survival of the business.

The Koch family of Wichita, Kansas, owners of a giant oil and chemical company and one of the wealthiest families in America, were the center of a family blow-up centered around their sons. Fred, the oldest, never entered the family business but became a patron of the arts in New York. (He was later disinherited by his father for that sin.) Charles, who was most like his hard-driving father, was followed into the business four years later by fraternal twins, David and Bill.

As a child, Bill envied Charles' athletic ability and considered himself "the family nerd." Their parents sent Charles away to boarding school at age 11 because, as his mother explained it, "We had to get Charles away because of the terrible jealousy that was consuming Billy."

When they grew up and Charles was running the company, Bill tried and failed to take control of the company. He was fired, after which he sued his brother and the company. One executive commented, "I don't think that the litigation had anything to do with money." Charles said, "I feel sorry for Billy. He has everything in the world—a big art collection, yachts, and consultants who fawn over him. Yet he is miserable. And he creates misery in his wake." Bill's final words on the matter were, "I wish I had left the family company a long, long time ago. The best thing that happened to me personally was to get fired. Before, my identity was subservient to Koch Industries and my family. Now I have my own identity, and I am doing my own thing."

Sometimes owners unwittingly exacerbate sibling rivalry by promoting open competition among family members in the business. Even among unrelated parties, the value of competition as a motivating force is questionable. Social psychologist Elliot Aronson observed, "The American mind in particular has been trained to equate success with victory, to equate doing well with beating someone. Studies, however, are proving, with astonishing regularity . . . that making one person's success depend on another's failure—which is what competition involves by definition—simply does not make the grade. Superior performances does not require competition; it usually requires its absence."[14]

Competition among siblings can't always be avoided, particularly when more than one child aspires to succeed the owner as boss; however, if the business is large enough, rivalry can be minimized by separation of roles, with siblings responsible for their own areas of responsibility. It may also be advisable to separate their jobs geographically if possible. This helps children to focus on their own jobs and not on those of their siblings.

Rewards, such as compensation and titles, should be defined on an objective basis, in advance, to reduce the emotional impact if one sibling should surpass another. Also, if you have an independent board of directors, their involvement can help to provide objectivity to important decisions such as major promotions and management succession, thereby reducing the emotional impact of a parent choosing among children.

Siblings themselves can prevent rivalry from becoming a destructive force by recognizing its capacity for harm and by agreeing on a code of behavior that recognizes their mutual dependence and establishes a process for resolution of differences, possibly with the help of the independent board of directors. This, of course, requires their commitment to put their personal agendas secondary to the best interests of the business.

One of the most publicized family business blow-outs of our time involved the Bingham family of Louisville, Kentucky, who owned a newspaper and television empire. After extended battles among his son and two daughters, Barry Bingham, Sr. sold the business. After the debacle he said, "In bringing up my children, I somehow didn't manage to get across to them that people have to make compromises."

An owner of a family business put it this way to his children: "We have a fine business. If you take care of it, it will provide you, your children, and your grandchildren with many of the good things in life. If you spend your time watching each other, rather than tending to the business, you'll destroy both the company and your livelihoods."

Family Strategic Planning

We believe that a family can improve its chances of success by planning its future together, establishing clear policies governing its relationship with the business, and delineating the responsibilities of family members. The process is called *family strategic planning*, and it can help families to approach their business in a unified way, rather than as a group of individuals who happen to be related. Such planning can be valuable both in building the business and in helping family members to cope with the inevitable stresses that go with the territory.

Family strategic planning consists of:

- Forming your family council.
- Addressing the critical issues relating to family involvement with the business.
- Articulating your family's policies and values in your "family creed."
- Monitoring your progress and maintaining regular communication through periodic meetings.

COMMUNICATION IS THE KEY

If there is to be open communication, the owner, from his position of authority in both business and family, must take the lead. Planning and communication, however, are not the long suits of many owners, who are often reluctant to rock the boat by bringing up sensitive family issues and possibly instigating unpleasant conflict. Often they "let sleeping dogs lie," unaware that many family conflicts, which may be resolvable in the early stages, can fester and escalate into full-scale family warfare in the future.

The secretive management styles of many owners can be frustrating to their families. We've seen adult children in the business who don't have a clue as to its sales volume, much less its profitability. One father constantly reassures his son that he's being groomed as his successor, but the son says, "I'm worried that I won't be in a position to replace him because he keeps me totally in the dark about this company. I run the second most profitable division, but I don't even set or control my own budget."[15]

The owner is often the principal victim of the close-to-the-vest style. Rather than sharing family-related business problems with his family and gaining their support in resolving them, he bears the burden alone. The kids, who love and respect their parent and would like to help, are precluded from raising questions for fear that their motives will be interpreted as being self-serving. Picture a child saying to the father, "Who are you going to leave your stock to when you die, Dad? . . . Dad? . . . Dad?"

In these circumstances, the charade goes on; speculation is often rampant, and frustrations and tensions build. John Bradshaw, an authority on family counseling, referred to these as "the open secrets. Everybody knows about them, and nobody is supposed to know that everybody knows."[16]

The mixture of family and business is difficult and complex in the best of circumstances, and impossible in the worst. However, if owners and their spouses meet with their children and share their thinking and if the children have a forum to express their views openly and participate in policymaking, many families can develop unified approaches to the business. Even if all family members don't agree on every issue, they at least have a voice in the process, and they understand the ground rules.

FORMING YOUR FAMILY COUNCIL

A *family council* provides a forum for family members to express their aspirations, views, and concerns (perhaps for the first time), and allows them to participate in policy-making. This doesn't mean that the business becomes a democracy or that the owner gives up his prerogative of having the final word. In our experience, however, family councils usually act responsibly, and it's rarely necessary for owners to exercise their veto powers. In this context, at least philosophically, it becomes a *family* business rather than "Dad's business." Family members are apt to gain a greater understanding of the owner's perspective and a greater realization that the business not only provides rewards but also demands responsibility.

In severely conflicted families where the blood is already flowing, the value of planning is generally limited by members' inability to communicate constructively. As one sibling put it, "How can we work out a plan? I can't stand to be in the same room with my brother." These families are usually better off getting help from a family business consultant or psychologist to resolve their differences before commencing the planning process.

"Normal" families, however, share a common bond of affection, are able to communicate with each other, and can resolve differences among themselves.[17] Family strategic planning offers these families a practical way to address their aspirations and concerns openly and to establish policy governing their relationship with the business. The chances of misunderstandings are greatly reduced when the rules are clear, and the rules are more apt to be respected when they are arrived at through consensus rather than edict. Open communication not only enhances a family's chances of preserving harmony, but it also forms a sound foundation for the business's strategic plan, which will be described in Chapter 5.

The composition of the family council is a matter of preference. Some prefer to limit inclusion to family members who are active in the business; however, unless there are strong reasons to the contrary, the council is most effective when both active and inactive family members *and their spouses* are members. Directly or indirectly, all family members have a stake in the business, and because spouses are usually going to find out what went on anyway, it's better that they get the story firsthand and accurately. One daughter-in-law who had a reputation as a troublemaker commented, "It's been an eye-opening experience for me. I never really understood what was going on."

Don't wait too long to get started. Family council meetings should start as soon as the kids are old enough to enter the business. In one instance, the owner's 27-year-old daughter had been in the business for five years. When her younger brother, who was in his junior year at college, indicated that he was interested in working at the business for the summer, his sister said, "It's OK, but don't touch my desk." The owner decided it was time to start.

A Family Retreat

An ideal way to start your family council is with a one-day family retreat at a quiet place away from the shop. This may be a good time to use the vacation cabin in the woods, or perhaps it's an opportunity to take the family away for a weekend vacation together. In addition to providing a relaxed environment for family members to discuss your future in a constructive way, the retreat provides a forum in which you can draft your *family creed*. (To be discussed later.)

A Facilitator Can Help

An experienced family business consultant can be helpful in getting your family council off on the right foot by facilitating the retreat. This provides an objective and seasoned perspective to guide the process and to set the tone for future meetings. The facilitator's role is to provide guidance and structure so that the retreat becomes a constructive and organized process rather than a bull or gripe session, and his experience can help the family in their choices of alternative paths of action. The decisions, of course, are made by the family.

The Meeting

The owner should make it clear at the outset that "anything goes" and that all family members are free to express whatever is on their minds. He should also make it clear that he is at the meeting as a participant and not as parent/boss. In this environment, family members have an opportunity to get pent up emotional baggage on the table, to dispose of it if possible, and to establish family policy. In our experience, this has never resulted in unpleasant confrontations or gripe sessions, and families have often been able to settle problems that they didn't know existed. In one session, two daughters, who were not active in the business, brought an extra supply of facial tissues because they were convinced that it would be a crying session. Although they were on the board of directors, they had never been offered the same opportunities in the business as their brother, and they resented his patronizing and "bullying" attitude at board meetings. Once allowed to surface, their concerns were addressed, and the family was able to get on the same wave length.

If you can reach agreement on the critical issues, your family will establish a strong foundation for future understanding. If not, you will at least have identified the issues and should be able to work toward future resolution.

The Critical Issues

In addition to issues unique to your situation, your family strategic plan should generally deal with the following questions:

The Family's Mission

- What are the family's aspirations for the business? Do we want to keep it in the family? Sell it eventually? Be acquired? Go public?

Management Standards for the Business

- In the management of the business, which should be paramount . . . the best interests of the family . . . the best interests of the business . . . or some combination?

Involvement of Family Members in the Business

- What should be the criteria for entry into the business?
- Should in-laws be allowed to enter?
- How should family members be compensated?
- How should they be evaluated?
- What if they don't perform up to appropriate standards?
- How will the roles of family members in the business be determined?

Ownership of Stock in the Business

- Who will be allowed to own stock in the company?
- Who should have voting control?
- Who should share in the future appreciation of the stock?
- What should be our dividend policy?
- What will happen to stock ownership in the next generation?
- Should we differentiate between family members who are active in the business and those who are inactive?

Management Succession

- What should be the criteria for selecting the next leader?
- When will the transition take place?
- What should be done if the choice is wrong?
- What are the owner's aspirations in retirement?
- How can we help him to achieve them?
- How can we insure the owner's financial security in retirement?

Relationships with Each Other

- What responsibilities do we have to each other?
- How can we best attain an atmosphere that enhances mutual respect and support?
- How should we deal with differences between family members?

Other

- Should we have an independent board of directors?
- If so, how should our family relate to it?
- How can we protect the security of loyal and valuable employees?
- What are our responsibilities to the community?

Your family's responses to these questions should be articulated in your family creed.

Your Family Creed

After the Revolutionary War, the wise money said that the United States wouldn't last a year. After all, the northern constituency consisted of industrial and nonslave states, and the southern constituency of agrarian and slave states, and it appeared that the new federation would quickly deteriorate once the bickering started.

The framers of the U.S. Constitution, however, had different ideas, and in their wisdom they were able to capture the common values and aspirations in the form of that ingenious document. A family, with the benefit of love, affection, and exposure to common values that accompanies growing up together, has an easier task. However, the need for the articulation of their aspirations and policies is just as great.

It can be captured in a document that we call *a family creed*, which spells out your family's values and basic policies in relation to the business and becomes your family's strategic plan. We recommend that it be reviewed at least annually and that it be subject to expansion and amendment as necessary. Many families, after a day-long retreat, are able to develop the first draft of their family creed, which is later ratified by all family members at a future meeting.

Here, with their permission, is the creed of a family that owns a newspaper business:

OUR FAMILY CREED

Preamble

From many open discussions among us regarding our family values and our aspirations for both our family and our business, most recently crystalized at our family retreat, we have agreed on certain binding principles and practices in the highest and best interests of harmony in our family and the opportunity for a brilliant future in the newspaper business for all those involved.

This Creed is drawn and agreed to in sensitive recognition of our Company's rapid growth, its loyal staff, its public responsibility, and the challenging fact that less than 15 percent of successful family businesses make it through the third generation. Our third generation is just now being born, and we want to allow them the same opportunities that we have enjoyed, should they so choose.

Our Agreement

Management Philosophy and Objectives

Our Company will be managed by a strategic management philosophy that combines the highest journalistic and business principles. Our highest priority will be the best interests of our customers.

We view our Company as a valued family heritage with immense potential for growth. We want to continue it as a family-owned business, with the understanding that our priorities lie more in honoring our responsibility to the public than the profit or economic return for family members. We believe that if we honor this trust and run our business properly the economic return will follow.

We will not compromise sound business principles for expediency in the family. The security of our employees and our family depends upon the integrity of this commitment, and each of us herewith commits, in good faith, *never*, for any reason, to place pressure on company officials or its board of directors for dividends, company jobs, or other benefits beyond what company

---

management and the board in its sole discretion feel are consistent with the above stated objectives.

Positions in the Company

Family members who have a great enthusiasm for journalism and who first gain at least one year's experience in another news organization will be welcomed to work full-time in the Company. Entry into the business will be an opportunity and not a birthright, and family members will be held to higher levels of commitment and performance than employees.

We agree that *no one, least of all a family member*, should be in this Company unless they have a passionate enthusiasm for their work and demonstrate excellence in their work. In the event that a family member's performance does not consistently measure up to this criteria, he/she may be requested to leave.

In order to limit the potential for future conflict, we hereby agree that, with all love and respect, no in-laws shall hold positions in the company.

Leadership

Selection of the next chief executive officer will be based on professional competence. It is our hope and desire that a family member will accede to this position, and we pledge our positive and full support to that person even if we may have preferred another choice. We have established that our next leader should satisfy the following criteria:

- Must have leadership qualities, the ability to command respect among employees and family members, and vision for the company's future.
- Must have solid newspaper experience and be an appropriate ambassador to our readers, the community, and the business world.
- Must have a proven track record of performance.

Compensation of Family Members

Family members who work in the business will be compensated on the same basis as their peers in the newspaper industry. They will participate in the same performance evaluation process that is accorded employees, including at least one annual written evaluation to be reviewed by the board of directors.

Voting Control and Stock Ownership

Only bloodline family members and their direct bloodline descendants may own stock in the Company or vote. Voting control will be vested *only* in family members who are personally active as employees in the business or in a voting trust. No stock in the Company may be sold or transferred by any family member, other than to direct bloodline descendants, without first being offered for sale back to the company at an independently appraised value.

Board of Directors

We support the principle of independent, outside members serving on our board of directors to provide objectivity, experience, and community representation to guide the company's growth. Outside professionals regularly retained to provide services to the Company shall not be board members.

Family members who serve in management positions in the company shall be eligible to serve on the board. Other bloodline family members who express interest may be invited as ad hoc guests to ask questions or make suggestions for board action. Any conflict among the family on any business issue whatsoever will be resolved by the sole and final judgment of the CEO and/or board of directors.

Communication

We will continue to have open and candid communication within the family. This will include at least one annual meeting of our "Family Council," which shall include in-laws and children who are ready to begin an understanding of the Company.

We will respect the opinions of other family members even if we don't agree with them. In the event of disagreements, we commit to constructive resolution that places the best interests of the Company and the family over our own preferences.

Our Employees

The success of our enterprise would not have been possible without our devoted, loyal, and hard-working employees. We are committed to the continuance of an environment that values their contribution, treats them with respect, and provides them with appropriate rewards and benefits.

Amendment of This Creed

We will together review this Family Creed from time to time (at least every five years) and will amend or modify it only by majority vote of family bloodline members over the age of 21. Although this is not a legally binding document, unless it is amended, we pledge to support it without reservation and to enforce it among our children to the best of our ability.

We agree that this Creed is adopted, effective as of this date.

Prevention and Resolution of Conflict

There are some who accept family conflict as inevitable. "People don't change," they say. Experts tell us, however, that while people themselves may not change, behavioral patterns *are* susceptible to change. Heavy smokers learn to quit, obese people lose weight, and people with hair-trigger tempers learn to control themselves.

Behaviorists tell us that in order for this to happen, these factors must be present: you must have a definite objective, you must commit to the objective, and you must be willing to confront the obstacles.

Conflict is inherent in the family-business scene, and there is often no right or wrong answer to differing viewpoints. The question is whether you manage *it* or it manages *you*. We believe that family strategic planning can help to establish an environment of openness, mutual respect, and cooperation that prevents or minimizes debilitating conflict, and that it can help a family to preserve the business so that they and future generations can enjoy the benefits of the hard work and sacrifice that made it possible.

Your family council can establish ground rules that family members can follow to resolve differences in a constructive manner. In the event that the differences are major and can't be worked out, a method of adjudication can be established, perhaps with the help of the board of directors or with the help of a family business consultant.

The Future
The retreat should be the beginning rather than the end of family communication. A timetable should be set for future meetings, which can be for two or three hours rather than a full day. Some families have annual day-long meetings with guest speakers. Responsibility for organization and leadership of the meetings can be rotated among family members, and you may want to invite the company lawyer, CPA, or insurance agent as guests to explain topics of interest. If you have an independent board of directors, a joint meeting with them can also be productive. In our experience, families that approach their future together, having clearly defined their goals and policies, have a considerably higher chance of success than those who just react to events.

SUMMARY

• Lasting family businesses are generally owned by strong families who usually share common characteristics.

• Father-son conflict is often a barrier to harmony in the family and continuity of the business into the next generation. Sometimes it is resolved by the passage of time and the happening of certain life events, and, if the willingness exists, it may be ameliorated by third-party intervention.

• Sibling rivalry is a common cause of conflict in the family. It may be controlled if siblings have an awareness of its potential for harm and are willing to compromise to prevent their personal feelings from damaging the business and disrupting harmony in the family.

• Family strategic planning is an organized process whereby a family can express its aspirations and orchestrate its relationship to the business. The establishment of a family council allows adult family members to participate in the process and helps to achieve a cohesive family approach to the business.

• The family's strategic plan can be articulated in a *family creed*, which spells out the family's aspirations and values, and delineates basic ground rules relating to the family's ownership and involvement in the business.

• The establishment of a family council and the development of the family creed can be effective barriers to conflict in the family by providing a forum for resolution of differences and the setting of clear rules of conduct for family members.

NOTES

1. Nick Stinnett and John DeFrain, *Secrets of Strong Families* (Boston: Little, Brown, 1986).
2. J. Davis, "The Influence of Life Stage on Father-Son Work Relationships in the Family Firm," dissertation, Graduate School of Business Administration, Harvard University, 1982.
3. J. A. Davis and R. Tagiuri, "The Influence of Life Stage on Father-Son Work Relationships in Family Companies," *Family Business Review*, Spring 1989.
4. Harry Levinson, "Consulting with Family Business: What to Look for, What to Look Out for," *Organizational Dynamics*, Summer 1983, p. 74.
5. Harry Levinson, "Conflicts That Plague Family Business," *Harvard Business Review*, March–April 1971.
6. Wilfred E. Calmas, "Increasing the Survival Rate of Family Business," Family Business conference at the Wharton School, Philadelphia, Pennsylvania, October 29–31, 1986.
7. Deborah L. Slobodnik, letter to Benjamin Benson, February 21, 1989.
8. L. B. Barnes and S. A. Hershon, "Transferring Power in the Family Business," *Harvard Business Review*, July–August 1976, pp. 105–14.
9. Segment of "Elegy for My Grandfather," from *The Diving Bell*, by Dabney Stuart, (A. A. Knopf, 1966) reprinted by permission of the author.
10. Lisa Gubernick and Ralph King, Jr., "The Ultimate Family Feud," *Forbes*, June 29, 1987, pp. 80–81.
11. Leon Danco, *Beyond Survival* (Cleveland: Center of Family Business, 1975), p. 53.
12. Adele Faber and Elaine Mazlish, *Siblings without Rivalry* (New York: W. W. Norton, 1987), p. 15.
13. Ibid.
14. Alfie Kohn, "How to Succeed without Even Vying," *Psychology Today*, September 1986, p. 22.
15. "The SOBs," *Across the Board*, May 1980, p. 28.
16. John Bradshaw, *Bradshaw on the Family* (Deerfield Beach, Fla.: *Health Communications Inc.*, 1988), p. 87.
17. F. Walsh, *Normal Family Processes* (New York: Guilford Press, 1982).

CHAPTER 4

FROM LIGHT BULB
TO ENLIGHTENMENT

At some time in the life cycle of virtually every organization, its ability to succeed in spite of itself runs out.[1]

Richard H. Brien

As a business matures and greater reliance is placed on employees, the CEO's management style must change to keep up with the differing needs of the business as it grows.

Individuals go through multiple stages of growth and development including birth, childhood, adolescence, adulthood, career, and retirement. Family businesses also go through predictable stages and are subject to many varieties of change. The changing life cycle of its products, competitive factors, the personal growth of the owner, and the family's changing needs all influence the outcome. Frequently, the most difficult hurdle is the need for owners to adapt their management styles to the differing needs of larger and more complex businesses. As will be described in Chapter 5, if the business is to flourish, "seat of the pants" management methods must be replaced with organized, planned methods of operation, and, as described in Chapter 3, the family's role must be carefully defined.

Management authority Peter F. Drucker put it this way, "The only things that evolve by themselves in an organization are disorder, friction, and malperformance. What is needed is a leader who recognizes that change is needed and who takes control of the process, rather than reacting to the inevitable crises."

Change does not come overnight or without some pain. Some owners intuitively adapt. Others, unable or unwilling to change, either limit the potential of their businesses unknowingly or preside over the decline of the businesses that they have worked so hard to build.

THE FIRST STAGE: LIGHT BULB

In this stage, the light bulb goes on; the owner has an idea and takes it to market. Frequently, the idea is an outgrowth of the owner's previous business experience. (What often distinguishes entrepreneurs is their ability to integrate experiences so that they see opportunity where others only see a sequence of events.)

For example, an entrepreneur managed a video rental store in a downtown mall. To diversify and increase revenues, he added personal computers to the rental inventory, anticipating that individuals might rent personal computers (PCs) for personal use as they did videos. The biggest renters of PCs turned out to be other small businesses in the same mall. The entrepreneur "sees" the light bulb: There's a market opportunity to sell PCs at wholesale prices to small businesses who can't afford retail prices.

Another example: Ray Kroc sees a multiple milk shake machine at a stand and wonders if hamburgers could be made that way. Voila! McDonald's and the fast food industry are born.

Everyone who has started a business understands the filaments of the light bulb stage. The founder:

- Identifies a market need (e.g., wholesale PCs and fast food).
- Develops/invents/constructs/buys a service or product to meet that need.
- Seeks and finds capital.
- Builds an organization to sell and provide the product/service.

This stage is frequently characterized by the following:

- *A small, dedicated owner-employee team who are tireless, committed, and excited.* (Survival is at stake, and nothing is taken for granted.)
- Focus on growing sales and generating revenue.
- Chronic undercapitalization.
- High levels of frustration and fun: "It's hard to get things done because we're figuring it out as we go. *But* what could be more fun?"
- Congenial chaos and disorganization. (Improvisation is the name of the game. However, the business is still small, and the chaos

is controllable because the owner is personally on top of everything.)

- A family feeling in the company (whether employees are family members or not); and shared highs and lows.
- Cohesion of the underdog: "We try harder; we're mean and lean."
- Absence of specialization. There are no job descriptions because everyone does everything.
- Ad hoc decision making: "We'll figure it out when we have to."
- Matchbook planning: "It's hard to figure out how today will end, impossible to plan for tomorrow."

Given a good idea, a receptive market, and enough capital to deliver the product and make the payroll, many businesses survive this first stage on pure gusto and adrenaline.

The Owner

In the first stage, the owner is frequently:

- Involved with every task, from negotiating a bank loan to sweeping the floor.
- Willing to take risks, make investments, bet the ranch.
- Afraid that the business will fail. This leads to high control, absolute hands-on management, and a belief that "if you want a job done right, do it yourself."
- Guilty about putting the family security at risk and not spending time with the family.

During this stage, owners will often focus on what they know best in order to reduce the tension. If their background is sales, they'll typically give highest priority to marketing and sales. If they're engineers, they're more apt to concentrate on product development. Often the founder's "taking comfort in the familiar" determines whether the business will be sales driven or product driven.

The Family

During this stage of growth, owners will often involve family members to bring them closer to the business. Their involvement at this point is often as a "helper" (e.g., a wife helps with the books or a husband helps with collections) rather than as a member of the management team. The family also shares in the owner's sacrifice as he becomes almost an absentee husband/father while he commits his life to building the business.

Surviving the Light Bulb Stage

Most entrepreneurs love the excitement and challenge of the light bulb stage. Here the "good old days', bad old days' stories" stories originate. It's the classic western movie, with the newcomer fighting the establishment and prevailing against heavy odds. But once established, where do you go from there? If the business is to achieve its potential, the survival methods that were so successful in the light bulb stage must be replaced with methods more suited to the needs of a growing business. The following changes are needed:

• *Activity to results.* It's easy and seductive to confuse activity with results in the early stages. Sales activity can cloud the fact that the profit margins are insufficient; overutilized equipment can mask an inability to move the product out the door; long hours make up for inadequate administration and accounting systems that were built by patchwork. In the next phase, the focus must change to *results.*

• *Chaos to organization.* Founders often start their own enterprises because they are repelled by the structure and bureaucracy of big business. Consequently, the "chaos" that is endemic to the first phase of growth can be a tonic to the founder: If something needs doing, you just do it without waiting for approval. There are no committees or forms, and everyone loves their image of being fast-moving.

With this mindset, it's no wonder that founders resist any attempt at structure (e.g., planning, job descriptions, budgets, and organization charts) which they see as bureaucratic trappings to be avoided at all costs. While excessive structure is inappropriate at this or any stage of growth, the owner cannot be on top of everything anymore, and there is now a need for more structure and organization.

• The future of the business should be charted in specific terms; an enlightened and constructive environment must be established to bring out the best in the employees; proper accounting systems established, and cost controls put into place. This will be discussed further in Chapters 5 and 6.

• *Hands-on to thumbs-on.* If the founder continues to wear all the hats in the business and insists on being involved with every detail, the business never develops beyond his/her own capacity to be personally involved.

Many founders have a low level of trust for the abilities of others to do the job right and are unable to give up the involvement with every task that characterized the first phase of growth. To get to the next phase, the founder must make the transition from hands on (i.e., "I do it all myself") to thumbs on (i.e., "I know about everything even if I don't do it"). Consider the alternatives: As C. D. Cavour put it, "The man who trusts other men will make fewer mistakes than he who distrusts them."

• *Family helpers to family contributors.* It's dangerous to keep family members on as helpers for too long. Helpers are perceived as having little value by others and are difficult to manage because they are volunteers. If you need a family member's skills, time, or "hands," make your expectations of them clear and compensate them for their work. In other words, in the next stage, family members should be treated on a par with other employees.

The first stage of growth is the most dynamic and often the most fun. Many businesses never grow beyond the first phase and become perpetual start-ups. This may satisfy all of the founder's needs, but if the business is to continue to the next level of growth, new methods are needed.

THE SECOND STAGE: BRIGHT LIGHTS

Business Implications
As the second stage of growth begins, it dawns on the owner that:

- "This is a real business!"
- "Employees, customers, vendors, and lots of people depend on me to make this business work."
- "This business can be a great opportunity for my kids."
- "Someday, we've got to get organized."

The "bright lights" of the second growth stage generally occur when the business has achieved financial equilibrium, sales have stabilized, and there is no longer week-to-week concern about meeting the payroll and paying suppliers.

Once the work force reaches approximately 20 to 30 employees, many of the previously effective procedures don't work any more, and they become organizational and management nightmares. For example, bills go out late, and collections lag. Employees don't appear to be motivated and mistakes are frequent. The owner can't watch everything as in the old days.

Some of the fun starts to disappear, and the owner realizes that something should be done, but what? He doesn't know any other way to manage, so he just works harder. As the sage said, "It's hard to remember when you're up to your ass in alligators that the reason you're there is to drain the swamp."

This stage is a crossroads; some businesses will organize for growth and set the foundation for the fourth stage, "enlightenment." Others who fail to adapt are candidates for the third, "dimming lights" stage, which often have the following characteristics:

• *Top line growth without corresponding growth in profit.* Many businesses in this stage focus on bringing in business with the mistaken belief that if you have enough sales, profit will take care of itself. Without a system to monitor profitability or control costs, the bottom line is often a disappointing revelation at the end of the year. "I can't understand it," an owner will say. "We sold a ton of product last year. Where did the money go?"

• *Overall lack of systems or structure.* Most businesses in this stage lack adequate organizational structures, regular communication, planning, budgeting, or effective human resources policies. This is probably the answer to the owner's lament about where the money went. There may be duplication of effort, confusion about responsibilities among employees, and inadequate cost controls, and nobody but the boss can make a decision.

• *Growth of the management group.* With the growth of the business, new managers are needed. Whether promoted from the ranks or hired from outside, talented managers seek an atmosphere where they will be granted authority and allowed to assume responsibility. Owners who develop talented managers can establish a framework that helps to carry the business to the next level. If not, the talented people generally leave, and the boss remains with the entire burden.

• *Attempts at expansion and diversification.* As founders gain confidence in the core business, many expand or diversify. Additional products may be added; the plant may be expanded, or perhaps new lines of business sought. Often, however, these attempts fail because there is insufficient management talent to successfully integrate the new endeavors.

• *Stabs at "professionalization" that don't work.* Advisors may convince the owner to develop a strategic plan or adopt more formalized human resources procedures. This smacks of bureaucracy to him, but to appease them he agrees to "give it a shot." Half-hearted attempts are made; the owner torpedoes them, and then says, "See, I told you that it wouldn't work."

• *Lack of clear long-term planning.* Still in the "survival" mindset, owners often immerse themselves in day-to-day operations. While their intuition, drive, and business smarts frequently allow them to exploit opportunities, they rarely take the time to conceptualize the future of their business. As one owner put it: "My idea of long term is tomorrow morning."

• *Lack of organization.* From the owner down, each manager is too busy "doing" to step back and determine how efficiently the organization is functioning. A manager with a clean desk who took some time to think about the bigger picture would be perceived as having taken a day off.

The boss's unwillingness to delegate creates bottlenecks at all levels. For example, Marv, a brilliant engineer with a talent for innovation, started a printing business 20 years ago. His ability to design new, innovative equipment has helped the company to become a leader in its niche, and the company's sales have reached the $10-million mark. However, foreign competition is intensifying; profits are declining, and there is excessive turnover among key people. It's not unusual to hear a manager say, "This place succeeds in spite of itself and in spite of the boss."

Marv's response is to cut back on advertising and marketing (just when the company needs it most) and to increase his time in the plant working on difficult orders and rebuilding and retrofitting equipment for new applications. "After all," he reasons, "this worked before, and it should work again." The rest of the business more or less manages itself, with nobody but Marv being empowered to make a decision. So despite the company's competitive advantage, the company's management deficiencies threaten its market position and perhaps its survival.

The owner is usually still doing what he likes and does best. The business has grown since the start-up phase, and perhaps he senses that it's out of control. His individual effort doesn't seem to be enough any more, and he often tries to assign blame: "My people don't know what hard work is. . . . If I want something done right, I have to do it myself." In order to deal with this perception, he exerts even more personal control than before, rather than taking the steps that would lead to improved management of the business.

The need is for the owner to change from "doer" to leader/manager and to recognize that his primary role is to establish direction, establish a committed and competent organization, and then get out of the way so that employees can do the job. Some owners are able to make this transition and proceed to build enduring and successful organizations.

Many, however, resist leaving their line activities because it's not as much fun and excitement as the "good old days" when the business was starting out. It's not unusual for some to sell the business and start over again.

The Kids Enter the Scene
Often, during this stage, the children have grown up and are starting to enter the business. With a more current grasp on rapidly changing technology, a more formal view of management technique, and new objectivity, they often push for more professionalized management, or as one child in this situation said, "emergence from the dark ages."

Sometimes the owner is receptive, and the company moves toward more organized management; sometimes it's a losing battle, and the children, if they don't leave the company, must wait until the owner retires or dies to institute the necessary changes . . . if the business lasts that long.

THE THIRD STAGE: DIMMING LIGHTS

This stage only applies to a business that has not gotten its act together in the second stage. *Although the momentum of the first stage and the talent and hard work of the founder may carry the business through the second stage, in the third stage the chickens generally come home to roost*. Even in the best of circumstances, a successful business suffers growing pains as growth tests its management ability, physical capacity, systems and controls, and the ability of its people to meet new and often more complex problems.

The alternatives are clear: if yours is a growing business and you don't plan for orderly growth and adapt your organization to the needs of a larger business, you'd better be good at crisis management because you'll have plenty of opportunity to practice it.

In the "dimming lights" stage, the situation often progresses from irritation and frustration to crisis as a way of life. Missed deadlines, deterioration in product quality, and indifference by employees now become apparent to the customer. In a small, new company, the owner may have been able to prevent these problems by his presence, but the size of the company no longer allows it, and he's not as young as he used to be. In the old days, customers may have forgiven a few glitches, but the business is now in faster company, and foul-ups are not as easily forgiven.

Rather than making the changes in management style that may solve the problems and allow the company to exploit its hard-earned market position, unfortunately the owner proves the adage, "When your only tool is a hammer, everything looks like a nail." He reverts to what used to work, intensifying his personal control, when what is really needed is a change of style. The informal methods of the past must be replaced with clearly articulated policies and procedures; effective financial controls must be introduced, and enlightened human resources policies instituted.

For example, one company, because of its unique market niche, is profitable despite autocratic management and lack of proper systems and procedures. Complacent with its position, the owner spent little time in planning for the future and derides attempts at organization as bureaucratic. His watchwords were, "Don't argue with success" and "If it ain't broke, don't fix it." Gradually changing market conditions, however, plunged the company into the dimming lights stage. As the needs of the market shifted and the company's most profitable product became obsolete, the company paid the price for its failure to plan.

Fortunately, the genius of the owner exerted itself, and an exciting new alternative product was quickly developed. It achieved quick acceptance, and orders poured in. Unfortunately, the owner had put his young, inexperienced son in charge of manufacturing and the obsolete plant was not able to produce the new product efficiently. Quality deficiency, slow delivery, and foreign competition all led to the dissipation of the company's lead, and despite the ingenuity of the owner and market demand, the company suffered the fate of many dimming lights companies—it became an also-ran.

Unlike the early stages when they were closely involved and responsive to their customers, dimming lights companies often lose touch with their markets. One company in this mode structured its warehousing and delivery operations to ensure next-day delivery, believing that speed was important to its customers.

However, the speeding up resulted in more errors, and while customers received next-day delivery, there were many mistakes. Alarmed by the loss of customers, it surveyed its customers to identify which service elements were important. Bingo. Very few customers felt it was important to get next-day delivery; however, *all* customers felt that accuracy was critical.

Characteristics of Dimming Lights Businesses

• Growth has outstripped physical, managerial, and often financial capacity. This often results in missed delivery dates, quality problems, erroneous billings, wrong shipments, unhappy customers, and low employee morale.
• Management spends most of its time in damage control rather than on planning how the company can become more profitable or achieve its next level of growth.
• Emphasis is concentrated on sales rather than on profitability. Financial controls are inadequate, and information may not be available until it's too late to take corrective action.
• There is a pervasive lack of management systems or procedures—no budgets, no planning, out-of-control hiring, unclear organizational structure, erratic compensation practices, and poor training and direction of employees.
• Managers from "the old days" are kept in key positions out of loyalty although they have not grown with the business and clog the compa-

ny's arteries by blocking the career paths of more able employees. This often leads to empire building resulting in tension and divisiveness between those who perform and those who don't.

• Younger, higher performing staff become demotivated by the organizational indigestion, lose faith in the future of the company, and leave. This adds to the bunker mentality of management which views the departures as "abandoning ship." Less talented replacements are then often hired.

• Management becomes preoccupied with its internal problems and loses touch with the outside world, its customers, and suppliers. The downward spiral is thus exacerbated.

Dimming Lights and the Family

The business owner and family are probably hardest hit during the dimming lights stage. The owner's frustration with being unable to lead the company out of the woods often spill over into family life with the following consequences:

• The owner and family experience high levels of stress and sometimes confusion about how to turn the company around. This stress often results in a search for the villain, resulting in "finger pointing" or blaming family members.

• Disagreement about management philosophy increases. Tensions rise as the kids push for change and the owner digs in his heels because he feels that he is under attack.

• Now that the business is no longer profitable, the profiles of low-performing family members in the business become higher, contributing to stress in the family.

• Because of the lack of professionalism in the business, family member roles, responsibilities, functions, and performance expectations are blurred. This creates additional conflict both in the family and the business.

• The personal security of family members becomes threatened, and they start to question whether the business will be able to meet their financial needs. It is during this stage that conversations commence about selling the business.

Treatment for the "Third-Stage Blues"

The biggest hurdle for you, the owner, is to recognize that change is necessary if your company is to survive. Many owners need the stimulus of pain to get their attention before they will accept change. If you're in a third-stage company, the pain is evidenced by high employee turnover, decreasing profitability, and customer dissatisfaction.

The first step is to admit that something is very wrong and that *you*, as the owner, are responsible. It's seductive to blame others and to fault external factors; however, it's your business and your problem, and it's up to you to deal with them. It may not be too late to start to "professionalize" the business. To do so calls for the following changes:

• Micromanagement to macromanagement. End your personal involvement with every aspect of the business and concentrate more on managing people. This transition will entail: relinquishing control, decentralizing responsibility by pushing it down to the lowest possible level, assigning increased accountability to other management staff, and engaging in participative (though not necessarily democratic) management decision making.

This does not mean that you should distance yourself from the trenches and become a distant bureaucrat but that you should assume a new role as leader and manager of people. It means getting out from among the trees so that you can see the forest. If you don't have the capacity to make this transition and if the next generation isn't ready, perhaps this is the time to hire a professional manager or think about selling the business.

• *Managing events to managing systems.* Organized systems are needed to reduce time and effort spent in continually reinventing the wheel. These systems include the following:

- An organizational structure with clear lines of responsibility.
- Strategic and operating plans that delineate the direction of the business, strategies, and allocation of responsibilities to "make it happen."
- Budgets and financial monitoring systems.
- Accurate and current management information systems.
- Regular and complete communication at all levels of the company.
- Formalized human resources programs, including performance appraisals, performance-based compensation, recruiting, and training and management development programs.

Family Involvement to Family Management

Unless steps are taken in time to reverse the dimming lights effects, the turmoil in the business spills over into the family, often resulting in finger pointing and conflict among family members. It's time to establish a planned approach to family involvement in the business. This can begin with the establishment of a "family council," as discussed in Chapter 3, to address all of the issues inherent in family involvement in the business.

Dimming lights is not an inevitable growth period like adolescence. It can be avoided altogether by professionalizing the business without waiting for a dimming lights crisis. However, if you're already a dimming lights company, it may not be too late to start instituting the necessary changes. Failure could mean that you will inevitably reach the "lights out" stage and the demise of the business.

THE FOURTH STAGE: ENLIGHTENMENT

After a business is successfully professionalized, it may enter the fourth stage: enlightenment. This is a period of integration: people, systems, and processes work *with,* rather than *against,* each other. Managers support each other; a management team emerges, and a lasting culture begins to take shape.

This doesn't mean that utopia has been attained or that the business won't experience setbacks and strains. But once the owner begins to *manage* as a way of life rather than being managed by events, the company experiences a cultural readjustment that encourages peak performance and allows the business to achieve new levels of growth and profitability. This doesn't mean that the business becomes a bureaucracy, only that it has become organized. Properly accomplished, the intuition and fluidity of action that made the business successful in the first place are retained and enhanced, rather than lost.

The owner and key managers are able to concentrate on strategically enhancing the business rather than in fighting operational fires. And, ironically, all of this success generally take less of the owner's time and effort than the earlier developmental stages and provides a high level of satisfaction to most owners and their families.

The "enlightenment" stage is usually characterized by the following:

• The owner, having shared responsibility with others, is free to *lead* the company forward. During this stage, a chief operating officer is often hired, and possibly a chief executive officer, so that the owner is freed to concentrate on his missions as visionary and leader.
• The owner's control resides in his confidence in others to manage their responsibilities.
• The owner manages the business; it doesn't manage him.
• Growth is controlled through strategic planning that establishes growth goals and provides for the marketing efforts, people requirements, financial needs, and the necessary facilities.
• The company's mission is clear, and a definable culture begins to evolve.
• Managers are held accountable for clearly stated and measurable goals; they are involved in the decision-making process and have begun to make decisions on their own, rather than just carrying out the owner's wishes.
• Communication is consistent, open, and clear.
• The company is positioned for profitable growth.
• Outside advisors (boards, accountants, and attorneys) play a more active role in helping the company develop and in brainstorming with the owners and management.

The "Enlightened" Family
Ideally, at this stage, the owner and active family members have also developed many of the skills and perspectives that are necessary both for their personal growth and harmony in the family. Roles of family members in the business are clearly defined; the family has developed acceptable processes for dealing with family issues in a business context and are able to resolve differences constructively and to reach consensus on important issues.

Communication in the family is open, and the family has begun to address the key issues that affect the continuity of the business—management succession and ownership of the corporate stock in the next generation.

SUMMARY

- In the start-up, or "lights on" stage, the scene is chaotic, but it's often fun and exciting. The owner wears all the hats and oversees every element of the business. Family members are often helpers in this stage.
- If the business reaches the "bright lights" stage, it now is an established business, and if it is to grow successfully, the owner must start to change from doer to manager. The children often become fully involved at this stage and may influence the outcome, either during the owner's lifetime or when they take over, if the business lasts that long.
- Unless the management of the business changes to meet the changing needs of the company, it may enter the "dimming lights" stage despite marketing or product advantages. This is often marked by customer dissatisfaction, rapid turnover in the work force, and tension in the family.
- When an owner is able to build an able and motivated work force, and create a planned view of the future, accompanied by a committed family with an organized approach to both business opportunities and responsibilities, the company is said to be in the "enlightenment" phase where the owner's dream has its best chance of coming true.
- The company can be deemed to be in the "enlightenment" phase when the owner is able to create a planned view of the future, both in the business and in the family.

NOTE

1. Richard H. Brien, "The Managerialization of Higher Education," *Education Record*, Summer 1970.

CHAPTER 5

SOMEDAY WE'VE GOT TO GET ORGANIZED

There are three categories of people in industry—the few who make things happen, the many who watch things happen, and the overwhelming majority who have no idea what happened.

O. A. Battista

If a business is to grow successfully, the loose methods of the start-up phase must give way to a more disciplined environment, and the direction of the enterprise must be plotted. The business needs to be "professionalized."

This chapter is about making things happen. As an owner of a business in today's world, you must deal with intense competition, rapidly changing technology, strict environmental regulations, changing market needs, complex tax laws, and the ever-present threat of litigation. Costs are escalating, and the margin for error is continually decreasing, yet the credo of the shoot-from-the-hip entrepreneur often continues to be Ready . . . fire . . . aim! Even without the complexity of balancing family involvement, it's a wonder that the mortality rates of family businesses aren't even higher.

Your business is unique. No other enterprise has the same characters, beliefs, values, experiences, and skills, and certainly nobody else has the same family. Nevertheless, both successful and unsuccessful family businesses, once they have grown to a point where the owners can't do it all themselves (usually when the approximately 20 to 30 employee level is reached), tend to share several key characteristics.

The Winners

- Strong, capable leadership that pushes responsibility and authority down to employees.

- Clearly defined goals. The organization functions as a team with management and employees committed to the same objectives.
- Committed employees. Turnover is low.
- Clear and consistent *two-way* communication at all levels.
- Timely and accurate reporting systems that allow management to take action to prevent crises, rather than dealing with them after the fact.
- Family members who work cooperatively.

The Losers

- Lack of direction. Nobody (perhaps including the owner) has a clear picture of the goals of the business.
- Autocratic management. The boss makes all of the decisions, and employees have little authority.
- Low employee morale. Turnover is excessive.
- Inadequate communication. The boss tends to be secretive, downstream communication is poor, and upstream communication is discouraged.
- Poor reporting systems. Information is late and often inadequate.
- Preoccupation with crisis management, rather than planning the future.
- Open conflict among family members.

A common thread of the winners is that they have graduated from the "hit or miss" approach that characterizes so many entrepreneurial enterprises, and have professionalized their businesses by planning for and controlling their growth through the use of strategic management methods, either consciously or intuitively. And owners have established a vision for the company that is widely shared. One authority on the topic said, "Vision is the linchpin of strategic management; there's no other conclusion you can reach after a while." In analyzing the difference between high and low-performing businesses, he commented, "The good ones had a vision. As for the bad ones, it was hard to tell why the people had to come to work in the morning."[1]

A growing business needs an organized approach for the integration of all of the parts of the business into a coherent and manageable whole. In this way, its financial resources, physical assets, human resources, reward systems, product development, and marketing strategy can be focused to create a unified purpose throughout the organization. The overriding purpose is to create a competitive advantage for the business, now and in the future.

Many companies even though they share a preponderance of the attributes of the losers are nevertheless doing well, perhaps in part due to a buoyant economy. This euphoria does not last indefinitely, and the reckoning is inevitable unless the owner makes the necessary changes . . . or the business lasts long enough for the next generation to make them. Thomas Watson, Sr., of IBM said, "Prosperity is more dangerous for companies than depressions. When things go badly, most companies are forced to do the right things. But when things are going well, overconfidence leads to mistakes that can wreck the business when adversity returns."

While not every aspect of this chapter applies to small businesses with few employees, many of the methods that are advocated in this chapter, principally strategic management and marketing, can be used effectively by most businesses, regardless of size. These methods are not based on esoteric theories but present a *practical* way to help fulfill the principal objectives of most CEOs, healthy growth and profit.

Although the benefits of strategic management have been clearly established, most owners of family businesses have not yet taken advantage of this logical process. According to the L&H entrepreneurial survey, only 34 percent of family businesses have strategic plans. Even among larger businesses with over 250 employees, less than half have developed such plans. This should not be surprising; the L&H/AMA family business survey indicated that only 59 percent even employ such rudimentary controls as annual budgets.

Some entrepreneurs will misunderstand and say, "Hold it, right now! Our greatest strengths are our intuition and flexibility of action, and we like it that way. If we add structure, we'll become bureaucratic like the giants." It should be clear that strategic management doesn't mean that you abandon the freedom of action that got you where you are or discourage innovation. It provides an orderly environment that helps you to channel these strengths so that everyone in your organization pulls their oars in the same direction.

W. S. Rukeyser, an authority on the subject, put it this way: "The challenge to think systematically about large, ambiguous questions is inherently daunting, and is one that many businessmen—activists by nature—may be reluctant to take up. But if businessmen are to manage events, rather than be managed by them, there is no alternative."

STRATEGIC MANAGEMENT

Once the business passes the survival stage, management must adapt to its differing needs. Every business has a limited amount of resources, capital, physical assets, and people. If the business is allowed to go forward without a clear direction, these resources may not be effectively utilized. Among successful companies, management doesn't allow the business to drift along but takes a proactive approach to managing the business.

An assessment must be made of the political, social, economic, technological, and competitive context in which the business will be operating in the future. Based on this assessment, goals are established, and strategies to achieve the goals are formulated. Finally, the management gets everyone in the organization involved in carrying out the plan. *The result is the integration of all parts of the organization —strategy, capital, human resources, reward systems, structure, and marketing—into a coherent and manageable whole, all pulling in the same direction.* It begins with a *strategic plan*. Once the plan has been formulated and your business is being managed according to its precepts, you're practicing *strategic management*.

THE STRATEGIC PLAN

Strategic planning is a road map for your business. The process requires that you get out of the trenches for a short time and look at the battlefield. This overview and the accompanying introspective look at your business can provide you with a new and fresh perspective, even if you never develop a strategic plan. Former president Dwight David Eisenhower put it this way, "The plan is nothing. Planning is everything." In our experience, both owners and managers who participate in the planning process find it to be an exciting and stimulating experience.

An insurance agency whose growth had slowed decided to develop a strategic plan to try to determine the reasons why. One problem that emerged was that its top people were too busy to follow up with profitable commercial customers or to call on potential sources of new commercial business. Analysis during the strategic planning process revealed that "Pareto's Law" was in effect with a vengeance. The law essentially states that 20 percent of the customers account for 80 percent of the sales, 20 percent of expenses account for 80 percent of the total, and so forth. (This law was named after Vilfredo Pareto, Italian economist, 1848–1923.)[2] Its commercial customers, who represented only 20 percent of its customer base, accounted for 80 percent of the profits while the residential customers, who only provided 20 percent of the profits, demanded over 80 percent of its time. Growth and profitability both increased dramatically when its priorities were reordered. Variations of Pareto's Law can easily sneak into any business and can go on unnoticed for years unless management steps back from the trees and looks at the forest.

Some owners feel that planning is futile because the future is unpredictable. Strategic planning doesn't attempt to predict the future; it scans the total environment in which the company will be doing business in the future. Alternative scenarios of future developments are also developed so that the company's future can be shaped to changing circumstances rather than being carried along with the tide and left to luck. The strategic plan is kept flexible so that it can be adjusted to changing conditions.

In a family business, you cannot create a strategic business plan without considering the family's interests. For example, if the family isn't committed to the long-term future of the business, or if it appears as though there is no solution to the management succession issue, it brings the continuity of the business into question—an issue that has a profound effect on the business plan. Conversely, a family plan committed to the perpetuation of the company lays an important foundation for the business plan.

The family strategic plan that was discussed in Chapter 3 is essential to the development of your business's strategic plan, and because your family's commitment is critical, we suggest that your family strategic plan be developed first.

Many small and medium-sized family businesses are lulled into a false sense of security by their progress, and rest on their laurels in the erroneous belief that planning is unnecessary and that somehow the future will reenact the past. Some major companies have made the same mistake. At one time, Volkswagen dominated the small car market with the most popular car in history; however, it didn't assess the situation properly or respond to the market situation, and its competitors left it far behind. How many of the familiar orange roofs of Howard Johnson restaurants do you see on the highway today?

In simple terms, strategic planning provides a structured approach for you to apply these questions to your business:

- Where are we?
- Where do we want to go?
- How do we get there?

It provides you with an organized way of dealing with the basic management tasks of planning, organizing, staffing, directing, and controlling; it recognizes the need of every business for carefully conceived planning and efficient systems to monitor performance; and it places proper emphasis on the need for highly motivated, competent, and committed employees.

While this may seem simplistic, in our experience, businesses succeed over time largely by executing the fundamentals properly. Professional football players, for example, after years of experience, practice the fundamentals over and over again. Winning teams are those that best execute the basics.

This process shouldn't be confused with typical long-range plans that are prepared by committees and which almost invariably end up in desk drawers, gathering dust. A strategic plan should be a living document that determines the direction of your business. According to Michael Kami, a prominent authority on the subject, "Strategic management begins Monday morning." We believe that the question to any business of substance is not whether it should undertake formal strategic planning, but whether it can afford not to. Here are the components of a strategic plan.

The Objectives

- Define the most important needs of the business in measurable and objective terms.
- Anticipate major problems and take preventive measures.
- Build commitment and orientation to a common purpose among the members of the business's senior management team.
- Ensure consistency in decision making and effective allocation of resources.
- Establish an objective basis for the evaluation of corporate and individual performance.
- Provide a management framework that facilitates quick responses to unexpected change.

The Process

While there are different approaches to strategic planning, we have found the following method effective with small and medium-sized businesses:

The Facilitator and the Retreat

The plan is often developed at a two to three-day retreat, at a place away from the business, possibly over a weekend. A facilitator, skilled in strategic business planning, can be important to the organization of the retreat and the development of the plan. The facilitator's role generally includes the following:

- Interview top management to obtain an overview of the company and to identify priority issues.
- Conduct personal interviews with key managers to obtain their individual perspectives about key issues.
- Based on the interviews, help management determine the composition of the planning group, and establish an agenda for the retreat.

- Facilitate the planning retreat so it moves toward the resolution of the established objectives, rather than evolving into a "bull session."
- Based on the discussions, develop the first draft of the company's strategic plan for management's review and approval.
- Follow-up implementation.

The Planning Team

All members of the key management team—owners and nonowners, and family and nonfamily—should participate. Participants will emerge with a better understanding of both the importance of the plan and their individual responsibilities. This will help to build the consensus and commitment that's vital to the success of the plan. If managers have not previously experienced similar involvement in decision making, the opportunity to express their views and to be involved in the process can be a real "turn-on."

Participation by those who'll be responsible for carrying out the plan is important. Major corporations recognized the value of the strategic planning process some years ago and created large planning staffs to develop these plans. Eventually they learned that the operating people who were responsible for implementation resented being dictated to by planners who had never had line management or profit and loss responsibility. Consequently, little attention was paid to their grand plans. Now, people who are accountable for implementation are usually involved in the formation of the plan. If you develop a plan in an ivory tower and pass it down to your people for implementation, you will probably have the same result.

Developing the Plan

Begin the process by taking a critical look at your company and the environment in which it operates in order to identify the strategic issues/decisions confronting the business.

The internal examination defines the following:

Strengths: Positive features of the company and factors which differentiate it from the competition. Example: Our product has a longer shelf life than that of competitors.

Weaknesses: Deficiencies of the firm or areas of competitive disadvantage. Example: We lack broad geographical distribution capability.

The external examination defines the following:

Opportunities: Positive conditions such as changing technology, new market needs, or demographics that offer potential opportunity to the business.

Threats: Negative conditions, such as government regulations, changing technology, and changing customer needs.

At the conclusion of the strategic diagnosis, the planning team should identify the critical issues to be addressed in the strategic plan.

The Plan

The basic components of the plan include:

- *Mission statement:* a clear definition of the business, its products, services, customers, and the primary purpose for its existence.
- *Goals:* measurable statements of what the business will accomplish in areas such as growth, profitability, and research and development.
- *Strategies:* broad initiatives to be taken to enable the achievement of the specified goals.

Mission Statement

A critical (and often difficult) element of the plan is to define the company's mission for the next three to five years, crystalizing the purpose of the business. Before attempting the mission statement, you should answer these questions:

- What business are we in?
  For example, if you had asked this question at IBM in the 1950s, the answer may have been "We're in the punched card data processing business."
- What business should we be in?
  At IBM the words *punched card* would have been replaced by *computer*. If not, IBM could have suffered the same fate as the buggy whip manufacturers.

- Who are or will be our customers?
- How do we want to be known by them?
  - For quality?
  - For service?
  - For something else?
- Why are we in business?
  - For profit?
  - To provide security and employment to family members and employees?
  - To fill an unmet need in the marketplace?

You're now ready to develop your mission statement, which should be market-oriented, feasible, motivating, and specific. Your mission represents the aspirations of your company; your strategic plan spells out how you plan to fulfill those aspirations.

Two examples of mission statements follow:

- To be the preeminent real estate firm in the Southwest, distinguishing ourselves by providing professionally managed properties for our rental customers, in order to generate superior returns for our investors and excellent career opportunities for our co-workers, and to achieve reasonable profits for our companies while being fair to all.
- To be a professionally managed manufacturer of customized forms and specialty products, recognized as the preferred supplier in the XYZ market, by providing superior delivery and service through a high-quality distributor network, with the purpose of achieving equitable compensation and job security for employees and a sound return on investment for the ownership.

Goals
The goals of the business are based on the strategic diagnosis findings, and spell out in crystal-clear terms what the business wants to accomplish over the next three to five years. A goal should be established for each critical issue area, usually resulting in between four to eight goals

Each goal should be measurable, as specific as possible, and should include a time frame. For example:

Goal Area	Goal Statement
Growth	Increase revenues from new customers by 20% annually over the next three years.
Profitability	Maintain pretax profit margins at 15% over the planning period.
Organization	Recruit and train a specific number of high-caliber people necessary to support planned growth.
Facilities	Expand plant to accommodate planned growth. Complete by December 31, 19__.

Strategies

Once the company's goals have been set, strategies should be established describing the methods to be used to accomplish each goal. For each goal in the strategic plan, the following should be specified:

- Action steps to be taken.
- People responsible for completing the step.
- Time frames for performance.
- Resources/assistance required to accomplish the step.

A sample format for an action program is presented below.

Goal	Strategies/ Tactics	Schedule		Lead Responsibility	Required Support	Additional Resources Required
		Start	End			

Commitment of Resources

Next, the planning team should review the newly defined mission, goals, and strategies to determine their effect on the resources of the business. Areas to be considered include:

Financial requirements: How much will it cost to implement the plan? If additional funds are needed, where and how will they be obtained?

People: Are human resources adequate? Will staff have to be added? Developed? Retrained? Replaced?

Facilities/equipment: Is our production capability sufficient? What changes will be necessary?

Organization structure: Is our organizational structure appropriate to the needs of the company?

The Plan Summary

The written plan should include an abbreviated outline that can be used for dissemination to the family and to selected employees who are not part of the planning team. It generally follows the following format:

I   *Executive Summary* (highlights mission, major goals and strategies)

II   *Strategic Diagnosis Findings*
   • Strengths
   • Weaknesses
   • Opportunities
   • Threats

III   *Strategic Direction*
   • Mission
   • Goals
   • Strategies
   • Action programs

IV   *Implementation Considerations*
   • Organizational structure
   • Policies and procedures
   • Human resources
   • Resource allocation

V   *Contingency Plans*

VI   *Financial Plan*
   • Sales/revenue/expense forecast
   • Exhibits
   • Reference material

Remember, while the development of the plan is a valuable process, it is of limited value unless it's implemented.

Implementation

To implement the plan:

- Develop operational procedures to translate the plan into specific goals of people who are accountable for its implementation.
- Evaluate progress regularly.
- Review and update the plan at least annually.
- Develop a new plan on a regular basis (three to five years).

A third generation manufacturing and distribution business, despite doing more than $20 million in annual sales, was barely breaking even. Although everyone worked hard, especially the family members, they couldn't seem to make any headway, and frustration ran high.

The owners decided to step back from the daily pressures of business and engaged a facilitator to help them develop their first strategic plan. During the retreat, the owners and managers were able to share thoughts and ideas in ways that had never been possible before. They were able to identify several market opportunities, agree upon key goals and strategies, allocate responsibilities, and establish implementation procedures. Their superordinate goals included improving profitability and changing the business mix. Key strategies included divesting themselves of one product line, revamping the compensation approach to make it performanced based, and naming the most qualified family member to be CEO for the business with fully defined authority and responsibility for running it.

As a result, for once all of the family members were pulling in the same direction—more important, they were working smarter, not harder. In the first full year after implementing the plan, sales declined $3 million—but it earned $1.2 million before taxes. A clear victory for planning.

If you've been "winging it," you may find that the discipline imposed by this system is uncomfortable at first; however, if you make the commitment and effort, the benefits will be evident, and after your organization makes the transition to strategic management, you'll wonder how a business can be managed any other way.

As management authority Peter F. Drucker put it, "The future will not just happen if one wishes hard enough. It requires decision—now. It imposes risk—now. It requires action—now. It demands allocation of resources and, above all, of human resources—now."

ORGANIZATIONAL STRUCTURE

Management genius Alfred P. Sloan, Jr., said, "Take my assets, but leave me my organization, and in five years I'll have it all back." Many entrepreneurs think of organizational structure in terms of names in neat, little blocks more suited to large bureacracies than small or medium-sized businesses.

In their view it's often simple; the owner makes all of the decisions. As a business grows, however, the owner can't be everywhere, and structure is needed if confusion, duplication, and waste are to be avoided. Structure should determine:

- How communication in the company will work.
- How decisions will be made.
- How operational rules will be established.
- How accountability will be determined.
- How performance will be recognized and rewarded.

Your organizational structure should follow the strategy established by your strategic business plan. *The right organizational structure does not evolve by itself—you must establish it by design. If you want to change behavior in your organization you must first change its structure.*

There are no absolute rules that fit all, and your structure should fit your unique needs; however, one principle generally applies: Authority and responsibility should be *decentralized to the lowest possible level.* Here are some of the many reasons why:

- Flexibility is improved with managers in the field empowered to move quickly to meet with changing circumstances.

- It tends to motivate personnel.
- Organizational depth is enhanced, minimizing dependency on the CEO.
- Perhaps most importantly, it frees the CEO from day-to-day pressures so that he can become a leader with both the time and perspective to plan for the future.

In our experience, most family businesses employ "garden rake" organizational structures; the owner is the pole, and everyone else the teeth, reporting directly to the CEO. The pushing downward of responsibility involves risk on the part of the boss; however, it encourages experimentation, problem-solving, and high performance by managers and employees.

Delegation of authority is not a blank check, and managers who accept authority must also accept responsibility and accountability. Neither does it mean that the CEO should become a distant, bureaucratic figure; it means an arrangement of job responsibilities that allows people to function at the highest level of their abilities.

For many owners, the most difficult aspect about delegation is in adjusting to the fact that others may do things differently; this doesn't mean that they'll be done wrong—just differently. Ultimately, if your business is to grow and flourish, you must depend on people with different backgrounds, experiences, and styles. If you select them carefully and allow them the latitude to develop, even if you make some mistakes in the choice of people along the way, you'll eventually build the foundation of an enduring organization.

Many CEOs of family businesses are unwilling or unable to apply the same organizational procedures to family members as they do to employees, and family roles spill over into the business, often causing tension and pain among those affected and confusion in the business. In the shop, some CEOs still play daddy and are excessively solicitous and patronizing of their children; others are overly demanding and overbearing. Some adult offspring are overly dependent and irresponsible; others are rebellious and unappreciative. Some spouses assume authority in the business by virtue of their relationship with the boss, regardless of their ability to contribute.

The roles of family members become further complicated when

there is confusion over "who does what." In smaller businesses, there is unavoidably some overlap among roles. The tension and confusion that can accompany family involvement in the business can often be minimized or avoided by clear divisions of responsibilities and, if possible, supervision of family members by nonfamily members.

In the final analysis, the right organizational structure is one that is simple, clearly delineates authority and responsibility, allows the people in the organization to function at their highest and best levels, and considers the unique issues caused by family members working in the business.

MARKETING

In Search of Excellence is one of the biggest selling business books of all time.[3] One of the chapters that created the most attention was titled "Close to the Customer." Its theme was that excellent companies tend to share these common attributes:

- They try to understand their customers' needs.
- They listen to their customers.
- They are close to their customers.
- They have an "obsession" with customer service and with the quality and reliability of the product.
- They find niches where they can be better than the competition.

None of this is exactly earth-shattering, and it would seem that most businesses would follow these fundamental concepts as a matter of course. Coauthor Robert Waterman recently said, "Cultivating the customer is a lot harder than most managers think." He recently gave the typical U.S. company only a 5 on a scale of 1 to 10 when it came to getting close to the customer, up from a 2 in 1982 when the book was written.[4]

This is a dismal commentary on a critical element of a business's reason for being, and obviously a major reason why the United States has lost so much ground to foreign competitors. Many small and mid-sized businesses, having carved out a place for themselves because of the ingenuity and hard work of the owner or because they have identified a market niche, limit their future opportunities because they fail to utilize even the most basic marketing concepts.

Recognize that marketing and selling are not the same. Marketing consists of identifying the needs of your market, developing the right products, and pricing, distributing, and promoting them effectively. Selling, the one-on-one job of convincing the customer that your product should be chosen over a competitor's, while very important, becomes much less difficult if the marketing job has been done effectively.

Allan Kennedy, founder/CEO of Selkirk Associates, Inc., and author of *Corporate Cultures,* put it this way: "At McKinsey, we . . . gloried in the competitive game, in people who did something really clever to beat out the competition, not in the end result of the game, which was making money. Now I have an entirely different viewpoint. Only a damn fool would try to beat out competition—the purpose of business is to avoid it altogether. Supply a real need nobody else is supplying. God forbid you should have competition; it only makes it that much harder."[5]

Even with the advantage of a well-conceived marketing approach, it's important that you have a strong *sales force void of order-takers*. For most of your customers, they *are* your company, and one of their most important jobs is to educate your customers so that you don't find yourself in the unhappy place of trying to compete only by cutting your prices. In *Guerilla Marketing* Jay Conrad Levinson says you should first ask the following questions about your product or service:

- Does my target market really want this product?
- Is it a real honest-to-goodness benefit?
- Does it truly separate me from my competition?
- Is it unique and/or difficult to copy?[6]

Storemaster, a north Kansas City company, went from concept to a 20 percent national market share of a special box product in 19 months. According to an interview of the company's managers in *Sales and Marketing Management* magazine, "The process started with a thorough analysis of the gang box market, including a look at such things as competitive products, pricing, terms, physical distribution, costs, and patterns, as well as internal capabilities. As a result of this environmental scanning, a plan was concocted which included a push strategy. The entire marketing effort was concentrated on reps and distributors, leaving to the distributors the marketing effort to the ultimate buyers."[7]

With the intensification of both domestic and foreign competition, many major companies have realized that they can no longer take their customers for granted. Richard E. Heckert, chairman of Du Pont, said "As the world becomes more competitive, you have to sharpen all your tools. Knowing what's on the customer's mind is the most important thing we can do." Techsonic Industries in Eufaula, Alabama, manufactures depth finders for fishermen. After suffering nine new-product failures in a row, management interviewed sportsman groups and found that they wanted a gauge that could be read in bright sunlight. "The customer literally developed a product for us." the chairman said. "The quality of any product or service is what the customer says it is."[8]

Planning to meet existing customer needs shouldn't inhibit you from identifying needs that are not yet apparent and developing innovative new products. For example, Stephen Jobs wasn't responding to existing customer demand when he set out to put a personal computer in every home.

A disciplined marketing approach can help you to do something that many CEOs find very difficult: refuse bad or unprofitable business. Jan Carlzon, CEO of Scandinavian Airlines (SAS), said, "The most important advice I ever got in business came from a colleague of mine who was quite a character. He said, 'Never forget, Jan, that the most difficult thing in business is to say no to bad business, the bad opportunities.' He meant that you must always decide who your customer is and what product you are going to present to your specific customer. And you should say no to every option that is not related to that customer's need or to that production or to that performance."[9]

As the competitive environment has intensified, there is now renewed emphasis on product quality and customer service. Unless you have no competition, this is often the area that distinguishes your company from the competition. According to one CEO, "We hear a lot about service these days—in the computer industry, the automobile industry, wherever. The fact is the products themselves are hard to differentiate; I can't tell one model car from another. . . . So the service relationship is important in that it ties the customer more closely to the producer."[10]

Top-drawer customer service not only keeps your customers happy and produces repeat business, it often leads to recommendations to new customers. Inadequate service produces exactly the reverse effect, and you may never even know that it's happening until it's too late.

Some suggestions:

• Develop a formal marketing plan for your products, commit to its implementation, and stay with it long enough to let it work. The plan should provide answers to these questions: What is the situation? What are our objectives and goals? What are our marketing strategies? Who has responsibility for implementing these strategies? What will they do and when? What will our marketing cost be and how will it be controlled?

• Commit to the philosophy that THE CUSTOMER IS KING. Drum this into everyone in your organization.

• Get your management people out into the field where they can "press the flesh," and listen to the needs (and complaints) of your customers.

• Recognize that your involvement shouldn't end with the sale. Follow-up not only cements relationships but it leads to repeat business.

• Consider the potential of foreign markets. Although many small and medium-sized businesses have exploited foreign opportunities, most have not explored the possibilities. The international division of the U.S. Chamber of Commerce is a good source of information and may be a good place to start (1615 H Street N.W., Washington, D.C. 20062).

The business graveyards are littered with the remains of companies that ended up with the wrong products at the wrong time, that didn't market their products properly, or took their customers for granted. In the final analysis, you can do business without many other things, but you can't do business without customers. Market your products with this in mind, and treat your customers with the thought that your survival depends on them.

MANAGEMENT REPORTING SYSTEM

An efficient management reporting system is an essential link in the strategic management chain, as accurate and timely information is necessary to make sound decisions.

Here are some suggestions:

• Start with your strategic plan. How will the organization's goals and objectives be measured? How often? Your management information system should be coordinated with your plan to routinely provide you with results to compare with projections and goals.

• Frequency of information should make sense for those who "need to know." For example, the shipping clerk may need to know the number of shipments scheduled and completed on a daily basis, but normally the CEO can rely on weekly or monthly shipping reports. Financial statements are an absolute necessity on a monthly/quarterly/annual basis but wouldn't make sense on a daily basis.

• Information should be timely. There isn't much that can be done about accelerating the collection of June's accounts receivable balances if the report isn't received until September. Comparisons of actual and budgeted expenses don't help management to deal with problems if they're received two or three months late.

• The system should be simple and practical, and shouldn't give you the history of the clock industry when all you need is the correct time. In the age of the computer, it's easy to produce reams of reports that nobody needs or reads. This tends to obscure meaningful information.

• The information should be easily understood. If comparisons are being made across periods or budget versus actual, are the differences expressed in both dollar amounts and percentages? Would a graph be easier to read than dollar amounts, a chart, or table? Remember that just because reports have always looked a certain way doesn't mean that is necessarily the best format.

• Include "warning signals" that flag departures from pre-established limits. For example, acceptable profit margins can be predetermined and "exception reports" prepared to quickly identify margin declines.

Computers are now cost-effective for almost every business. Get the necessary help, and make the necessary investment to get the right system (with the right software) installed; it will pay for itself many times over.

COMMUNICATION

Picture a football coach trying to inspire his team at halftime:

COACH:

"We can win the game if we all pull together as a team."

PLAYER:

"It would help, coach, if we knew where the goal line was."

COACH:

"Don't worry; I'll let you know when you're getting close."

PLAYER:

"But we don't even know the score."

COACH:

"You don't have to know. Trust me. You're doing terrible."

It sounds ridiculous, doesn't it? Yet versions of this scene are being played out daily in countless family businesses. Ask the owner about his views on religion, politics, or sex, and you're apt to get a candid answer. Just don't bring up any forbidden topics such as the company's financial statements.

Of course, this behavior doesn't apply to all CEOs. Many are able to build open, effective organizations; however, many others play it close to the vest. Perhaps they fear that competitors would benefit if they had access to inside information. Maybe they're concerned that employees would leave if they knew how bad business was. Or possibly they're concerned that employees would want a bigger piece of the pie if they were aware of the profitability of the business.

Some owners feel guilty about accumulating a disproportionate amount of wealth as compared to their employees. The owner risked his capital, bore the responsibility for managing the enterprise, and was probably the driving force for the success of the business. Yet many feel guilty about it. As Léon A. Danco, the noted authority on family business, put it, "You'd think that they're smuggling cocaine."

The penchant of many owners for secrecy relates to a large extent on their inordinate need for control. When the business is in its infancy, control is achieved by the boss's involvement in every aspect of the business, down to the smallest detail. When the business gets too big to allow that level of involvement, control is partially maintained by being the almighty source of information—the "keeper of the secrets."

While this may make the owner feel important, such behavior prohibits the team-building that is essential to creating a lasting business. In every business, people need information to do their jobs properly. In many companies, this information is inadequate, and employees must function without it or depend on the company grapevine with all its distortions. In well-managed businesses, communication is the glue that holds it together, and information is complete, timely, straightforward, and widely disseminated.

In our experience, the secretive approach eventually leads to low employee morale, substandard performance, and, ultimately, the loss of high performers who tire of mind reading and guessing games.

While the egos of many owner/managers prevent them from sharing the dream, glory, or authority, others would change their management styles if they realized how destructive such styles were to their enterprises and their families. As Theodore Roosevelt put it, "People ask the difference between a leader and a boss. . . . The leader works in the open, and the boss is covert. The leader leads, and the boss drives."[11]

One CEO of a growing company didn't realize how insulated he had become until some of his employees had a few beers at the company picnic. "I learned more about what's going on in my company in two hours," he said, "than I've learned from reams of computer printouts for months."

Even the leaders of the Soviet Union, with perhaps the most secretive society in the world, finally realized that these policies are counterproductive and instituted its "glasnost" policy to create more openness. By comparison, the owner of a family business has an easy job.

Some owners may be secretive because they have something to hide. Perhaps they've become wealthy by underpaying employees. Maybe they use unethical or illegal practices. In our experience, most owners don't fall into these categories, and upon examination, their concerns usually are groundless. Would employees really run to competitors with damaging confidential information? Do employees really expect to be co-owners? Would the kids be more demanding if they knew how well the business is doing? In most instances, the answer is no, yet many owners rationalize their bunker attitudes by projecting dire results from the sharing of information.

Charles J. Bodenstab, CEO of Battery & Tire Warehouse Inc. (a $12-million company in St. Paul, Minnesota), in order to "set up a few systems that would make me feel—and act—accountable to people outside the company," decided to send quarterly financial reports and an annual business plan to each member of his board, the company's banker, and major suppliers. He observed, "Not only have these systems kept me on my toes when I'd prefer to have my head in the sand, but the feedback they provide has been invaluable. . . . It might strike you that the disclosure of all this information is risky; I am discovering that my fellow business owners are very reluctant to share company data. But personally, I don't see where the risk lies. If a competitor obtains some of this information, so what? As far as I'm concerned, the only really confidential data we have is our customer list."[12]

According to management authority Fernando Bartolome, "Given the natural obstacles to trust and candor, managers need to make the most of whatever opportunities they have to increase subordinates' trust. Trust is not easy to build in the best of cases, and the kind of trust that concerns us here has to grow on rocky ground—between people at different levels of authority. There are six principal factors that affect the development of trust and candor: communication, support, respect, fairness, predictability, and competence."[13]

A story in *Inc.* magazine tells about Springfield Remanufacturing Center Corporation: Its management system is based on the premise that business is essentially a game—one, moreover, that almost anyone can learn to play. As with most games, however, people won't bother to learn it unless they get it. That means first, they must understand the rules; second, they must receive enough information to let them follow the action; and third, they must have the opportunity to win or lose. . . . And that's exactly how the company is run. . . . From top to bottom, people in the company really understand what the business is about—what it takes to be successful, what role everybody plays. Management and workers set the targets, work together to meet them, and share in the rewards. You've got to see it to believe it."[14]

If management is the process of getting other people to do the work that has to be done, communication is the very essence of man-

agement. In one instance, a $15-million manufacturing company experienced trouble in balancing timely shipments with production quality. When shipments were timely, quality slipped, and returns skyrocketed. When the process shifted to emphasize quality, late shipments caused customer complaints. Ultimately, the problem was discovered: Mixed signals were reaching the shop floor, and the production supervisor was responding to the loudest voice. Once the situation was addressed and a clear message conveyed, both product quality and customer satisfaction increased substantially.

Roger Smith, CEO of General Motors, tells about the massive restructuring he undertook in 1981: "If I had the opportunity to do everything over again, I would have made exactly the same decision. . . . But I sure wish I'd done a better job of communicating with GM people. I'd do that differently a second time around and make sure they understood and shared my vision for the company. . . . If people understand the *why*, they'll work at it. . . . I never got all this across. There we were, charging up the hill right on schedule, and I looked behind me and saw that many people were still at the bottom, trying to decide whether to come along. . . It seemed like a lot of them had gotten off the train."[15]

Here are some suggestions:

• *Open up*. If you review your "secret" information objectively, you'll probably find that, in most cases, there's no real reason for playing it so close to the vest. The damage of excessive secrecy to your own organization probably far exceeds any that could be caused if the information reached your competitors.

• *Share your goals*. Communicate your strategic plan with your employees, starting with the full plan for highest level employees to condensed or summary versions for others, depending on their levels. You'll be surprised at the excitement it will cause in your organization and the impact that it will have on team-building. Issue periodic progress reports, and have periodic meetings to discuss both the ups and downs.

Keep your communication *clear, consistent, and meaningful*. An owner might say, "We have wonderful communications. We even have a newsletter." While a newsletter featuring the latest "new baby and dead fish" information may meet a need, it doesn't provide information about what's really going on. Meet periodically with employees, and elicit ideas about how you can both build a better company. You might be surprised how much you can learn from them and how this approach can help to build proprietary attitudes among your employees.

• *Encourage two-way communication.* Employees can be a valuable source of information to a CEO; however, there first must be an atmosphere of trust and candor. One business was experiencing a sales decline, and the boss, who hadn't been in the field since "the old days," felt that the solution was to "pound leather, and work harder." Members of the sales force, who were close to their customers, knew that the market's needs had changed but couldn't tell the boss. "He doesn't want to hear anything that conflicts with his view of the situation," lamented a salesman.

When the chairman of Allstate Insurance took over, he announced his intention to reorganize the company. And then he did an even more remarkable thing: He asked the employees how to do it. The responses allowed the company to eliminate an entire layer of management and make the company more customer-responsive.

• *Listen.* It's estimated that our work time is spent 9 percent in writing, 16 percent in reading, 30 percent in speaking, and *45 percent in listening.* If you asked an employee about the most important quality of a good manager, he'd probably say, "He listens." You can't be a good listener if you're dominating the discussion.

SUMMARY

• When the business grows beyond the ability of the owner to be on top of every activity, there is a need for a more organized approach to business management called *professionalization.*

• An ideal way to commence the professionalization of a business is through *strategic management,* which commences with the development of a *strategic business plan.* Strategic management can have a profound effect on your business if it becomes part of your basic discipline—a way of thinking about your business, the people, and its environment.

If you're "just too busy," remember Alan Harrington's statement, "Watch out when a man's work becomes more important than his objectives, when he disappears into his duties."

• Your organization structure helps to determine how things get done, primarily establishing clear lines of authority, responsibility, and accountability. Successful organizations tend to push authority and responsibility down to the lowest possible levels.

• A business's reason for existing is to serve its customers. The customer's needs should drive the marketing process, which is dedicated to developing the right products and getting them to the right markets at the right price. This doesn't eliminate the need for effective one-on-one selling to the customer. Customer satisfaction should be the ultimate goal of every business.

• Every business should have an effective management information system that delivers useful and accurate information on a timely basis to help management in decision making.

• Communication should be open, timely, and complete enough so that employees can do their jobs properly. The sharing of goals and results throughout the organization and the encouragement of two-way communication can elevate morale and stimulate employees to better performance.

If you have 20 to 30 employees or more, here's an unscientific self-evaluation quiz to help you determine how well you have professionalized your business:

	Agree	Disagree
You, the Owner		
Your workload prevents you from taking regular vacations.	—	—
You often feel overworked and "stressed out."	—	—
In your view, planning is a low priority.	—	—
Most of your time is spent dealing with crises and problems.	—	—
You wish you had more time to devote to your family.	—	—
You can't immediately name your top three current work goals.	—	—
You believe in giving subordinates only the information they need to do their specific jobs.	—	—
You rarely ask your subordinates for their opinions.	—	—

It's hard for you to accept someone else's
  ideas.   —   —

Your People

Too many good people leave the company.   —   —

They don't have regular performance
  appraisals, in writing, with goals and
  periodic reviews.   —   —

They don't make many decisions without
  consulting you first.   —   —

They wouldn't work hard if you weren't there
  to push them.   —   —

They rarely come to you with new ideas or
  new ways of doing their jobs.   —   —

They aren't aware of the business's mission
  or goals.   —   —

They rarely "open up" and tell you what
  they really think.   —   —

There are no structured training programs
  for employees.   —   —

Recruiting policies are "hit or miss.'   —   —

Compensation policies don't encourage
  performance.   —   —

Poor performers are tolerated.   —   —

Your Organization

No one seems to know what's most important.   —   —

You don't have a written strategic plan for
  the next three years.   —   —

Confusion frequently arises about areas of
  responsibility.   —   —

Your management information system
  doesn't give you current, accurate
  information.   —   —

Decisions, even minor ones, are usually
  made at high levels of management.   —   —

Everyone in the organization reports to you.   —   —

Criticism is more common than praise.   —   —

Communication is mostly from the top down.   —   —

The idea of "participative management" is
  seen as soft-headed.   —   —

There are no clearly articulated marketing
  plans.   —   —

If you agree with many of these statements, it probably indicates that your company is, or has the potential to be, a loser as defined at the beginning of this chapter. It professionalizing your business makes sense to you, help is available. Major accounting firms maintain consulting departments with expertise in organizational development, strategic planning, and human resources management, and there are consulting firms that also specialize in this area. *Make sure, however, that your consultant is experienced in serving businesses of your size; preferably family businesses.* Industry specialization, while helpful, is secondary.

Source: This quiz was adapted from a book by James M. Jenks and John M. Kelly, *Don't Do. Delegate!* (New York: Franklin Watts, 1985), pp. 25–28.

NOTES

1. Donald Povejsil, "Coming of Age," *Inc.*, April 1989, p. 42.
2. Quoted in *The Official Rules* by Paul Dickson (New York: Dell Publishing, 1981), p. 142.
3. Thomas J. Peters and Robert H. Waterman, Jr., *In Search of Excellence* (New York: Harper & Row, 1982), pp. 156–99.
4. Patricia Sellers, "Getting Customers to Love You," *Fortune*, March 13, 1989, p. 49.
5. Allan Kennedy, "Coming of Age," *Inc.*, April 1989, p. 45.
6. Jay Conrad Levinson, *Guerilla Marketing* (Boston: Houghton Mifflin, 1984), p. 22.
7. William A. Cohen, *Winning on the Marketing Front* (New York: John Wiley & Sons, 1985), p. 22.
8. Patricia Sellers, "Getting Customers to Love You," *Fortune*, March 13, 1989, pp. 38–39.
9. George Gendron and Stephen D. Solomon, "The Art of Loving," *Inc.*, May 1989, p. 37.
10. Regina McKenna, "Coming of Age," *Inc.*, April 1989, p. 56.
11. Leonard and Thelma Spinrad, *Speaker's Lifetime Library* (West Nyack, N.Y.: Parker Publishing, 1979), p. 152.
12. Charles J. Bodenstab "The Case For Accountability," *Inc.*, June 1988, pp. 129–30.
13. Fernando Bartolemé, "Nobody Trusts the Boss Completely—Now What?" *Harvard Business Review*, March–April 1989, pp. 135–42.
14. Bo Burlingham, "Coming of Age," *Inc.*, April 1989, p. 99.
15. Roger Smith, "The United States Must Do as GM Has Done," *Fortune*, February 13, 1989, pp. 71–73.

CHAPTER 6

COACHING A WINNING TEAM

The employer generally gets the employees he deserves.

Walter Gilbey (1901)

No matter how brilliant and hard-working you may be, the success of your business depends on your ability to attract quality people and to provide an environment that encourages them to do their best work.

You hear it over and over again, "People are our most important asset!" However, it's often lip service; too many CEOs take their people for granted and devote far less attention and time to the vital area of people management than it deserves and needs. In well-run companies, the management of people is a top priority.

PepsiCo, acknowledged to be one of the best run and most admired companies in the country, ranks first in its industry in attracting and developing good people. Wayne Calloway, its CEO, attributes the company's success to what he calls the three Ps: "people, people, people." He says, "We take eagles and teach them to fly in formation." This attention pays off. Calloway, who estimates that he spends 40 percent of his time on people issues, personally reviews his top 550 managers.[1]

Most CEOs of family businesses, with considerably fewer people to worry about, devote much less time and thought to management of people. As one CEO put it, "Dealing with people is not my strong suit. It's easier to manage 'things' because they don't have feelings and they don't talk back." Another said, "I seem to find every excuse in the book to avoid confronting people issues. I hate confrontation. I'm afraid I'll screw it up." He continued, "Going into this business, I never realized just how much time the people side of my organization required or how little I knew about what was really involved." Yet most CEOs of successful businesses consider people to be their most important priority.

Many owners find a market niche and obtain the money, facilities, and equipment necessary to create a successful business—yet they ultimately fail because of their inability to manage the people side of their businesses with the same planning, care, and attention they give to finances and bricks and mortar.

Many successful CEOs see their roles, not as bosses, but as "enablers" who help their people to succeed in their jobs. As noted management authority Peter F. Drucker put it, "A manager develops people. Through the way he manages, he makes it easy or difficult for them to develop themselves. He directs people or misdirects them. He brings out what is in them, or he stifles them."

WHAT EMPLOYEES WANT AND NEED

If you asked most CEOs about their perceptions about the needs of their employees, they'd probably say more money, promotions, and job security. However, a study by Rutgers University asked employees from several companies what made them willing to do their best work. They named respect for them as people, allowance for their own individual preferences and needs, information about what their company was up to, and the reasons behind decisions and policies.[2]

In another study, when both bosses and employees were asked what mattered most, employees answered "freedom to decide how to do their work." Only 37 percent of their bosses guessed that this was the highest priority.[3] As Roger Ward Babson said,"The outstanding mistake of the employer is his failure to realize that he is dealing with human material."

Management authorities Thomas J. Peters and Robert H. Waterman, Jr., put it this way: "Treat them with dignity; treat them with respect. Treat *them*—not capital spending and automation—as the primary source of productivity gains. . . . We are not talking about mollycoddling. We are talking about tough-minded respect for the individual and the willingness to train him, to set reasonable and clear expectations for him, and to grant him practical autonomy to step out and contribute directly to the job."[4]

If you want to bring out the best in your people, you must find out about their needs and concerns. Try convening small groups and asking questions such as:

- What does management do that *helps* you most in your job?
- What does management do that *hinders* you most in your job?
- What would enable you to do your job *better*?

If the atmosphere in your company allows your employees to answer these questions truthfully without feeling threatened, you might gain new insights into how to stimulate your people to higher levels of performance. General George C. Marshall put it this way: "If you want a man to be for you, never let him feel he is dependent on you. Make him feel you are in some way dependent on him." The best way to do that is to help him stand on his own feet. As the philosopher Lao-tze said, "When the best leader's work is done, the people say, 'We did it by ourselves.'"

THE NEED FOR TEAMWORK

In today's business environment, teamwork is not an elective method of operation—it's a business imperative. The ability of the Japanese to function cooperatively is one of the principal reasons for their economic miracle. And don't make the mistake of assuming that this is only possible because of their culture or that this only applies to giant companies. Every business needs teamwork

Here are some pointers:

• *Establish and communicate your mission as a business.* Employees have a need to know where the organization is headed and how their role fits into the greater picture. For example, a work group was in the bottom 50 percent of the performance ratings before it became part of the team to build the first manned spacecraft to land on the moon; 18 months later they were in the top 15 percent. When asked why, the leader responded, "I've been a piece of furniture in my job for years. Do you know what it's like working 40 to 60 hours a week and not knowing whether your work makes a damn bit of difference to anybody? . . . Want to know my secret? I've got a mission—something that matters to me, something we can sink our teeth into and be proud of."[5]

While your business may not be as exotic as building a spacecraft, the same principles apply. Many CEOs are so preoccupied with day-to-day operations and putting out the daily fires that they don't have a clear picture of their company's mission themselves. "You don't understand," they'll say. "That's for big companies. I haven't got time for that fancy stuff." And the employees continue to work because they have to feed their families, and the business operates like an eight-cylinder automobile with four cylinders out of commission.

An old but appropriate story tells of two bricklayers, one with twice the production of the other. In order to determine why, the supervisor asked what they were doing. The low performer answered. "I'm laying bricks." The high performer said, "I'm building a cathedral."

• *Emphasize teamwork in your value system.* Teamwork doesn't result from pep talks or lip service. You must build it into your organizational structure and reward system. Although individual accomplishment should be recognized, in winning companies everyone is dedicated to fulfilling the goals of the business. For example, the Boston Celtics professional basketball team was an also-ran until "Red" Auerback became coach and developed a teamwork-oriented philosophy that resulted in their becoming one of the most successful professional sports franchises of all time. Players who are traded to the Celtics from other teams often make comments such as: "I love playing for the Celtics. On other teams the players' emphasis is on minutes played and points scored. Here the only thing that counts is how we contribute to team victories." Players who don't subscribe to this spirit are quickly traded or released, no matter how talented.

• *Teams need autonomy.* Teamwork encourages employees to step outside of the bounds of the traditional boss-worker relationship, to find better ways to get the job done, and to assume responsibility for their efforts.

THE NEED FOR SUPERVISION AND TRAINING

If you look at your financial statements, you'll almost surely find that your payroll constitutes the largest expense. Despite this, and the importance of people to the success of a business, many CEOs take supervision and training for granted.

In describing his company's policy, one owner proudly exclaimed, "We just throw them into the water and see if they can swim." While some employees survive in this type of environment, others often flounder or fail to achieve performance levels that would have been possible with proper supervision and training. As a result, potentially valuable employees, acquired at significant cost, quit out of frustration. A two-year study of American business practices conducted by the Massachusetts Institute of Technology concluded that one of the reasons why the United States lags in productivity is poor training. Workers learn by "following Joe."[6]

John McCormack, cofounder of Visible Changes Inc., a chain of hair salons based in Houston, Texas, tells how employees reacted to a training program that was instituted 10 years ago: "People told us they thought it was punishment to have to come to the office and learn. They resented it. Recently we had them vote on all our benefits, and they voted our training program number one. . . . They want us to provide standards so they can get better."[7]

Effective supervision is also crucial to a healthy work environment. At Mary Kay Cosmetics, they have a saying, "The speed of the leader is the speed of the gang."[8] Good supervisors lead by example, share their experience, and train by showing rather than telling.

If you want your employees to perform at high levels, establish structured training programs, and provide for effective supervision of every employee.

HOW'RE WE DOING?

Most employees want to be high achievers. They want to know what is expected of them and want feedback on how they're doing. If this is done constructively, areas of positive performance can be reinforced and areas that need improvement can be identified. Family members have the same needs as employees so don't make the mistake of limiting this important process to employees.

Performance evaluation consists of:

• The development of a written "performance description" of each job, containing the job title, primary reporting relationship, primary responsibilities, and qualifications. Unlike many "job descriptions," this is not intended to be a limiting document but to establish a clear understanding of what the job entails. This is augmented by the establishment of *measurable* goals *in writing* that are agreed to by both the employee and supervisor. (It's often desirable to ask the employee to establish his own goals, subject to the approval of the supervisor.)

The goals should be challenging, yet realistic and achievable. For example, a credit manager could establish his own goal of reducing bad debts by 8 percent and reducing the average period for receivables from 60 days to 50 days.

• Periodic reviews. The employee and supervisor meet periodically and review the employee's progress. Criticism can be devastating to an employee and should be packaged into a "sandwich," beginning with acknowledgment and reinforcement of the employee's accomplishments. Areas that need improvement are then identified, and constructive suggestions given. It's important that criticism be focused on the issue or problem and not on the person. Finally, the positive qualities of the employees should be reiterated and agreement reached about the future.

For example, a sales manager might say to a salesperson, "You've worked hard to open new accounts and have done an excellent job; however, some of your existing customers aren't being serviced properly. I think you need to manage your time more effectively and I would like to help you balance your priorities better. With your talent, I'm sure that you can do both."

In many businesses, while criticism about a specific failure is usually swift to follow, all too often, after a year's hard work, the only acknowledgment that the employee gets is a hurried "good job" comment by his boss, if that. The fact that you take this process seriously and are willing to take the time to make it work makes a statement to the employee that you care. Remember loyalty is a two-way street, and contrary to many misconceptions, you can't buy it with a paycheck.

PROMOTION POLICIES

In his book, *Coaching for Improved Work Performance*, Ferdinand Fournies says, "Suppose that you worked for an airline, and one day the boss called you in and said, 'I'm promoting you to be a pilot.' Very likely your response would be 'Thanks, but first teach me how to fly a plane.' And yet every day, in businesses throughout the country, bosses tell employees, 'You're such a good worker; I'm going to make you a manager.' Typically, the response is not 'Thanks, but first teach me how to manage.' Instead, the worker simply says, 'Thanks,' and the boss says, 'Great. Now go out there and manage.'"[9] The "Peter Principle" of Professor Laurence Peter, that people tend to be promoted until they reach their level of incompetence, is still alive and well.

In a family business it becomes more complicated, and owners should resist putting unqualified family members in managerial positions. This sets the family member up for failure and can be demoralizing for employees. Consider the following steps in establishing promotion policy:

- Define objective criteria for the performance of managers and supervisors.
- Develop objective standards for promotion.
- Apply those standards equally to all employees, including family members.

Effective management of people is hard, demanding, and time-consuming work, but is there any other element of your business that is more important?

EMPLOYEES IN A FAMILY BUSINESS

Why would anyone want to work for a family business anyway? An employee can't aspire to ownership, may be in the middle of family squabbles, and, after spending years to achieve management-level responsibilities, finds that the boss's kid becomes his superior.

There are advantages, however, in working for a family business. Employees can interact with the decision maker, get responsibility sooner, and work in a personal, less formal environment than in large, public companies. They generally recognize and accept that the future ownership and management of the business will probably rest in the hands of a family member.

While many family businesses enjoy the benefits of highly motivated and dedicated nonfamily employees, others are unable to attract and retain high performers. In our experience, the common denominators of the successful companies are:

- They are meritocracies. Family and nonfamily members are evaluated by the same standards, which are objective and well communicated.
- Nonfamily members have adequate opportunity for career and financial growth.
- Demoralizing family battles, if they exist, are kept out of the shop.
- The owner has established a management succession plan and communicated it to the employees. (Their futures depend on the continuity of the company.)
- The contribution of nonfamily employees to the success of the business is openly recognized. (This may be done through job titles, awards, compensation, and verbal acknowledgment.)

One business limped along for two generations and then boomed when the third generation brought in a new group of talented, industry-trained managers to service a fast-growing market segment. With responsibility for marketing and operational decisions and a performance-based compensation system that rewarded both corporate and individual performance, the managers brought a new level of know-how and enthusiasm to the business. When asked how this worked in a family business, the CEO said, "Sure this is a family business. That's what makes it work. But we couldn't possibly succeed without more dedicated, experienced people than the family can provide. My greatest challenge is to make our managers feel like part of the family, with all of the responsibility—and reward—that being family implies."

HIRING THE RIGHT PEOPLE

This is where it all starts. Your company will perform better, and your life will be less stressful if you hire the right people.

One owner reflected on the many failures he had experienced in hiring managers. "I just don't understand what happens," he said. "I meet candidates; they come well-recommended; their résumés look great, and they say all the right things. But more than half of them, once hired, never meet my expectations, and I have to start over again. . . . I've lost confidence in my ability to pick people."

If you are typical, your hiring process may be as follows: Résumés are gathered, either through an employment agency or from a newspaper advertisement. The most impressive are sorted out and invited for interviews. Untrained in interviewing technique, you interrupt your busy workday and ask the usual questions. Many of the candidates, skilled at résumé preparation and prepared for these questions, give you the answers you're looking for, and you make this possibly expensive decision principally on "gut feel," perhaps choosing the most physically attractive, charming, and extraverted candidate.

While your intuition may be correct, all too often, after making an investment in training the new hire, you learn that you made a mistake. Perhaps you terminate the employee and start over again, or you rationalize, "I don't like to fire people, and I hate like hell to start over again, and the employee isn't all that bad, so we'll just go along with it for now." And the initial error becomes compounded.

In many ways, hiring people is like drilling for oil. There is a substantial initial investment in finding and hiring people, another cost in training them, and a further cost (in the form of poor performance) if they aren't right for the job. Some employers bite the bullet when they realize that they've made a mistake, and they start over again. Others, feeling that "the devil you know is better than the one you don't know," stay with their mistakes and, over time, burden their businesses with mediocrity. The difference between these employers and the wildcatter is that the wildcatter quits when he encounters a dry hole and knows how much it costs.

David L. Birch, president of Cognetics, Inc., reflected, "I guess I've learned the lesson in that Kenny Rogers song, 'You've got to know when to hold 'em, know when to fold 'em, know when to walk away, know when to run.'" That's a very, very useful piece of advice, and I never fully appreciated it. I guess I was much more inclined in the beginning to hold onto people with some notion that somehow, eventually, they would work out. I'm much more inclined now to say, 'Let's look at it for six months, and if it works, it works, and if it doesn't, let's quit.' I think I should have come more quickly to judgments about people than I did."[10]

A retired founder of a uniform supply company that is now experiencing its greatest growth under his daughter/successor said, "Our company was very paternalistic. We never fired anybody. My daughter tells all new employees that the first few months is a trial period to see if we're right for each other. With low performers constantly being weeded out, I've never seen such productivity."

Finding and selecting the right people is a tough job under any circumstances. It's even tougher when the task is approached haphazardly. If the cost of hiring the wrong people appeared as a line item in your financial statements, and you realized how much it costs to have low performers in your organization or how expensive it is to train new hires, perhaps hiring would get the attention it deserves. You should ask yourself three important questions before you make a new hire:

- Is this person able to do the work? (Does he have the skills?)
- Is this person willing to do the work? (Will he make the commitment?)
- Will this person fit into our organization? (Will he fit in with our culture, and can he be managed?)

The Hiring Process

It's estimated that as many as 50 percent of new hires nationally are terminated within six months. Much of this is caused by sloppy hiring practices. To maximize your chances of success, the hiring process should consist of the following procedures.

Define the Job
Many hiring mistakes occur because of lack of understanding about the job. Think it through, and define the job in specific terms, in writing, so that there will be no misunderstandings.

Establish the Requirements
Define which technical skills are "must haves" and which are "nice to haves." Too many "must haves" may limit the field of acceptable candidates.

Define the educational and experience requirements Again, excessively high requirements may limit the field.

Define the important personal qualities. The candidate should share the basic values that guide you and your business and be able to march to the same drummer as the rest of your organization.

Expand the Pool of Candidates
It stands to reason that the more candidates you have to choose from, the better your chances will be of finding the right person. Build a candidate list from among your own employees, business associates, business acquaintances, outside directors, and business advisors. Consider people who work for competitors. If they aren't personally interested, they may know of other qualified candidates.

You may also want to place advertisements in appropriate newspapers and trade journals or work with employment agencies. While some agencies do an effective job of screening, their fee depends on the placement, so they may be lesss than objective. If you work with an employment agency, take the time to check them out with others who have used them. Quality employment agencies take the time to understand your needs and do an effective job of screening candidates. They may be particularly helpful if they specialize in your industry or in the functional skill area that is your area of need.

If you're looking for a high-level manager or for a unique skill, you may want to use an executive recruiter or "headhunter." They normally have industry contacts and seek out prospects who are not necessarily looking to change jobs. The fees can be over 30 percent of the annual salary of the position, and while some executive recruiters are only paid if successful, many are on a "best efforts" basis so that they are paid regardless of their success in producing an acceptable candidate or whether you hire someone on your own. For more information on finding a search firm that meets your needs, you might contact the National Association of Personnel Consultants in Washington, D.C., or Paul Hawkinson, the editor of the search industry's leading newsletter, *The Fordyce Letter*, published in St. Louis, Missouri.

The Interview

Résumés and telephone conversations will yield just enough information for you to decide whether to invite the candidate to an interview. The candidate's résumé may indicate that he's the world's best at his job and that you'd be lucky to have him, but remember that many résumés would win awards at creative writing contests.

One CEO, when confronted with a large number of résumés, screens them by writing to the most promising applicants and asking them key questions in advance. The written responses enable him to select only the best qualified candidates for interviews.

Now that you've screened the résumés and invited the candidate to an interview, your goal is to get an accurate picture of his ability to do the job; his is to impress you.

Here are some techniques to help:

• The interview is a two-way street that's intended to share information, not put the candidate on the witness stand. Set the right tone for the meeting by putting the candidate at ease. Greet him personally, shut off telephone calls, and request his permission to take notes. Sit with the candidate rather than behind your desk which can act as a barrier.

• You want to learn more about the candidate. Can he do the job? Does he have the right work habits? Are his personal qualities consistent with the culture of your company? The best way to elicit information is to ask carefully thought-out questions. For instance, Chris Eugenis, a sales manager at an automobile agency in Highland Park, Illinois, asks candidates to name three things that they like about their present jobs, followed by three things they don't like. "I get more out of the answer to that single question," he says, "than I used to get out of the entire interview."[11]

• The use of both open-ended and closed-end questions can be valuable in helping you to get an accurate picture. You're apt to get more insight from open-ended questions which require expanded answers and frequently start with the words *how, why,* and *what.* Closed-end questions are used when a specific answer, frequently yes or no, is sought.

> *Examples of open-ended questions*:
> • If I were to call your previous supervisor and ask about your greatest strengths, what do you think he would say? Explain. How about your weaknesses? Explain.
> • Describe the perfect job for yourself?
> • Give some examples of times that you've been criticized? How did you react?

> *Examples of closed-end questions:*
> • Do you get along well with your peers?
> • Can you accept criticism easily?
> • Does your employer know that you are seeking other employment?

• *Listen! Listen! Listen!* You can't learn while you're talking. Give the candidate as much information as is necessary, ask questions, and listen. Ask follow-up questions. According to psychologist/personnel consultant Kurt Einstein, "At a certain point in the interview, ask the applicants to help you understand their past achievements. Ask them to name three accomplishments they're most proud of. Then invite them to take you on a journey through each experience, from start to finish in as much detail as they can give."[12]

• Describe situations that the candidate may encounter in your company. Ask candidates how they would approach each situation. Evaluate their answers in light of your standards and expectations. Listen to your gut. If the candidate gives you all of the right answers, but it doesn't feel right, go with your intuition. Inquire about the candidate's personal goals and probe as to the candidate's understanding about what it's like to work in a family business.

• An interview with a high-level candidate should probably take at least two to three hours and may require follow-up sessions, possibly with other managers who are experienced in interviewing techniques

• Under the law you may be subject to charges of discrimination if you ask improper questions, including inquiry about the candidate's race, color, religion, national origin, sex, marital status, spouse, or children. For example, you can't ask where the candidate's spouse works, inquire about the ages of the candidate's children, or ask about child care arrangements. Familiarize yourself with the rules.

Check References and Background.

Unfortunately, all that glitters is not gold. Experience has taught us that we can't accept a candidate's representation of skills experience, education, and accomplishments at face value. Degrees and licenses can be verified by sending letters to college/university registrars and to licensing and certification bodies.

In today's litigious society, many feel that contacting previous employers is a waste of time, as they won't tell you anything negative. Character witnesses are apt to be less than objective and have probably been prepared to expect your call. Still, you may be able to gain considerable information by conducting a thorough reference check. Here are some pointers:

• In addition to the candidate's previous supervisors, talk to their subordinates and peers. Consider contacting outside parties such as CPAs, bankers, and legal counsel.
• Prepare for the discussion. Describe the position for which the person is being considered. Define the "must haves." Ask about technical, people, and communication skills; personal characteristics; and strengths and weaknesses. Would the reference source be willing to hire/work with this person again?
    Drug abuse is an increasing workplace problem and it's estimated that at least one out of ten people are drug or alcohol abusers. As this affects job performance, it's well to inquire about the candidate's work habits and attendance record. Verify employment dates to make sure that there are no unexplained gaps. Listen to the tone of the response, and be sensitive to what the source avoids as well as what they say.
• Assure confidentiality. Respect the confidence of each reference source. Don't make the mistake of putting written reference reports in the personnel file. Most employees have access to their files.

By following this approach, you will be surprised at how much information can be obtained; however, in today's environment, you cannot take it all at face value.

Gain the Candidate's Acceptance

The hiring process is, of course, mutual. Once you've selected a candidate, it cannot be assumed that he will accept. In the interview, you should have obtained a clear understanding of the candidate's objectives, and you may have to do some selling to convince the candidate that your company can help him to meet those objectives. It's to your mutual interests that the employee have a clear, complete, and honest picture of your needs as misunderstandings can lead to dissatisfaction that will necessitate starting the entire process over again. The keys are:

Explain the Job

Candidates will be interested in your responses to the following questions:
• Does the job provide the challenge and opportunity that the candidate seeks?
• Is the job structured so that it's possible for him to succeed? (For example, will the authority that goes with the job be commensurate with the responsibilities assigned?)
• How will the candidate's performance be measured? Are the expectations reasonable?

Describe Your Company

• Provide descriptive information about your company—its products, history, management group, customers, competitors, revenues, and (if the candidate is not local) your community. If you have company sales brochures or other written material about the company, they can be helpful. Describe the business and personal qualities that are important to your firm, and discuss the values that drive the business.

Describe Your Compensation and Benefits Package

In today's climate, candidates for management positions usually look for:

• Base compensation levels and opportunities comparable to those available for similar positions in your industry and in the applicable labor market.

• Benefits (health and life insurance as well as retirement, savings, and profit-sharing plans) which are in line with benefits provided by similar employers.

• Additional compensation plans which provide opportunities to supplement base compensation based on company and/or individual performance.

• Perquisites (e.g., car allowance, expense reimbursement policies, club memberships, and the like) which are typically available to incumbents in jobs at similar organizational levels.

• Relocation cost reimbursement if applicable.

You needn't offer the highest compensation in town to attract and keep good people. And don't necessarily try to match benefits plans of much larger companies. Remember that a candidate will be attracted to a company the size of yours for many reasons. It's the total opportunity that counts, and while compensation/benefits are just one part of the picture, you probably won't attract and keep the best people unless your package is competitive.[13]

MOTIVATING YOUR EMPLOYEES

A customer writes to the president of a bank, "When I entered the bank, it had a totally different feel than most branches. It was evident the people enjoyed what they were doing, knew how to do their jobs, and cared about their customers."[14] If you asked these employees why they are so highly motivated, they would be unlikely to respond, "Because I'm well-paid" or "The benefits are great." They would probably answer, "Because I love my job." This is the key. It has been said that "all motivation is self-motivation." While it may be true that motivation must come from within, you can help to kindle and encourage it.

Some CEOs still think that the way to motivate people is with the carrot of financial incentives and the stick of penalizing failure. The only advantage to this approach is its simplicity, which is probably why it's so popular. Jan Carlzon, the CEO who turned Scandinavian

Airline Systems (SAS) from a losing operation into one of the most successful airlines in the world, said, "In my experience, there are two great motivators in life. One is fear. The other is love. You can manage an organization by fear, but if you do, you will ensure that people don't perform up to their real capabilities. A person who is afraid doesn't dare perform to the limits of his or her capabilities. . . . But if you manage people by love—that is, if you show them respect and trust—they start to perform up to their real capabilities because, in that kind of atmosphere, they dare to take risks. They can even make mistakes. Nothing can hurt."[15]

According to Frederick Herzberg, a prominent authority on motivation, "If I kick you in the rear (physically or psychologically), who is motivated? *I* am motivated; you move! Negative KITA (kick-in-the-ass) does not lead to motivation but to movement."[16] It's been well established, however, that most people have a psychological need to work and want achievement and responsibility.

Herzberg identified the principal motivating factors, in order of importance, as the need for "achievement, recognition, the work itself, responsibility, advancement, and growth." These are the "satisfiers" that are intrinsic to the job and motivate people to their maximum effort. He indicates that there are other elements in the job picture that can be "dissatisfiers," if negative, but don't in themselves motivate. These are extrinsic to the job and include: "company policy and administration, supervision, interpersonal relationships, working conditions, salary, status, and security."[17] San Francisco-based organization consultants Dennis T. Jaffee and Cynthia Scott, authors of *Take This Job and Love It* (Simon & Schuster, New York) make five suggestions to help unleash the natural desire of your employees to do their best work.[18]

- *"Cut them loose to solve problems."* Encourage them to improvise and use their own judgment.
- *"Let work groups decide how to get the job done."* Allow employees to have input as to how their jobs should be done.
- *"Keep people informed about what is going on."* When information is supplied, it helps employees to feel respected and helps them to resolve problems.

- *"Offer flexible work rules to fit individual needs."* This helps to focus on results rather than on when the job takes place or how long the job takes.
- *"Stretch jobs to offer variety and growth."* This helps to offer new challenges, encourages the personal growth of the employee, and helps to avoid staleness.

An Underutilized Weapon: The "Attaboy"

One of the most valuable motivational weapons in your arsenal costs nothing; it's the "attaboy." Many companies build their entire people management programs around recognizing high performers. This can include prizes, acknowledgment in company publications, and most of all, a word of praise from the boss for exceptional accomplishment.

One CEO inspires his employees to extraordinary effort by telling them, "You're the best. I know you can do it." On the other hand, some CEOs seem to be constitutionally unable to acknowledge successful performance or pay a compliment. One said, "What's the big deal? They're paid to do the job." Another said, "If I tell someone that they're doing a good job, they'll want more money." One top manager, after resigning to join a competitor, said, "They paid me well, but there was no psychic reward. When I'd come in all excited after a particularly big win, he wouldn't even acknowledge it. It really took the wind out of my sails, so I finally said the hell with it."

The need for recognition is a major motivating factor, and you'll probably find that judicious use of attaboys will make your employees feel appreciated and pay off in their performance. One employee said, "My foreman thinks I have more ability than I think I have, so I consistently do better work than I thought I could do."[19]

Who's Running This Shop Anyway?

"Wait a minute," you might say. "This is all about meeting the needs of my employees? Shouldn't this be the other way around, with them meeting *my* needs?" The answer is that under the carrot-stick method they'll work hard enough to keep the paycheck coming, but don't expect innovation or the extra effort that comes with caring. And don't think that the suggested approach constitutes coddling your employees or allowing the "inmates to run the asylum." Everyone knows who's boss. The objective is to find the best way to get the job done. When you give an employee more authority in determining how the job is to be done, the employee should also assume the responsibility for the results.

Here are some practical steps you can take:

- Try to structure work responsibilities so that an employee can follow the task through *from beginning to end*, assuming complete responsibility.
- Set the employee up for success. Provide the necessary training, direction, authority, tools, and budget for the job to be done right. Augment with encouragement.
- Provide clear goals, and make it understood that the employee is accountable. If goals are not achieved, provide constructive criticism; if they are, recognize it. Lee Iacocca said, "Over the years I've regularly asked my key people—and I've had them ask their key people, and so on down the line—a few basic questions: What are your objectives for the next 90 days? What are your plans, your priorities, your hopes? And how do you intend to go about achieving them?"

This approach is not only effective, but it also makes working in your business more fun for both employees and family members.

Incentive Compensation

Short-Term Incentive Plans
It's the last 10 days of the month, and the sales manager knows that if the quota is made he'll have achieved his sales goals. The production manager knows that if they can get the product out he'll have made his production goals. Both know that this means incentive compensation, and both make the extra effort to get the job done.

While money in itself has not been proven to be the major motivating factor, many CEOs have found that the recognition and monetary reward that come with incentive compensation can be effective motivators. It's reported that 75 percent of employers now use at least one form of nontraditional pay plan—and 80 percent of the plans have been adopted in the past five years.[20] Most share two common characteristics: They put more of the employee's pay at risk, and they link that pay closely to performance. This places a higher emphasis on results. As entrepreneur James J. Ling said, "Don't tell me how hard you work. Tell me how much you get done."

As these programs may encourage emphasis on individual rather than company goals, some employers tie them to team rather than individual goals. These short-term (usually annual) incentive plans are generally applicable to high-echelon employees, but they can be used at virtually every organizational level. One CEO said, "Incentive pay is the cheapest, most risk-free dollar I'll ever spend because it's already earned before I pay it." Perhaps the most extreme (and successful) example is Lincoln Electric in Cleveland. "Rather than paying an hourly rate, Lincoln rewards its factory workers on a piecework basis: For each acceptable piece they produce, employees receive so many dollars. In addition, each worker receives a yearly merit rating (based on his or her dependability, ideas, quality, and output) which serves as the basis for a year-end bonus. Employee bonuses average 97.6 percent of regular earnings. The payoff to Lincoln is 54 years without a losing quarter, 40 years with no layoffs, and according to a study . . . up to three times more productivity than their counterparts in similar manufacturing settings."[21]

A short-term incentive plan should:

1. Clearly define the measures of performance.
2. Set performance goals which are attainable and which will result in a meaningful reward if achieved.
3. Measure employees only on performance factors that they can directly control.
4. Be as simple as possible.
5. Be communicated effectively.

If an incentive plan is working effectively, it should create excitement. People should know more about what's going on in the company and talk more about their participation in helping to meet the goals. Be careful, however, about setting the goals so high that only a few high achievers can aspire to them. This is apt to demotivate the other employees.

Solar Press Inc., a family business in Naperville, Illinois, with 375 employees, has tried various versions of incentive compensation programs, starting in the 1970s, when it had fewer than 20 employees, before it settled on its present arrangement. Here is the evolution of its incentive program, along with management's perceptions of the various approaches:

Informal Bonuses, Companywide (1977–84)

Upside: No promises; easy to administer.

Downside: Employees didn't know what they were being rewarded for; no motivational effect.

Production Bonuses, by Team (1984–86)

Upside: Stimulated output and creativity.

Downside: Sets off rivalries among departments and individuals; created equipment and quality problems; administrative nightmare.

Profit Sharing Bonuses, Companywide (1987–present)

Upside: Simple to understand; emphasizes teamwork and interdepartmental coordination.

Downside: More difficult for individuals to influence.

Most people think that the present arrangement is working well. The plant supervisor said, "People know that if the company does well they'll get a share of it. They also know that if the company doesn't do well, the checks stop coming."[22]

Long-Term Incentive Plans

Most family businesses limit stock ownership to only family members. Suppose that you subscribe to that policy and that a key manager says to you, "I feel that I'm responsible for much of the success of the business, and I believe that I've earned the right to a piece of the action." There's merit to his argument and reason to believe that unless he can be satisfied he'll leave the company. If you don't want to take the risk of losing him, here are some options:

• Offer him restricted stock in the company, which is the same as all other stock except that it's required to be offered back to the company when the employee leaves or before it can be sold. However, this gives the employee all of the rights of a minority stockholder, and many owners are reluctant to subject the business to this exposure.

• Establish a "phantom stock plan" which derives its name from the fact that no new stock is issued. It's a deferred compensation plan that provides the recipient with a share of the future appreciation of the company. For example, the value of your company is $2,000 per share, and you issue a key manager the equivalent of 100 shares in the future growth. If the value of stock reaches $3,000 per share by a pre-determined future date, he becomes entitled to $100,000 in cash.

From an income tax viewpoint, because no real stock changed hands, there is no taxable event when the phantom stock is issued. When the cash is paid to the employee, it is treated as though it were compensation—deductible to the business and taxable to the employee. The employee will have taken no risk, and he will have shared in the growth of the company as though he were a stockholder.

A SELF-EVALUATION OF HUMAN RESOURCES IN YOUR COMPANY

Here's an unscientific quiz that may help you determine whether your company's policies are conducive to the selection, motivation, and retention of your employees.

	Agree	Disagree
1. For the most part, our employees are highly motivated and happy to be working for our company.	—	—
2. Our employee turnover rate is within reasonable limits. We don't lose an excessive number of employees that we wish to retain. (If you answered yes to the first question and no to this, how do you reconcile it?)	—	—
3. We treat our employees with respect.	—	—
4. Our employees participate in determining how their jobs are to be done.	—	—

	Agree	Disagree
5. Our employees have a clear picture of our company's mission and their roles in fulfilling it.	—	—
6. We encourage upstream communication even if it's critical of company policies.	—	—
7. Our value/reward system encourages teamwork.	—	—
8. Our employees are given the maximum possible authority and responsibility for their jobs.	—	—
9. We have an organized program to train and supervise our employees.	—	—
10. Criteria for promotion is clearly established. Family members are promoted on merit only.	—	—
11. Our hiring process is organized and thorough.	—	—
12. We don't allow family conflicts to overflow into the business.	—	—
13. Within the past two years, we have compared our base compensation levels against the job market(s) from which we draw our employees, and made necessary adjustments.	—	—
14. Outstanding performance is recognized, both through our reward system and by other means.	—	—
15. The criteria for salary adjustments are clearly enunciated in writing.	—	—
16. Family members are compensated at market levels.	—	—
17. We have written current performance descriptions which accurately reflect the major duties and responsibilities of each job.	—	—
18. We set measurable performance standards annually for the key responsibility/results areas of each job.	—	—
19. We periodically review each employee's performance against mutually agreed standards, acknowledging strengths and offering constructive suggestions for weaknesses. This includes family members.	—	—
20. There are no lifetime jobs in our company. Low performers are replaced.	—	—

If you answered "disagree" to five or more of these questions, you probably have serious weakness in your human resources policies and changes should be made. In the event that you need help, consider engaging a consulting firm that specializes in this area. Most major accounting firms have consulting divisions that specialize in human resources management.

If you follow the suggestions in this chapter, managing your people will probably entail more structure than you're accustomed to. The informal approach can work if your business is small enough for you to be personally involved with every activity. If, however, you have employees who must function on their own, you probably need more organized methods.

This doesn't mean the establishment of a bureaucracy but that the management of your people is too important to be treated haphazardly. This structure, rather than limiting the creativity and flexibility that is a strength of most family businesses, should enhance it. If you're not already employing organized human resources practices, then using these tools will add to your workload. However, if you agree that a business is successful because of its people, then this will probably be the highest and best use of your time.

SUMMARY

- Successful companies are generally unanimous in the view that people are the key. Considerable time is invested in the attraction, motivation, and retention of quality people.
- Employees who are treated with respect and who are allowed to influence how their jobs are to be done tend to be happier and more productive.
- Teamwork is important. Productivity and employee satisfaction are both enhanced when management shares its goals and the results with employees and where the environment encourages cooperation.
- Employees seek autonomy in the performance of their jobs and tend to perform at higher levels when they have authority, responsibility, and accountability.
- Training and supervision are important to effective job performance. Both should be structured rather than left to chance.
- Employees have a need to know what is expected of them, and they need feedback on their performance, which includes recognition for

accomplishments and constructive suggestions as to how they can improve their performance. Family members who work in the business have the same needs.

• Criteria for promotion should be clearly established in advance so that every employee, including family members, will be considered for promotion on an objective basis.

• The hiring process is critical to the attraction of quality people, and it requires a careful, structured approach to be most effective. The firing process is also important, and low performers should be terminated if employee quality is to be maintained.

• The carrot-stick method of motivation is ineffective compared to environments which allow the employee to find satisfaction in the content of the job, with recognition for superior performance.

• Incentive compensation is becoming more common as a means of motivating improved performance and relating rewards to results.

NOTES

1. Brian Dumaine, "Those High-Flying PepsiCo Managers," *Fortune*, April 10, 1989, pp. 78–86.
2. Dennis T. Jaffe and Cynthia D. Scott, "Bridging Your Workers' 'Motivation Gap,'" *Nation's Business*, March 1989, pp. 30–32.
3. Paul B. Brown, "What Employers Want," *Inc.*, November 1988, p. 18.
4. Thomas J. Peters and Robert H. Waterman, Jr., *The Search of Excellence* (New York: Harper & Row, 1982), p. 238.
5. Charles Garfield, *Peak Performers* (New York: William Morrow, 1986), p. 24.
6. John Hillkirk, "USA Firms—Easy Target in 'Slow Lane'," *USA Today*, May 3, 1989.
7. John McCormack, "Coming of Age," *Inc.*, April 1989, p. 63.
8. Mary Kay Ash, *Mary Kay on People Management* (New York: Warner Books, 1984), p. 65.
9. Ferdinand Fournies, *Coaching for Improved Work Performance* (New York: Van Nostrand Reinhold, 1978), p. 6.
10. David L. Birch, "Coming of Age," *Inc.*, April 1989, p. 39.
11. Bruce Posner, "Hiring the Best," *Inc.*, April 1989, pp. 169–70.
12. Ibid.
13. For more on selecting the right people, see Robert Half, *On Hiring* (New York: Crown Publishers Inc., 1985), and Martin John Yate, *Hiring the Best* (Boston: Bob Adams, Inc., 1987).

14. Cover of 1988 Annual Report of First Pennsylvania Corporation.
15. George Gendron and Stephen D. Solomon, "The Art of Loving," *Inc.*, May 1989, pp. 35–46.
16. Frederick Herzberg, "One More Time: How Do You Motivate Employees," *Harvard Business Review*, January–February 1968, pp. 53–62.
17. Ibid.
18. Jaffe and Scott, "Bridging Your Workers' 'Motivation Gap'," pp. 30–32.
19. "My Job and Why I Like It," quoted in "Points to Ponder," *Reader's Digest*, November 1988, p. 131.
20. Nancy Perry, "Here Come Richer, Riskier Pay Plans," *Fortune*, December 19, 1988, pp. 51–58.
21. Ibid.
22. Bruce Posner, "If at First You Don't Succeed . . . ," *Inc.*, May 1989, p 132

CHAPTER 7

HELP FOR THE LONELY CEO

No man is so foolish but he may sometimes give another good counsel, and no man so wise that he may not easily err if he takes no other counsel than his own. He that is taught only by himself has a fool for a master.

Ben Jonson

There is one thing all boards have in common. . . . They do not function.

Peter F. Drucker

An outside board of directors and competent professional advisors can help CEOs with valuable, objective support and advice . . . if they're willing to take it.

"The owner . . . of a business has one of the loneliest, scariest jobs in America. Nobody understands my problems," says Clayton L. Mathile of the IAMS Company in Dayton, Ohio.[1] In a family business, it's even more difficult than in a traditional corporate environment. Not only must the owner/CEO cope with the responsibilities of the business but also with the emotional elements of family involvement.

An article in the *Harvard Business Review*, "The Loneliness of the Small Business Owner," reports the results of a survey by David E. Gumpert and David P. Boyd on CEOs of small businesses. When asked whether they "frequently feel a sense of loneliness," 52 percent responded in the affirmative. "Moreover, this same group reported a much higher incidence of stress symptoms than those who said they do not feel lonely. In fact, we found that a respondent's perception of loneliness was closely correlated with his or her total stress score. . . .

Not surprisingly, loneliness was also strongly correlated with these disorders—back pain, headache, impaired digestion, and insomnia —the entrepreneurs commonly exhibited."[2]

Entrepreneurs have a tendency to keep authority in their own hands, rather than hiring effective managers and delegating authority to them. This is a principal contributing factor to these statistics; 68 percent of the respondents indicated that they had "no confidant with whom they could share their deep concerns."

This sense of isolation may be reduced considerably through greater sharing of authority and responsibility, as described in Chapters 4, 5, and 6 and by increased communication with your family, as discussed in Chapter 3. You can also make an important step in this direction by adding new advisors who understand your business, who are committed to its success, and who will tell you the truth. These are the people who you can share your ideas with and who can help you manage and shape the future of your company—in other words, an independent (outside) board of directors.

DO FAMILY BUSINESSES NEED OUTSIDE BOARDS?

According to management authority Peter F. Drucker, "A business enterprise must have a government. In fact, it needs both an organ of overall leadership and final decision, and an organ of overall review and appraisal. It needs both a chief executive and a board of directors."[3]

In public companies, the CEO is accountable to the board of directors, who have the responsibility to monitor his performance. This forces the CEO to prepare his plans carefully, to defend them against the critical analysis of board members, and to be responsible for the results. The wisdom and experience of the board can also be used as a sounding board for ideas.

Independence and objectivity are important strengths of independent boards. Without reliance on directors' fees as a meaningful source of income, and not emotionally involved with either the business or the family, the board may be the owner's only source of totally objective counsel.

Drew Lewis, former secretary of transportation and a board member of American Express, tells how CEO James Robinson III proposed going into business with the Japanese. "He threw out the idea," Lewis recalls, "and we sort of demolished it the way it was presented. He brought it back at the next meeting, somewhat modified, and came to the third meeting with a plan we were all basically happy with. I think the board made a real contribution."[4]

If asked about his views about an independent board, the typical CEO would probably say, "Hell, I created this company and built it. I control all of the stock and make all of the decisions. Why would outsiders want to be involved with my company, and why would I want them?"

This is consistent with the common misconception that independent boards apply only to large, public companies. Many owners of family businesses, who tend to function in an atmosphere of informality and secrecy, view the board strictly as a legal requirement. The board often consists of the legal limit of three people: the owner, his spouse, and the company attorney, perhaps supplemented by other honorary family members.

This "phantom board" has little to do with the management of the business, and its principal function is to sign minutes attesting that a legally required meeting took place, although the meeting never occurred.

According to the L&H entrepreneurial study, only 18 percent of family businesses have one or more independent (outside) members on their boards. We believe that the low percentage is not the result of owners weighing the trade-offs of an independent board but because they don't understand its value.

Most of those who have tried it, however, have found that independent boards are valuable. John L. Ward and James L. Handy conducted a survey (the Ward-Handy survey) of CEOs of privately controlled companies inquiring about their experience with their boards of directors.[5] When asked about the value of outside boards, they responded as follows:

Tremendously valuable	18%
Very valuable	49
Useful	29
Not as valuable as expected	10
Not worth it	2
	100%

George Y. Clement, CEO of Clement Communications of Concordville, Pennsylvania, said, "Bringing outside members on to a small company's board of directors is a lot like giving up smoking. Once you have done it, you will be telling everybody else to do it, too." Clement, the third generation CEO of a business (with $10 million in annual sales) founded by his grandfather, had concerns about whether he would measure up under the scrutiny of a board and whether he would lose control. Nevertheless, he went ahead and created a board comprised of himself and four outsiders. Within a year, it had prodded him into instituting significant cost-savings procedures, helped to improve financial reporting, and discouraged some acquisitions that were not advantageous. He says that informing the board about his business and determining how the board can best help him has made him a better CEO.[6]

As described in Chapter 5, many CEOs are secretive by nature, and the thought of sharing confidential business information and airing the family's dirty laundry may be threatening; however, this is one of the trade-offs that must be made if the benefits of an independent board are to be obtained.

HOW AN INDEPENDENT BOARD CAN HELP

The CEO of the typical family business, as the ultimate authority, and without an independent board, operates without the checks and balances of a more disciplined environment. Many owners prefer informal management styles, which frequently result in sloppy operational procedures, inadequate accounting systems, and little or no formal planning for the future. While the business may get by while the owner is on top of every detail, it suffers when management methods don't keep pace with the growth of the business. In another environment, the board of directors would focus on these deficiencies;

however, in most family businesses, without a board, there is no impetus for change if it isn't initiated by the owner.

For an independent board to work, the CEO must have the emotional maturity to depart from his comfort zone as supreme ruler of the business and be willing to subject his stewardship of the business to the scrutiny of outsiders. The process forces him to remove himself from the fray long enough to develop programs for the future that he can present to the board. Even if the board provided no further input, this would be valuable, as few CEOs take the time to articulate their objectives in the specific terms that are needed for effective management.

Common objections to outside boards are that they limit flexibility and that they represent a step toward bureaucracy. These arguments don't stand up under scrutiny. Getting the benefit of experienced advisors does not limit the CEO's flexibility or ultimate authority as owner, and while an effective board may require more formal management methods, these often are needed to impose needed disciplines rather than bureaucracy. One CEO said, "Your outside board can be the inside sparring partner who tests your perceived strengths and weaknesses before you get to the main arena—the marketplace."[7]

Outside board members cannot know the business as well as the CEO; however, they bring a perspective that helps him to see the forest for the trees. Business mortality statistics include many once glamorous start-ups that skyrocketed to almost instant success, only to expand beyond their resources and self-destruct. J. Bildner & Son of Boston, Massachusetts, identified the need in the marketplace for gourmet delicatessens that could satisfy the needs of upscale working couples. After gaining market acceptance, and buoyed by the unchecked excitement and enthusiasm of its founder, the company went public and engaged in an expansion binge far beyond the capacity of its resources. It has since lost most of its capital and was forced to close most of its stores despite its winning marketing strategy. Strong, involved boards often can prevent debacles such as this.

OUTSIDE VERSUS INSIDE DIRECTORS

Outside boards tend to bring a new dimension of experience, objectivity, and candor that's usually not found among family members or employees.

When the Ward-Handy survey asked CEOs with outside boards what they would do differently if they could, results indicated that 49 percent would increase the number of outsiders, 29 percent would get better expertise and balance into the board via more outsiders, and 17 percent would give the outsiders more influence.

To obtain the most benefit from a board, honorary positions should be eliminated, and, almost certainly, you'll be required to ask family members to relinquish their seats. This requires sensitivity. Make it clear that they aren't being "kicked off" the board for any transgression but that you need the help that an independent board can provide. Sometimes this is more difficult than it appears.

Not every business would obtain enough benefits from an independent board to justify the time, effort, and cost. Normally a board is not justified unless the following two questions can be answered in the affirmative:

- Is the CEO committed to making it work? Will he give the board the information that they need, and will he value its advice and guidance?
- Is the business substantial enough so that the board's input can make a difference, and does it have the resources to take advantage of the board's recommendations?

THE NONBINDING COVENANT

In a public company, the board represents the shareholders. The CEO serves at the board's pleasure and can be replaced if it isn't satisfied with his performance. In a family business, however, it's the reverse. The CEO is usually the owner, with the power to appoint and fire board members. An old cartoon had the CEO saying at a board of directors meeting, "All those who disagree, please signify by saying 'I resign.'"

When independent members serve on the board, there is a subtle and not legally binding covenant. In working with the board, the CEO is "primus inter pares," first among equals. He is not obliged to accept the advice, counsel, and direction of the board; however, the independent board members have a final weapon if they believe that their input isn't valued. They can resign. They never asked for the job in the first place, and they don't need it.

One CEO of a $12-million business put it this way, "My board members are people I know I cannot con or manipulate. It's true that they don't own stock and they can't dismiss me for poor performance, but they are people I respect. And they serve my purpose perfectly, which is to have a group of people with whom I can discuss a problem—and then be too embarrassed to show up at the next meeting without having tackled it."[8]

He continues, "During this past quarter, for example, I admitted that while our sales were well above last year and on target, our profits were running under plan. That forced me to think through the reasons why—and what we were going to do about our tight gross margins and high operating costs. Comfortable? Hell, no! But I feel it is a lot better to answer these questions at this point than to face our irate creditors a year from now because we hadn't coped with the issues in time."[9]

There is a Turkish proverb, "Whoever tells the truth is chased out of nine villages." In the CEO/board relationship, however, honesty is essential. "It is a partnership in which each side is completely open with the other," said J. Peter Grace, CEO of W. R. Grace and a member of six other boards. "It is a partnership in which each side is completely open with the other—no secrets and no fooling around. If you give any director the slightest feeling that you're not telling the whole story, that's when trouble starts." He adds that the most successful CEOs are "more upfront when things go bad than when they're normal."[10] This doesn't mean that the CEO must tell the board *absolutely everything* but that he must keep the board well enough informed to do its job.

ROLE OF THE BOARD

It's important that board members understand that their role is to ask questions, advise, and recommend—not to tell the owner how to do his job. The director should be "an observer and coach—not a full-time 'player' coach but one who is willing, occasionally, to talk about how to do things."[11]

The usual responsibility of a board centers around the company's short and long-term objectives, the strategies for meeting those objectives, allocation of major resources, major financial decisions, mergers and acquisitions, and evaluation of top management. The board is also responsible for oversight of the company's compliance with laws and regulations. This is increasingly important in today's highly regulated environment, as the penalties for violation of many of these rules can be severe.

According to Robert K. Mueller, an authority on corporate governance and formerly chairman of Arthur D. Little, in a family business, the outside director is called on to play the following roles:

- *Arbitrator* capable of handling family disagreements, hostilities, and other emotional stresses or conflicts. (This does not mean that board members are decision makers in resolving family disputes but that they may act as mediators, helping the family to achieve their own resolution.)
- *Gap-filler* when owners lack time or expertise to cope with the difficulties of managing a family firm in a dynamic environment.
- *Resource* to the board or top management, who can supplement internal resources and provide freedom from group and insider thinking when key decision makers are advocates of a particular view or beneficiaries of a particular action.
- *Father confessor* with whom owner, directors, and managers can talk confidentially and share concerns, hopes, or troubles.
- *Devil's advocate* who can pinpoint the defects in the evidence or presentation when a family-dominated board needs a champion of the worst cause or case.
- *Catalyst* who can provoke the need for significant shifts in the conduct or objectives of the enterprise—going public, making a divestiture or an acquisition, or changing top personnel.
- *Image asset* who as a talented or distinguished person adds credibility to the firm by his or her association and identification with the enterprise.
- *Corporate networking agent* whose network of potential sources of capital, new business, technology, information on economic trends, international contacts, and connections in industry, government, and educational centers can benefit the family firm.[12]

A working board can be important in the event of the death or disability of the CEO. When one owner suffered an untimely death, rather than his unprepared widow being saddled with responsibility for the business, the board took over, hired a professional manager, and the business continued in an orderly way until one of the owner's children was ready to assume leadership.

It's important that board members establish a relationship with the CEO's family, as their confidence in the board can be important and there may be times that the board will be involved in helping the family to resolve its problems. However, if the board sees its mission as including the arbitration of family squabbles, it may be perceived as favoring one side or the other. A board that is respected and trusted by family members can help to defuse potentially dangerous situations. In one instance, co-owners were engaged in a disruptive conflict about management policies that degenerated into name-calling and personal abuse. The board was able to influence the situation by pointing out the consequences of continued conflict, providing a forum for the presentation of both viewpoints, and assisting the co-owners to focus on the issues rather than on personalities. The board didn't take a position on the merits but helped the brothers to work out an accommodation. Most importantly, the board's involvement allowed both brothers to save face, with no clear winner or loser.

In another situation, the board helped the owner to see that none of his children was capable of succeeding him as CEO and that other alternatives for the future should be explored. They then helped to identify the options, assisted the owner in evaluating them, and guided the owner through the eventual sale of the business.

THE NEED FOR A *WORKING* BOARD

According to management authority Peter F. Drucker, the kind of board member who is needed "makes sure that there is effective top management, . . . makes sure that management thinks and plans; . . serves as the 'conscience' of the institution; as the counsel, the advisor, and informed critic of top management."[13]

To be effective, a board should gain an understanding of the company's business, get actively involved in the formation of company policies, and challenge management with fresh perspectives and new ideas. You want a board that's not afraid to get its hands dirty and who'll visit your shop, learn about your business, and do its homework. At the Follett Corporation in Easton, Pennsylvania, outside directors rotate an annual "day in the box," walking through the plant, asking questions of employees at all levels, and gaining an overall better understanding of the business. It's also important that your board meet and establish rapport with your family. They are important to each other, and they should work toward building an atmosphere of trust between them.

Replacing passive family members with equally passive outsiders will not help. Lord Boothby described the duties of such directors as follows: "No effort of any kind is called for. . . . You go to a meeting once a month in a car supplied by the company. You look both grave and sage, and on two occasions say, 'I agree,' and say, 'I don't think so' once, and if all goes well, you get $1,440 a year. If you have five of them, it is total heaven, like having a permanent hot bath."

The development and operation of a working board can take considerable time, particularly in the formative stages. Don't even start unless you are willing to make the commitment that's needed to make it work, and don't continue it if it becomes a bureaucratic formality rather than a vital element of your company's management.

WHY DIRECTORS SERVE

Why would anybody want to serve on the board of directors of a family business anyway? The ideal candidates are busy, successful people and are not apt to be motivated by the relatively nominal fees that you can offer. Yet many highly qualified people accept directorships and find them to be rewarding experiences. Serving on the board of a successful company brings with it a feeling of eliteness and power as well as status in the community. Although not generally altruistic by nature, directors are often challenged by the opportunity to be of help and are apt to enjoy the satisfaction that comes with being an important influence in a growing, successful company. Directors can also find the role to be a stimulating and learning experience that helps them to run their own businesses more effectively. One director compared the role with being a grandparent, "You have a brief visit and then you leave while someone else deals with day-to-day problems."

COMMON BOARD PRACTICES

Size of the Board

According to Charles Wolf, Jr., director of RAND Graduate Institute, "Major actions are rarely decided by more than four people. If you think a larger meeting you're attending is really 'hammering out' a decision, you're probably wrong. Either the decision was agreed to by a smaller group before the meeting began, or the outcome of the larger meeting will be modified later when three or four people get together."[14]

The board should be large enough to allow divergent viewpoints yet not so large as to be unwieldy. A small business might want to start with just one outside director. As the business grows, and additional skills and perspectives are needed, an additional director or two may be added. A company with up to 100 employees probably doesn't need more than two or three outside directors; companies with 100 to 500 employees can do well with three to five, and only the largest companies need as many as seven directors.

Compensation of Directors

Compensation is an essential, but subtle, element of the covenant between CEO and directors. Both parties recognize that directors' compensation is an expression of appreciation rather than a fee for services. However, compensation should be significant enough to express the seriousness of the commitment by both parties. For most family businesses, the fees per director run from about $2,500 a year to $8,500, depending on the size of the business and the number of meetings that are required.

According to Donald Perkins, former head of a large retailer, "I have always looked at the board as a very inexpensive way of getting very useful information. People work as directors for fees they wouldn't think of working for as consultants."[15] Compensation may be based on a fee per meeting, an annual retainer, or a combination of both, plus travel and meeting expenses. Sometimes there are special circumstances that require more active participation by the board. Perhaps the company is engaged in a major merger or acquisition, or going public. Maybe the board is called upon to assume closer supervisory responsibilities due to the death or disability of the CEO. In these circumstances, a readjustment of fees is indicated, perhaps to much higher levels than those indicated for regularly scheduled meetings.

Term of Office

Although the majority of existing boards tend to favor unlimited terms for board members, there are advantages to establishing limits which would allow for the board's rotation. This would protect against directors getting stale, provide for new skills to meet the changing needs of the business, and provide a discreet way of parting with ineffective board members. It can also be a selling point to board candidates who may be reluctant to assume responsibilities for an unlimited time frame.

Preferably the terms should be staggered so that the continuity of the board is not interrupted. If there is an extensive learning curve in your business, a one-year term may not be sufficient for the board member to reach a point of maximum contribution. Depending on the circumstances, consider electing directors to terms of up to three years.

SELECTING OUTSIDE DIRECTORS

Establish the Criteria

Above all, you will want directors who are intelligent, analytical, honest, and well-respected and who will not be rubber stamps but will challenge you and offer constructive advice. Strive for a balance among your directors, considering industry and business experience, functional skills, and just plain, common sense.

Chemistry is important. Will you enjoy mutual respect and rapport? Will you be able to engage in the give and take that's necessary for effective board performance? While this poses no problem when the candidate is a long-term associate, it's worth spending some time with new candidates to assure that your personal relationship will be conducive to working together.

If you've ever served on a business or not-for-profit board, you've probably observed that some members, even though they have extensive credentials, just sit there seldom participating. The relatively small size of your board doesn't allow the luxury of honorary or passive members. Try to select members who will not be afraid to rock the boat and who will challenge you and not just tell you what you want to hear. Try to choose board members who will get along well together, but remember that the board is not a "good old boys" club.

What skills and experience can the director bring that will complement those in your company? Consider a candidate with a track record for success, and preferably a CEO of his own company, who faces the same challenges, frustrations, and trade-offs as you. Maybe you have a need for more sophisticated financial expertise that a banker or venture capitalist could provide. If marketing expertise would help, consider a member of a reputable advertising or public relations agency. Seek a balance that will bring new and valuable skills to your business.

If you're contemplating going public, it's a good idea to have a board member who has gone through the experience. If mergers or acquisitions are in your game plan, consider someone with a background in the area.

It's generally preferable to have professional consultants (i.e., your lawyer, accountant, insurance agent, and employees) in advisory positions, rather than as members of the board where their objectivity may be questionable.

Retired people may have the time and the experience to make a valuable contribution; however, some CEOs shy away from them as board members. One owner said, "This is a fast-moving world, and people who are no longer in the mainstream lose touch with the way things get done." Another expressed concern that the director's fees might become overly important to a retired person living on a pension and might color his objectivity. Not every retiree fits this description, however, and retirees can bring experience and expertise that is not otherwise available.

Develop Board Guidelines

Establish *written* guidelines which describe how the board should function. While these may be susceptible to change once the board is formed, the guidelines will help you to clarify your own thinking, help in your recruiting of board candidates, and help prevent future misunderstandings.

Include a brief history of the business—its objectives, its position in the marketplace, the principal challenges that confront it, and its financial history. Present brief biographies of family members and current directors as well as information about stock ownership in the company.

The role of the board should be delineated as well as information about directors' fees, terms of office, and the frequency of regular board meetings. You may want to spell out your expectations of board members, possibly including language such as this:

• Your responsibility is to provide guidance and support to the CEO. This requires that you express your views even if the CEO isn't receptive to conflicting viewpoints.
• You *do not* have a responsibility to set strategy or to run the company. That is the CEO's job.
• One of your important functions is to require the CEO to present his plan for the future of the company for the next three to five years. What are the company's objectives? Its strategies? How will its resources be allocated? How will its achievements be measured?
• Do your homework. You can't be an effective director unless you understand what's going on in the company. Insist that the CEO prepare properly for board meetings and that you get the necessary information in advance so that you can prepare for meetings properly.
• Avoid ego trips and conflict with the other directors. While disagreement can be healthy, make sure that the best interests of the company are paramount.
• Inquire whether the CEO is planning for transition to the next generation. Is he planning for management succession? Is his estate plan up to date? Is it conducive to the long-term health of the business?
• Inquire about the company's compliance with the applicable laws

and regulations. For example, are the human resources practices appropriate? Is the company in violation of environmental laws?
• Get acquainted with the CEO's family. If necessary, help them to sort out emotional issues relating to the business, and recommend the use of outside specialists if needed. Avoid taking sides in family squabbles. Your real and perceived independence are important to the performance of your job.
• Help other board members to give the CEO a constructive (and sensitive) evaluation of his job performance. This may be one of your most important responsibilities.

Finding and Attracting the Right Candidates

Once the size of the board and director profiles have been established, prepare a list of people who you know with the necessary qualities. Ask your lawyer, accountant, banker, and people in the business community about potential board members. If you've served on local business, civic, or charitable boards, consider other board members who have been effective participants. Be careful about including close, personal friends or people who do business with your company because the necessary objectivity and independence of thought could be lacking.

Once you've identified the candidates, it's important that you check their references, discreetly and sensitively, in advance. According to Gardner W. Heidrick, cofounder of Heidrick Struggles Inc., the international executive search firm, "The best predictor of future success is past performance. Subjects for review include attendance, participation, and quality of contributions on the boards of other for-profit organizations. If the prospect has not held such a post, he or she may serve on the board of a charitable organization. Indeed, since such service is typically on a volunteer basis, it may provide an even better insight into the candidate's level of commitment to assumed responsibility."[16]

The right candidates are busy people, and they are not seeking the role, so you must do a selling job if you're to convince them to accept The fact that you have developed board guidelines will be evidence of your seriousness of purpose and that you have thought the matter through. Share your dreams for the future. Explain how the candidate's participation can not only be valuable to you and your business but also a valuable and interesting learning experience for him. Your invitation should be flattering to the candidate, as it indicates your confidence in his ability and is a gesture of respect.

Your first selection may be particularly important, as later candidates may be influenced by the acceptance of an individual with high personal stature in the community.

LEGAL LIABILITY AND THE ADVISORY BOARD

We live in a litigious society, and lawsuits against boards of directors have reached crisis proportions. While these have been primarily directed to boards of public companies, directors of family businesses are not immune, particularly from lawsuits by family stockholders who are not represented on the board.

In general, directors are responsible for the management of the company and are required to exercise the "care that an ordinarily prudent person in a like position would exercise under similar circumstances." At this time, however, courts have adopted a "business judgment rule," with the result that "in the absence of fraud or self-dealing directors are rarely found liable for errors, mistakes, or simply bad judgment."[17]

Nevertheless, it's possible that the corporate veil may be pierced, and directors may find themselves personally liable, either for their actions or failure to exercise due care. Board members who view their responsibilities as honorary and who don't get involved may be in for a rude awakening. According to one observer, "The board is something like the captain of an ocean liner who walks around watching and taking salutes to show he is on the job. But is he really keeping an eye on things, or is he simply taking salutes? That is the question a director has to be prepared to answer in court."[18]

Outside directors are understandably reluctant to assume such risks in return for being Good Samaritans, and they are entitled to be protected. The corporation should agree to indemnify them from any costs resulting from litigation, and it should purchase directors and officers liability insurance in a sufficient amount to provide them with peace of mind.

Directors should be able to avoid personal liability by following two precepts: First, all decisions should be made on an informed basis, with documentation sufficient to withstand a challenge in court. Second, the interest of the corporation should always come before personal interests. To these general guidelines should be added one piece of procedural advice: A director who concludes that the board is making an imprudent or illegal decision should dissent and make certain that the negative vote is recorded. Otherwise, silence will be construed as consent to the action, and this in turn can lead to liability.[19]

The Advisory Board

Some companies seek to insulate directors from liability by utilizing two boards of directors—the *legally constituted board* and an *advisory board primarily constituted of outside directors*. To our knowledge, this approach has not yet been tested by the courts; however, it can be expected that courts will go to the substance of the situation and say that "if it looks like a duck, walks like a duck, and talks like a duck, it's a duck." There is also the risk to outside advisors that they would be treated as consultants and therefore possibly be liable for bad advice.

Fred A. Tillman, professor of legal studies in the Department of Risk Management and Insurance at Georgia State University, advises, "To avoid being treated either as a board of directors or as its alter ego, an advisory group must be separate from the board and must function only on an advisory basis." He suggests that it be named an advisory "council" rather than "board" and that careful documentation be maintained delineating the responsibilities and actions of the council, as differentiated from the board.[20]

EFFECTIVE BOARD MEETINGS

Regular board meetings should be scheduled in advance, usually about four times a year, with each meeting lasting from a half day to a day In order that the time be used effectively, the CEO should prepare a written agenda and send it to the directors *in advance*, accompanied by up-to-date financial information and supporting data for agenda items, so that they can plan for the meeting. Minutes of the preceding meeting should be referred to by exception only rather than wasting time in reading them in full.

The CEO's role, as chairman of the board, is to present the issues to the board for consideration, requesting its evaluation and advice rather than expecting it to take the lead. Open, candid discussion should be encouraged, and the CEO should not get defensive if the board is critical or disagrees with his viewpoints. If everyone always agrees, the board doesn't serve any useful purpose, other than satisfying the statutory requirements.

OUTSIDE PROFESSIONAL ADVISORS

Lawyer, Accountant, Insurance Agent

A survey by *Venture* magazine asked respondents to rate their advisors on satisfaction for services rendered. Only 44 percent were satisfied with their lawyers, 51 percent with their accountants, and 42 percent with consultants. Bankers were rated lowest, with 31 percent rated low in effectiveness, 35.5 percent in the medium range, and only 19 percent getting high marks.[21]

If you weren't familiar with this scene, you might ask a naive question of those who weren't satisfied: "Why do you stay with them?"

Although professional advisors can play a critical role in the success or failure of the business, the company lawyer is often Uncle Willie, who needs the business, and the CPA is good old Charlie, the owner's golfing buddy. The insurance agent provides routine coverage and has never made a suggestion as to how costs may be cut, but he's been with the company since day one, and there is such a thing as loyalty.

If the owner examined their professional capabilities, he might find that Uncle Willie's practice consisted principally of personal injury cases and that he is Charlie's biggest client, the next most substantial being the local convenience store. It might also come out that insurance coverage could be enhanced and costs lowered if the insurance agent took the pains to find the best approach.

Many owners are reluctant to change professional relationships and often stay with professionals who either are not competent to meet the needs of the business, too busy, or indifferent. Thus, they continue to be victimized because it's too inconvenient to change.

Some owners, erroneously assuming that all professionals are equally competent, hire those with the lowest fees. Many retain professionals because of personal relationships although the business may have long since outgrown the capacity of the professionals to service it properly.

What a mistake. In today's complex business environment, professional advisors can have a great impact on the success or failure of a business, and a prudent CEO should periodically evaluate the capabilities of his outside professional advisors. If a change is indicated, considerable care should be exercised because it's a lot easier to hire professionals than to fire them. In hiring a new professional, consider the following:

• *The human element.* If it's a large firm, who will be in charge of your account? Do you have the right chemistry? Do they appear to understand your needs? Will they *really care* about your business, or will you just be another account? One owner chose a particular firm because the partner, in presenting his business card, wrote his home telephone number on the back and said, "You can call me if you ever need help outside of business hours."

• *Competence.* A common error is to assume that all professional firms are equal in ability. Nothing can be further from the truth. In every profession, there are firms that may have special talents to service your needs. Perhaps they are specialists in your industry or in a given functional area such as taxation, strategic planning, or human resource consulting. Perhaps they possess that extra, rare dimension of creativity that distinguishes them from professionals who will merely help you to comply with the rules and regulations. In evaluating your own professionals, ask yourself whether they just go through the motions, responding to your requests for service and complying with the rules and regulations. Or, in addition to the routine matters, do they come up with valuable new ideas and suggestions? If you're not getting this type of creative service, don't assume that nobody else is either. Ask your business associates and colleagues about their relationships with professionals, and try to affiliate with firms who can make a meaningful contribution to your company even if it means departing from comfortable relationships of long standing.

Make it a practice to visit with your professionals periodically even if there are no immediate problems. Don't worry that the meter is running. Tell them what's going on. Challenge them to come up with new and creative ideas. One CEO who has made this a habit said, "I can't remember a time that one of them didn't come up with at least one suggestion of value."

• *Fees*. If you want to buy a product from a supplier, it's easy to get competitive bids. Professional services, however, usually don't fall into this category, and it's often difficult for you to determine how much time a particular project should take or whether the fee is fair. Some professional firms, in order to get your business, will "lowball" their initial fees, even to the point of losing money on your account. You might pride yourself on your negotiating ability, but will you get the same level of service as profitable accounts? And will they try to make up the shortfall in the future?

Of course, you want to control the cost of professional fees, but it's often poor economy when you're buying a blind item to hire the lowest bidder. This does not suggest that you write a blank check. Professional services are based on time. Ask for fee estimates in advance. While it may not be possible to pinpoint the exact amount, it's usually possible to estimate a range. Insist that if, during the work, unexpected problems arise that will necessitate a higher fee, you be notified *in advance not after the fact*. In the final analysis, if you settle for less than the best because of fees, it'll probably be an expensive bargain.

Banker

Your relationship with your banker is also important, and many owners treat it too casually. Does your banker take the pains to really understand your business? When was the last time that he visited your shop? Do you encourage close rapport and keep your banker fully informed about your business even if you don't need a loan, or do you only see him when you need money? Because there is frequent turnover among loan officers at many banks, some CEOs make it a point to be acquainted with higher-ups.

It's to your best interests that your banker understand what's going on in your business. If you really want to impress your banker, share your strategic business plan, as discussed in Chapter 5, with him. It will impress him and allow him to understand your business and your aspirations better. This can make a big difference when support from the bank is needed.

Remember also that bankers hate surprises. If you see some bad news on the horizon, your banker should be the first to know. They're used to dealing with adversity and may be able to help. Schedule routine visits during the year to keep your loan officer up to date even if there's no staggering news. Above all, remember that one of the most important elements in your relationship is the banker's confidence in your integrity. If your bank doesn't express the interest or isn't willing to take the time to understand your business and work with you, perhaps it's time to find another bank.

Consultants

Many CEOs are reluctant to hire consultants. Their fees may appear to be high in relative terms, and some CEOs describe consultants as "someone who borrows your watch and then tells you what time it is." Yet, when you don't have the expertise within the company for a specific task, it often makes sense to engage a consultant to help.

From a cost viewpoint, consultants are not added to your payroll, nor do they become entitled to benefits. When their task is completed, they leave. If they've been effective, you get an ongoing, long-term benefit that would not have otherwise been possible. Before you engage consultants, check their professional credentials, and talk to others who have used their services. Insist that the scope of the engagement and the fee arrangement be clearly spelled out in writing in advance.

A family business consultant can help you to develop and implement your family strategic plan, as described in Chapter 3; a specialist on strategic planning can help you develop your strategic business plan, as described in Chapter 5; and a consultant can help you to improve your human resources practices, as discussed in Chapter 6.

Your Advisors and Your Family

Your professional advisors can have a profound influence on events that affect both your business and family. Consider involving family members who are active in the business in your discussions with them. You may also want to invite them to selected meetings of your family council as discussed in Chapter 3.

SUMMARY

Independent Board of Directors

• An independent board of directors can provide valuable advice and can constitute a check and balance to owners who are willing to submit themselves to its review.

• The board can bring new dimensions of objectivity, experience, candor, and networking connections to the family business.

• A major benefit of the board is the discipline it imposes by requiring CEOs to articulate their programs and defend them under scrutiny.

• The board does not manage the company. It provides a sounding board to management, reviews the long-term plans of the company, reviews the allocation of the company's resources, and can provide an evaluation of the management of the company.

• The board can be a valuable resource to the family by providing an objective forum for the resolution of family differences; however, it must remain impartial.

• Criteria for selection of the board should be established carefully, depending on the needs of the company. Compensation, term of office, size of the board, and frequency of meetings depend on the circumstances.

• Board members should be indemnified against legal liability by the company and protected by insurance. In some companies, the board serves in an advisory capacity, rather than as the legally constituted board, in order to provide further insulation.

Outside Professional Advisors

• Outside professional advisors are important to the success of the business, and their selection should be based on competence.

• Professional relationships should be periodically evaluated to determine whether the business is getting the proper level of service. This includes creative suggestions by the professionals.

• In choosing a professional, the owner should consider personal chemistry, the commitment of the professional to service, his competence, and the fairness of his fees.

• Banking relationships should involve periodic and open communication, with the banker apprised of the company's plans for the future in addition to the current situation. If the bank doesn't express sufficient interest, perhaps another relationship should be sought.

• When additional expertise is needed, the right consultant can help. Although fees are high in relative terms, it's usually more cost-effective than a permanent hire, and there can be long-term benefits if the job is done right.

NOTES

1. Clayton L. Mathile, "A Business Owner's Perspective on Outside Boards," *Family Business Review*, Fall 1988, p. 231.
2. David E. Gumpert and David Boyd, "The Loneliness of the Small Business Owner," *Harvard Business Review*, November/December 1984, pp. 18–24.
3. Peter F. Drucker, *The Practice of Management* (New York: Harper & Row, 1954).
4. Richard B. Stolley, "How to Fire the CEO," *Fortune*, August 31, 1987, p. 39.
5. John L. Ward and James L. Handy, "A Survey of Board Practices," *Family Business Review*, Fall 1988, pp. 289–308.
6. Sharon Nelton, "Bringing an Outside Board Aboard," *Nation's Business*, May 1985.
7. Ibid.
8. Charles J. Bodenstab, "The Case for Accountability," *Inc.*, June 1988, pp. 129–30.
9. Ibid.
10. Richard B. Stolley, "How to Fire the CEO," pp. 38–48.

11. Thomas L. Whisler, "The Rules of the Game (Homewood, Ill.: Dow Jones-Irwin, 1984).
12. Robert K. Mueller, "Differential Directorship: Special Sensitivities and Roles for Serving the Family Business Board," *Family Business Review*, Fall 1988, p. 240.
13. Peter F. Drucker, "The Bored Board," *Wharton Magazine*, Fall 1976, p. 25.
14. Paul Dickson, *The Official Rules* (New York: Dell Publishing Company, 1979), p. 187.
15. Richard B. Stolley, "How to Fire the CEO."
16. Gardner W. Heidrick, "Selecting Outside Directors," *Family Business Review*, Fall 1988, pp. 271–77.
17. Cindy A. Schipiani and George J. Siedel, "Legal Liability: The Board of Directors," *Family Business Review*, Fall 1988, pp. 279–85.
18. Walter Olson, book review of *Board Games* in *Fortune*, March 13, 1989, p. 143.
19. Ibid.
20. Fred A. Tillmad, "Commentary on Legal Liability," *Family Business Review*, Fall 1988, pp. 287–88.
21. Echo M. Garrett and Webster E. Williams, "Choose Me," *Venture*, May 1988, p. 16.

CHAPTER 8

MAKING A PERFECT FORWARD PASS

YOUTH

They will sit where we are sitting,
and when we are gone, attend to
those things we think are important.
We may adopt all the policies we
please, but how they will be carried
out depends on them. They will
assume control of our cities, states
and nations. They are going to build our homes
And take over our churches,
schools, and corporations.
All our work is going
to be judged, praised or condemned
by them. The fate of humanity is in
their hands. So it might be well to
pay them some attention.

Anonymous

The owner has committed his life to building the business. It's his baby, and he loves his role as its leader. However, if the business is to survive, he must provide for someone else to take his place.

The locomotive hurtles down the tracks at high speed. In the cab, the engineer busies himself with the instruments. There are warning signals, but they don't imply an immediate threat, so he turns them off.

Far ahead, a bridge is down, and the gorge beneath it is filled with the ruins of other trains that have preceded his. Although there is still

time to take corrective action, he is oblivious to the threat and continues at full speed to his rendezvous with disaster. This is often the story
of succession in family business.

THE CHALLENGE OF SUCCESSION

If you're the owner of a family business, it's probably your dream to
continue your business into the next generation and hopefully even to
succeeding generations. (Over two thirds of the respondents of the
L&H/AMA family business survey indicated that they wanted to keep
the business in the family.) You've probably dedicated your life to the
building of your enterprise, and what better monument could you have
than to see your creation carried on by your family.

Unfortunately, many businesses never grow beyond the shadow
of their founders, because they cannot solve the complex problem of
management succession. This issue is especially critical now as the
founders of many businesses in the post–World War II era near retirement age.

Your business may be regenerated by competent and committed
members of the next generation, or your departure may signal the beginning of the end of the enterprise that you worked so hard to build.
To a great extent, the outcome depends on you.

Generally, the alternatives are clear: Succession either takes place
gradually, in an organized way, or suddenly when the owner dies or
becomes ill. In the first case, a prepared successor grows into the role
under the direction and guidance of the owner; in the second, an
unprepared spouse or child is suddenly thrust into it. Family business
mortality statistics are grim evidence of how often the second case
prevails.

FORCES THAT WORK AGAINST SUCCESSION

Approached rationally, succession should be a planned and evolution-
ary process. After all, we are all mortal, and it's axiomatic that a leader
has a responsibility to identify, train, and install his successor during

his lifetime. Unfortunately, many owners don't address this important responsibility. Professor Ivan Lansberg of the Yale School of Organization and Management, in examining the changes required by the succession process, said: "These changes are anxiety-provoking and create a need to resolve some of the uncertainties surrounding the future of the family enterprise. At the same time, resolving these uncertainties makes it necessary to address many emotionally loaded issues that most people would prefer to avoid or deny."[1]

Successful management succession often requires that the following barriers be overcome:

The Owner

• *Denial of mortality*—It is inconceivable to many founders that they won't always be around to run their beloved businesses or that someone else can replace them at the helm. One owner said, "Planning my succession was like participating in my own wake."[2]
• *Unwillingness to change roles*—The owner is accustomed to being in charge and is apt to be most comfortable when he's in total control. To most effectively develop a successor, he must change from "doer" to teacher and mentor, gradually giving up the control that he covets as his pupil assumes more responsibility. Many owners are incapable of assuming a mentor role or of allowing their successors the independence that they need to develop as leaders.
• *Inability to choose among the children*—Family values dictate that children be loved and treated equally. Business values, however, dictate that the selection of a leader should be based on competence. Many owners view the selection of one child as preferential treatment and are unable to do it because they fear hurting the others.
• *Bias against planning*—Successful management succession is generally the result of an extensive planning process that commences many years before the transition occurs. The management style of many owners, however, discourages formal planning, which they may perceive as restrictive, and the owners prefer to manage by "the seat of the pants." Without thoughtful preparation, both parent and child are forced to deal with the transition on a crisis basis.
• *Inability to face retirement*—Many owners are threatened by the prospect of retirement. The following concerns are common·

- I built this business, and it needs me. Nobody else could run it as well.
- The business is my baby and an important part of my life. Giving it up would be like abandoning a child.
- What will I do with my time if I retire? I've devoted my life to the business, and I have few outside interests. How much time can I spend on leisure activities?
- I'm now the decision maker, an important person. How can I retain my self-esteem if I give up my authority and involvement in the business?
- Most of the assets that will support me and my spouse in retirement are tied up in the business. How can I turn it over to an unproven successor?
- I'm now the family patriarch. Will my central role in the family be diminished if I cease to be the source whence all blessings flow?
- If I give up my role as boss, will I lose the status that I enjoy in the community and among my business associates?

The Owner's Wife

- Many wives, after a lifetime of competing with the "mistress" that is their husbands' business, encourage their husbands to expedite retirement so that they may both enter a new and more relaxed phase of life. Some, however, oppose it. A wife may feel that in her position as the boss's wife she is a *very important person*, and this may be a significant part of her identity. She may fear that her importance will be diminished if her husband relinquishes control of the business.

The Children

- There is a taboo in our culture, rooted in childhood fear, that prohibits discussing the death of parents. This is particularly true when it deals with financial matters because a child who raises this discussion would appear to be selfishly interested in his inheritance rather than his parent's longevity

  Although the childrens' future may be profoundly affected by Dad's succession philosophy (or lack thereof), they normally must depend on Dad to take the initiative Usually they admire and love their father, and aren't apt to push for his retirement because it would make them appear to be unappreciative and greedy.

Sibling rivalry, which is discussed in Chapter 3, can make the owner's choice of a successor more difficult and can be even more destructive when the owner leaves a power vacuum by neglecting to plan for orderly succession.

Father-son conflict, which is also discussed in Chapter 3, commonly inhibits the succession process, with fathers experiencing powerful feelings of rivalry and jealousy toward potential successors.

The Employees

• During the building process, the owner probably has earned the respect and the loyalty of the employees. He is *the boss*, a source of strength, who can be depended on as a leader. They know the owner's ways and are comfortable with them. How can they accord the same trust to an unproven kid who will probably try to change everything? Employees can be obstacles to succession, even though the continuity of the business is in their best interests.

THE OWNER'S DILEMMA

Some owners look forward to the day when the next generation will take over so that they will be able to pursue other interests and to "smell the roses," unfettered by day-to-day responsibility.

Others, however, have a dilemma: "Should I initiate the process that will ultimately require me to leave the leadership position that I covet? Or should I continue in my role as long as I can and let the future take care of itself?"

It's usually not an immediate problem. The penalties for failure to plan succession are generally not felt until the owner dies or is physically unable to continue in his management role, so the issue is avoided, and the owner retreats to his comfort zone of putting out the daily fires in the business. "Someday," he says, "I'll address it when I have more time." Of course, that time rarely comes, and eventually the Grim Reaper settles the issue. As C. Northcote Parkinson put it, "delay is the deadliest form of denial "

An owner may be motivated to address this vital issue if he views the business as a monument to his values and accomplishments and if he realizes that the survival of his business, the well-being of his family, and the security of his "extended" family, his employees, depend on his providing for the continuity of the business. Sadly, many owners don't view succession in this perspective.

KEYS TO SUCCESSFUL MANAGEMENT SUCCESSION

With all of these obstacles, many families are able to solve the succession puzzle, some of them for several generations. Dr. Léon Danco said, "If we could be both immortal and celibate, then most of these problems wouldn't come up." For those owners who don't fit this description, here are the keys that may help you to deal with the issue constructively.

The principal components of successful succession usually include: *a unified family*, committed to the continuity of the business; *an owner* who initiates the process early and who guides it to completion; *an able and committed successor*; and a willingness by all participants to work together to preserve a valuable family asset.

Someday you're going to leave your business. The only question is whether you'll leave it *vertically* and gracefully, having provided for competent management in the next generation, or *horizontally*, dumping your responsibility onto an unprepared spouse or other family members. (See "How to Make Your Widow Hate You" in Chapter 11.)

Some owners wait until they are jolted into reality by a life-threatening event, such as a heart attack or an automobile accident. You will improve your chances of success if you don't wait for this to happen, and start *now* to plan for management succession while you have time. If you fail to guide the process through to completion in your lifetime, someone infinitely less qualified will be forced to do it for you. This may result in a bonanza for the tax collectors and lawyers, and trauma for your loved ones. It may also signal the end of the business that you labored so hard to build.

Remember, the ability of a football quarterback to throw a successful forward pass is dependent on the ability of a receiver to catch it. In a family business, the development of a pass-catcher should start early.

The Training Process

Children's viewpoints are colored by your attitude toward the business during their formative years. If they hear you constantly complaining about the "jungle out there" and all of its carnivorous inhabitants, rather than the positive and exciting aspects of the business, why would you expect them to enter it? A cartoon has one owner telling his young son: "The tax people are hounding me; my customers don't want to pay their bills; the employees don't want to work, and someday, son, this will all be yours."

A son who chose not to enter the family business writes about growing up in a family where it was a "silent expectation" that the family business would survive through the generations and his father never quite understood his son's decision to become a writer, rather than to carry on the business. In the son's formative years, the business was rarely discussed at home, and the son's exposure was limited to menial tasks during summer vacations, without his learning what the business was about or how his work contributed to it. His father never expressed the feeling that he enjoyed his work, or that it was fulfilling to him.

The son recalls one of the few conversations he had with his father on the topic when he was 10 or 12, and his father had suggested that someday he might take over the business:

> "Oh, I don't think you'd want that," I said. "Why not?" my father asked. "What would you possibly do with the business that would upset me?" And here, with a kid's insight, I got closer to the differences between us than I probably ever will again. "I'd sell it," I said.[3]

Contrast this with the story of Linda Johnson-Rice who, at age 29, was named by her father to be president and chief operating officer of Johnson Publishing Co., the largest black-owned company in the United States, with annual volume of over $175 million. According to

Business Week, "She has been training for her new job since the age of seven. That's when her mother began taking her on biannual trips to Paris, clothes-hunting for the family company's traveling fashion show."[4]

Should They Enter the Business?

If your child isn't cut out for the business, you do him no favor by creating a job for him and allowing him to become a lifelong dependent. It robs him of his self-esteem and can deter him from pursuing a personally rewarding career elsewhere. One owner's son wanted to be a school teacher but couldn't live on a school teacher's salary. The owner solved this dilemma by providing a subsidy for the difference in pay. This made everyone happy. Make it clear to your children that they are welcome to enter your business, but that if they choose another alternative, you will accept it and be supportive.

Don't assume that they will want to enter the business. After all, the business is *your* baby and an important part of *your* life. And don't expect them to be interested if it doesn't present economic opportunity for them. One of the most frequent, and tragic, errors of owners is to create jobs for children who are not suited to the business. This can result in an unhappy working career for the child and can be demoralizing to the others in the business.

Encourage Them to Be Eagles

One father compared children to eagles that soar away when they learn to fly and to ducks that stay at home. His view was that if you allow children to be eagles, they may find other opportunities and never return to the business, while if they're ducks, they'll stay. It's worth the risk. Encourage your children to gain outside experience before joining your business. If they return as eagles they'll almost certainly be better for the experience. If not, it's their choice, and you should be happy that they have found satisfying careers.

Many owners are authoritarians, more accustomed to giving orders than acting with the restraint that the training process requires. Inexperienced as teachers, they try to train impatient pupils who may have inflated opinions of their own capabilities. What is called for is patience, patience, and more patience with a commitment by both teacher and pupil to make it work. Encourage two-way communication, and listen, really listen to your child. You have much experience and know-how to share, but if your relationship becomes an extended lecture, you'll risk turning them off.

A "Preemployment" Agreement
Sometimes, despite the best of intentions, it doesn't work out. Maybe the child isn't meant for the business. Maybe you just can't work together. If you both view the relationship as an irrevocable commitment, chances are that it will be a lose-lose situation for everybody. Discussing this possibility in advance and agreeing on an escape clause might help to avoid misunderstanding and perhaps animosity. It's not unusual for a child to leave the business for a period of time and then return to develop a successful relationship after both parent and child have done some more growing.

Clarify Work Habit Expectations
Joining most family businesses usually demands hard work and long hours, and children entering the business should understand this commitment. Discuss the working hours, possible seasonal demands, and travel requirements.

One of your child's most demanding challenges is to earn the respect of employees, so avoid preferential treatment for family members and don't allow them to treat the business as a country club. One father said to a son, "I think you're Jewish on Saturday because you observe the Sabbath; on Sunday you're Catholic—you observe the Sabbath; but after three o'clock during the week, I want to know what religion you belong to that you can't be around."[5]

From Parent/Disciplinarian to Teacher/Mentor
During your children's growing-up years, you were parent/disciplinarian. They are now adults and should be treated that way without being shielded from the hard knocks that are necessary to the learning experience. Become their teacher and mentor. As William Arthur Ward put it, "The mediocre teacher tells. The good teacher explains. The superior teacher demonstrates. The great teacher inspires." Share your experience and wisdom, and be available for counsel, but also listen to

them. Encourage them to express their ambitions and ideas. Give them no special favors; they have a need to earn their own way. Above all, challenge them to build on and improve your creation, rather than just to continue it.

Because of the emotional involvement, fathers can be the worst teachers. Remember when you first tried to teach your child to drive? Encourage your child to find a mentor in the organization other than you so that his performance will not be colored by his childhood or family implications. When Armand Hammer, of Occidental Petroleum, hired his grandson, he told the latter's boss to "work his butt off. If you don't, your butt is out of here."[6]

Rotate childrens' jobs throughout the organization so that they can learn the business firsthand. Grant them increasing independence, working toward their assumption of responsibility and accountability for their own profit centers as soon as possible. There is no substitute for this kind of experience, out from under Dad's wing. And remember that each generation has a different language and can't learn what former generations knew until it has been translated into their words.[7]

How did you learn your role? Almost certainly, you learned by perseverance, mistakes, and possibly some luck. You probably had one or more mentors who took you under their wings. Allow your children the same opportunity. One owner put it this way, "I won't put my son in a position to make a mistake that could threaten the business, but he'll never learn to assume total responsibility unless he's allowed to make his own mistakes on a smaller scale. When there's a victory, it's *his* win. When there's a screw-up, it belongs to both of us."

If your child makes a mistake, view it as a learning experience; point out what happened and give constructive advice, but don't second-guess. One child complained: "I keep looking over my shoulder because he'll be along to correct everything I do. If he makes every decision, I might as well let him do my job. And he thinks he's helping me." Another who despaired of pleasing his father said, "Every time I get the ball down the field, he moves the goal line." In General George S. Patton's words, "Never tell people how to do things. Tell them what to do, and they will surprise you with their ingenuity."

Introduce your successor to your banker, key customers, important suppliers, and your outside professionals, such as your lawyer and CPA. In addition to being a learning experience for the successor, it is comforting to those who depend on you that you're farsighted enough to plan for the continuity of the business.

Define Their Roles
It's important that the role of each family member in the business be clearly defined, as conflict over roles can be a major cause of tension. In larger businesses, this can be resolved by separation of responsibility for differing segments of the business. A common and generally successful approach is when one child is "Mr. Inside" (production) and another is "Mr. Outside" (sales). If the business lends itself to it, geographical separation is usually desirable. One owner observed, "my kids seem to get along together better when there's 500 miles between them."

Sometimes, in a smaller business, a clear separation of work may be inefficient, and some overlap is necessary, but the "everybody does everything" approach can be a breeding ground for conflict. Establish the responsibilities of each role in writing. Provide procedures on how overlap will be handled. Tension can be prevented by the existence of established policy that is clearly understood by everyone involved.

Establish Goals and Provide Feedback
When your child enters the business, establish *achievable and quantifiable* goals that are mutually agreeable. As discussed in Chapter 6, employees, *including children*, have a need to know what is expected in their jobs. They also need feedback about their performance, including recognition for accomplishments and constructive advice on areas that need improvement. This should be done regularly and in writing. Change the goals and objectives as the child progresses.

Don't practice the commonly used evaluation system—"If you don't hear from me, assume that you're doing all right. If you screw up, I'll let you know."

While it can be valuable for a child to learn every job on the way up, make sure that it is a legitimate learning experience rather than a way to make him "pay his dues." There is a great difference between 10 years of experience and one year of experience repeated 10 times.

You Can't Clone Yourself
Some owners view succession like a cloning process. They believe that as soon as they train their children to be duplicates of themselves, then

maybe they can think about retiring Of course, this doesn't happen The child has his own ideas and is impatient to try them, but Dad may stand in the way with the traditional defense: "This is how we always did it." He continues to justify his failure to phase down and delegate authority by concluding that "the kid is just not ready yet." In these circumstances, what could be an enriching and broadening experience for both generations becomes a battlefield. One son said, "My father thinks that the only way to get on first base is to get a hit, although there are several other ways."

For better or worse, your children are not you. They grew up in a different environment, probably had different educational backgrounds, have different aspirations, and are entering a business that is quite different from when you founded or entered it. The father of noted anthropologist Charles Darwin once wrote to him, "You care for nothing but shooting, dogs and rat-chasing and you will be a disgrace to yourself and your family."

Your children have their own ideas and, just as you did, will express them in their own ways. However, this does not mean that you should turn over the business that it took you a lifetime to build to untested heirs. It means that you should share your experience, provide counsel, and help them to grow according to their own abilities.

Don't assume that your children understand what you have in mind. Encourage ongoing and extensive *two-way* communication so that you can plan your futures together. And listen, really listen to them, even if you don't agree with their ideas.

Henry Ford refused to entrust his son Edsel with more management responsibility because he lacked "toughness." As a result, he gave his son the driver's seat but didn't give him the keys. Hindsight proved that a change in management style was just what the company needed at the time and that this was another father-son blunder.

Pay Them Fairly
Some owners pay their children far below their true worth, and conversations such as the following are common:

Child:

> Dad, I'm having a hard time getting by, and I'd like an increase in salary.

Owner

> What are you worried about? Someday you're going to own the business. You should be happy that you've just been named executive vice president

This is called a TILOP (title in lieu of pay).

Other owners go to the opposite extreme and pay children far beyond their value to the business, in effect providing an extension of the allowances that they used to get as children. While this may provide the kids with a tax-deductible lifestyle that they could not otherwise have afforded, it can be unhealthy for both the child and the business as it can make the child into a lifelong dependent.

Excessive compensation can provide a lifestyle that the child couldn't otherwise afford, thus locking him into the business. One son in this unhappy position said, "I really hate this business and the way Dad treats me. I'm 32 years old, and I already have ulcers, but if I left, we'd have to give up our beautiful home, luxury cars, and private school for the kids, and I'd have to start over. I can't do it to my family."

In our experience, the healthiest compensation method is to pay family members the market value of their jobs, as though they were working for another company. It allows them the dignity of relating their incomes to merit, provides them with the sense of independence that would allow them to leave if they chose, and bases their salaries on objective criteria, rather than on subjective and emotional factors that can lead to conflict. In these circumstances, a child who is a shipping clerk can hardly expect to be paid the same as a sibling in charge of a segment of the business.

PLANNING FOR TRANSITION

Establish a Succession Plan

Consider appointing a succession task force, consisting of key trusted employees and selected family members, and work with them to develop a succession plan. This doesn't mean that succession will necessarily be a democratic process, or that you'll give up your prerogatives; however, it provides an opportunity for all concerned to discuss their thoughts, fears, and concerns openly, and it should help to reduce negative emotional reaction in the family by providing a forum for the issue to be discussed openly and objectively. Express your ideas as to the criteria for the choice and the timetable that you have in mind.

You may have assumed, incorrectly, that everyone wants the job. Find out who aspires to it, and how they'll deal with the disappointment if they don't get it. All too often the discussion is confined only to the top job, which is only part of the process. Get their ideas about the constitution of the management team in the next generation and their places in it. Gather your conclusions into a succession plan.

Communicate your plan to your family, your employees, and to outsiders with a stake in the continuity of your business, such as your banker, customers, and suppliers. This will give everyone time to plan for a smooth transition and it will prevent the ambiguity that frequently leads to misunderstanding and conflict in the family. It will also announce to the world that you're far sighted enough to plan for your company's future.

Involve Your Family

Many owners silently agonize over succession rather than discussing it with their families. As a result, the children worry about it while waiting, almost interminably, for the other shoe to drop when the owner finally makes *the decision*. One owner tells about three sons in his real estate business, all hard-working and committed. "I'm ready to make my life easier and phase down," he said. "And I know that I have to select one of my sons as boss. My youngest son is more capable of managing the business than his brothers, but he has an abrasive personality, and I doubt that they would accept it. If he had a choice between entering a room by smashing the door down or by merely opening it, he would smash it down every time." The father agonizes over the decision but has never talked about it with his sons. A conversation with one of the sons, however, reveals a different perspective. "We know what Dad is going through," said his oldest son, "and I'm sure we could work it out if we addressed it together. But Dad refuses to talk about it."

As discussed in Chapter 3, if you discuss succession openly and candidly with your family, you may find that many fears and concerns, both yours and your children's, may be alleviated or resolved.

Get Outside Help

Many owners feel that they must be almighty and have all the answers. The best leaders, however, recognize their limitations and are not reluctant to seek help. Management transition requires decisions that you probably make only once in your career, and therefore you don't have experience in managing this difficult process. Perhaps you can benefit from others who have experience in this area, such as a family business consultant, your lawyer, or your CPA.

If you have an independent-working board of directors, as discussed in Chapter 7, it can provide a valuable source of objective guidance without the emotional overtones that so frequently accompany this process.

THE CHANGING OF THE GUARD

Choosing Your Successor

You may be in the difficult position of having to choose between the best interests of the business and harmony in the family. This is more likely to be true if you have allowed family values to dictate your business behavior, and it may be late in the game to change your family's expectations. If you have involved your family in an open planning process, there should be no surprises and less likelihood of family trauma.

In evaluating a candidate, important questions must be asked. Is the candidate committed to your company's mission? Does he exercise good judgment? Does he possess the skills needed by the business? Does he have the interpersonal and leadership skills that motivate others? As Henry Ford said, "The question 'Who ought to be boss?' is like asking 'Who ought to be tenor in the quartet?' Obviously, the man who can sing tenor."

One owner, talking about his two sons, said: "John, my older son, is a tough, capable businessman, and I know he can run the business.

Eric is not a leader, and he's not as motivated as his brother, but he's a considerate and caring son while John probably wouldn't notice if my wife and I dropped off the planet. Although it's difficult and I hate to hurt Eric, I believe that it's in the best interests of both the business and the family that John be my successor."

The "Logical" Successor

Sometimes the choice is easy. There may be a single successor who is both able and committed, and who naturally gravitates into the role. In one family, a son-in-law was the natural leader, and although he never owned stock in the company, he commanded everyone's respect and was the principal architect of its growth. In another instance, the younger of two daughters in the business was named as successor. The older sister commented, "she has always been a leader, and I've been a follower. I'm very comfortable with her becoming the successor."

The Fixed Rule

In some families, although there may be more than one potential successor, the rule of primogeniture prevails, and the oldest son is automatically the first choice. While this eliminates uncertainty and jockeying for position among the children, it may result in the naming of a lesser qualified leader as compared to other candidates.

Daughters as Successors

Don't overlook your daughters. As discussed in Chapters 2 and 3, daughters often have unique qualifications for the CEO role, unencumbered by traditional father-son conflict. When Hugh Hefner was looking for a new president in 1982, his daughter Christie pulled no punches in telling him what was wrong with the company, and he gave her the job. She has proven herself to be a creative and able executive who has transformed the company

In-Laws as Successors

As discussed in Chapter 2, in-laws as successors involve unique issues. In many instances, they are valuable and committed family members who provide next-generation leadership that would not have existed otherwise. Divorce is an obvious concern What happens if a son-in-law is running your business and a divorce ensues? The risk of a potential divorce against the benefits of an in-law in the business must be weighed. There are no easy answers.

In-laws have an additional hurdle in that many families restrict stock ownership to bloodline family members. So, from this quasi-family position, the in-law must more than prove his worth to be considered for the top job.

The Board of Directors Chooses

When there is an independent-working board of directors, as discussed in Chapter 7, it may assume the responsibility for choosing a successor. This provides an independent, objective assessment of the candidates, free of the emotional burden that the owner carries when a choice must be made among his children. Also, an unpopular choice may be more readily accepted by the family if it is made by objective third parties. Allowing the board to choose can be a "cop-out" by a CEO who is reluctant to make a difficult decision.

The Kids Choose

Sometimes the children are given the opportunity to select a successor from among themselves. While this could result in a popularity contest rather than a choice of the most competent leader, a successor chosen in this way would at least enjoy the support of his siblings. However, allowing the children to choose is normally an abdication of the owner's responsibilities and is not a frequently used method

Shared Management

Elliot Lehman, chairman and an owner of Fel-Pro, Inc. (a family-run car parts and sealants maker), when faced with the problem of naming a president from among the owners' children named three "Titles aren't very important to us," he said.[8] In our experience, however, most businesses need one leader with ultimate authority. Some owners, unable to reach a decision on which child should be the successor, allow them to fight it out, usually with destructive results. There are circumstances, however, when shared management can work, but they are extremely limited, and generally this style only lasts until a new or expanded cast of characters gets involved.

Under this style of management, there is no "boss" in the traditional sense but a partnership among the owners with decisions made jointly. For shared management to be effective, there must be a high degree of trust among the owners. It helps if each owner is relatively equal in ability and responsible for differing segments of the business. It's also important that the owners have the ability to compromise and reach consensus in decision making. One of two brothers who built a highly successful business said: "We've been disagreeing successfully for 25 years."

The parties should agree on a method of resolving impasses, should they occur. This may involve a third party who enjoys the trust and confidence of all the participants, or it can be by a "swing voter" who owns a minority of the stock. Shared management is most apt to be successful when there are a limited number of owners. Each additional owner exponentially reduces its changes of success.

One of six siblings who own a textile manufacturing company said, "We all take care of our own responsibilities, and we trust each other. If a major decision is involved, the majority prevails, but I don't remember the last time we actually had a vote. I don't know how it happens, but we just work it out and eventually agree. There's a lot of love in our family." In this situation, however, there's also Mom's strong presence. Consensus management works because Mom provides a cohesive force and is present as a tie breaker in case of an impasse. Project this scene into the next generation when she isn't around, and 15 or 20 cousins, all with equal voting control, are involved, and you have a prescription for chaos.

L. Vaughn Company, a woodworking company in Warwick, Rhode Island, survived for five generations until, with its stock split among several cousins, dissension practically caused its ruin. A CPA sent in by the bank to help diagnose the company's problems said: "The family could never decide who was leading the parade. Major decisions were held up because of all the second-guessing. There was a serious authority problem."[9]

Management Rotation
Some founders try ill-conceived compromises such as rotating management among the children. By the time one learns this difficult job, his term is over. This is a contrived device to avoid making a decision, and there are few known examples of its being successful.

When There Is No Competent Successor

Perhaps rivalry among the children is so intense that none of them would accept a sibling as leader. Perhaps none of them has the ability to run the business. If you assess the situation realistically and conclude that the chances of successful succession to the next generation are not favorable, you may save your family and your business by not forcing it. Here are some alternatives.

Divide the Business
If sibling conflict prevents the children from proceeding together, consider dividing the business and allowing the children to inherit different segments and continue independently.

Sell the Business
While selling the business may result in income taxes that might have been avoided if the business stayed in the family, it may protect both peace in the family and your financial security. (For more on selling the business see Chapter 10).

Engage Professional Management
Many families opt to hire professional managers if a family member is not capable of running the business. While this is no guarantee of success, at least the family can be assured that the helm is in experienced hands. With this step away from family involvement, the need for an independent-working board of directors becomes intensified.

Appoint an Employee
Sometimes the selection of an able and trusted employee is indicated. Perhaps the owner's children aren't old enough or experienced enough for the role, and the employee can serve in a transition capacity. For example, the owner's children may be just entering the business while the employee is in his mid-50s. By the time a child may be ready, the employee will have reached retirement age.

Few owners are inclined to choose employees as successors. In the L&H/AMA family business survey, owners were asked what they would do if none of their children were capable of succeeding them: Of these, 41 percent said that they would sell the business; 19 percent would appoint a professional manager; 17 percent would appoint an employee, and 23 percent had other responses or didn't know

MAKING A GRACEFUL EXIT

Prepare Yourself for Retirement

You are more apt to be successful if you prepare for your later years by gradually relinquishing your responsibilities. Think about how you can best use your newfound leisure time, possibly the first time in your adult life that you will have such a luxury. Retirement can be a terrifying experience, or it can be a time when you can enjoy the fruit of your labor. Experts say that this phase of your life is more apt to be successful if you are retiring *to* a new life with interesting activities that you never had time for, rather than *from* your old one, which connotes that your productive and useful days are over.

Walter L. Jacobs, who founded the rental car industry, became president of Hertz. Five years before his contemplated retirement, he told everyone of his timetable and gradually turned over authority and responsibility to younger people. Applying his experience, he started developing real estate and banking interests in the town where he intended to live after retirement. The result? He became involved in his new activities and enjoyed a long and happy retirement while Hertz prospered under new, well-trained leadership.

Many owners pass off operating responsibility to their successors and assume new, productive roles in the company. One took on the responsibility for expansion into international markets. Another took over the strategic planning function, and a third dedicated himself to new product development.

Contrast this with Charles Vergos (64) who owns a successful rib joint restaurant in Memphis and runs it with his sons and daughter: John (41), Nick (37), and Tina (33). Charles tells people, "I'm going to live to 100, and when I die, I'm not going to lie down; they're going to have to screw me into the ground." He has tapered down from his traditional 80-hour week and his children have assumed more responsibilities, but there's little doubt about who's boss. Nick said, "It's my father's restaurant. That is just a plain and simple fact."[10]

The Myth of "Semiretirement"

Many owners, unwilling to face the reality of leaving, try to find a middle ground called "semiretirement." This means Dad takes extended vacations and enjoys more leisure time while he boasts that the kids are really running the business. However, he's in daily telephone contact and probably has a fax machine at his vacation home so as not to miss anything. While this allows the kids more latitude to run the business, everyone knows that he is still boss, and the succession issue remains unresolved.

When asked about it William Rosenberg, then 72-year-old founder and chairman emeritus of Dunkin' Donuts, said, "Who said they retire? They call me up or I call them up. You're still involved. You walk in Dunkin' Donuts and if it's not run right, you're still going to yell like hell. You never change."[11]

Exit Gracefully

By the time your children are in their 40s, they expect leadership roles. Confronted by a father who refuses to let go, many children leave the business to pursue other opportunities. Others stay on because they're not financially in a position to start over again, but the situation is replete with resentment. It can be even more complex when there is father-son conflict, as described in Chapter 3.

The Owner's Departure Style

Jeffrey Sonnenfeld, in his book *The Hero's Farewell: What Happens When CEOs Retire*, classified CEOs into the following four departure styles:

- *Monarchs* don't leave office until they are forced out through death or an internal revolt.

- *Generals* are forced out of office but plot their return and quickly come back out of retirement to "save" the business.
- *Ambassadors* leave office gracefully and serve as postretirement mentors. While they may remain on the board of directors they don't sabotage their successors.
- *Governors* rule for a limited term of office, retire, and shift to other vocational outlets, maintaining limited contact with the business after departure.[12]

You will never be able to teach your children everything that you know, but hopefully you can help them to reach a point where they can manage the business. Don't hang on until you're viewed as an obstacle. You may assume a new role as chairman of the board where you can provide the guidance and the moral support that they need. However, don't succumb to the temptation to use this role to control operations.

For some, there will never be a right time to retire. An old story had a son inquiring about his father's retirement plans. "Don't worry," replied the father. "Your time will come. You're just not ready." The son replied, "But, Dad, I'm 67 years old."

It's only natural that you feel some ambivalence in letting go, and it's only natural that you'll feel sad about it. Be proud of the legacy that you're leaving, and celebrate your new life without the day-to-day responsibilities of the business.

Some owners become bored with retirement and return to the business where they get in everyone's way, vainly trying to recreate the old days. If this impulse should occur, try to find new sources of interest, and don't put your children in the unwelcome role of having to humor you.

SUMMARY

During Your Children's Growing-Up Years
- Share your dream. Tell them about the challenges and interesting experience as well as the negatives.
- Take them to the shop with you *if* they want to go. Let them be exposed, even if it means sitting at your desk with their coloring books.

• Share your business experiences. Remember that your attitude toward your business will color how they view it.
• Encourage them to work in the business during summer vacations. Try to find meaningful work for them to do. Explain how their jobs contribute to the company's objectives.
• If possible, take them with you to selected meetings and business trips.

When They've Completed Their Schooling
• Let them know that they are welcome to join the business, but that you will understand and be supportive if they pursue other careers.
• If they are interested in joining the business, encourage them first to consider employment elsewhere for an extended period.

If They Enter Your Business
• Let if be understood that working in the business is a privilege, involving special commitment rather than a birthright, and that it does not automatically include lifetime tenure.
• Explain that your business is run by sound business standards and that family membership does not exempt them from these standards.
• Provide them with the training that will allow them to achieve their highest level of potential. Allow them the latitude to grow in their own way and make their own mistakes.

Announce Your Retirement Plan
• At the earliest possible time, establish your retirement target date far enough in advance so that everyone can plan for it. Select your successor as soon as you can. Put your plan in writing, and let it be known to your family, employees, and the people with whom you do business.

When It's Time to Step Down
• Do it. Give up daily operations, and go on to a new, and hopefully enjoyable, phase of your life.

In the final analysis, the business is yours, and you can either help to provide for its regeneration or establish the groundwork for its destruction. The choice is yours.

NOTES

1. Ivan S. Lansberg, "The Succession Conspiracy," *Family Business Review*, Summer 1988, p. 121.
2. Ibid., p. 124.
3. Daniel Paisner, "The Family Business," *New York Times Magazine*, October 5, 1986, p. 86.
4. Lois Therrein, "A Nice Graduation Present: Johnson Publishing," *Business Week*, July 13, 1987, p. 32.
5. Paul C. Rosenblatt, Leni de Mik, Roxanne M. Anderson, and Patricia A. Johnson, *The Family in Business* (San Francisco: Jossey-Bass, 1985), p. 163.
6. Stewart Toy, "The New Nepotism: Why Dynasties Are Making a Comeback," *Business Week*, April 4, 1988, p. 106.
7. Edward F. Murphy, *Katherine Butler Hathaway: The Crown Treasure of Relevant Quotations* (New York: Crown Publishers, 1978), pp. 318–19.
8. Buck Brown, "Succession Strategies for Family Firms," *The Wall Street Journal*, August 4, 1988, p. 23.
9. Joshua Hyatt, "Splitting Heirs," *Inc.*, March 1988, pp. 102–10.
10. Megan Rowe, "Letting Go Gradually at the Rendezvous," *Restaurant Management*, November 1987, p. 42.
11. Mary Sit, "Retirement: Dirty Word to Most Top Executives," *The Boston Globe*, August 7, 1988.
12. Jeffrey Sonnenfeld, *The Hero's Farewell: What Happens When CEOs Retire* (New York: Oxford University Press, 1988), pp. 58–79.

CHAPTER 9

WHEN I GROW UP, I WANT TO BE PRESIDENT

ADVICE TO MY SON

To Laertes:
There, my blessing with you!
And these few precepts in they memory
See thou character. Give thy thoughts no tongue,
Nor any unproportion'd thought his act.
Be thou familiar, but by no means vulgar.
The friends thou hast, and their adoption tried,
Grapple them to thy soul with hoops of steel;
But do not dull thy palm with entertainment
Of each new-hatch'd, unfledg'd comrade.
Beware of entrance to a quarrel; but, being in,
Bear't that the opposed may beware of thee.
Give every man thine ear, but few thy voice:
Take each man's censure, but reserve thy judgement.
Costly thy habit as thy purse can buy,
But not express'd in fancy; rich, not gaudy:
For the apparel oft proclaims the man;
And they in France of the best rank and station
Are most select and generous chief in that.
Neither a borrower nor a lender be:
For loan oft loses both itself and friend;
And borrowing dulls the edge of husbandry.
This above all, to thine ownself be true;
And it must follow, as the night the day,
Thou canst not then be false to any man.
Farewell: my blessing season this in thee!

Polonius; *Hamlet*, Act I, Scene III

This chapter is directed to children in family businesses, who have a lot to prove—to employees, to the outside world, and to themselves. Most of all, they have to prove to the owner that they're capable of building the business and won't ruin his creation *

If you grew up in a family business, it probably had a profound influence on you during your growing-up years. Dad may have shared his dream and enthusiasm with the family at the dinner table. Your first exposure to the business may have come when, as a young child, you accompanied him to the shop with your coloring books. Maybe you worked there after school or during summer vacations.

IS IT A "CAN'T WIN" SITUATION?

Many young people with entrepreneurial aspirations find it more attractive to enter the already established family business than to go through the pain of a start-up without adequate capital. However, some people in your position feel that working in a family business is a can't win situation. They're concerned that if they succeed people may say, "Why not, look what they started with?" If they fail, they'll have destroyed a family legacy that was handed to them on a silver platter.

You may be a member of "The Lucky Sperm Club," but it wasn't your choice; just make the best of your opportunity. Many of the success stories of our era were created by second or later generations. IBM achieved its greatness under Thomas Watson, Jr. Henry Ford II saved his family's business. The Marriott Corporation started as a root beer parlor. Bill Marriott, the son of the founder, started with summer jobs waiting on customers in their family restaurants and became the

---

*This chapter, more than any other, refers to the owner as a male. While women are now starting businesses at rapidly escalating rates, men were responsible for most of the business formations in the post–World War II era. As the founders are now at or approaching retirement age, management succession is particularly relevant. We hope women readers will understand that to portray a balanced male/female approach to the owner would, for the most part, be inconsistent with the realities.

driving force that created a hotel empire with over $5 billion in annual revenues

THE TWO SIDES OF NEPOTISM

Ultimately, if the family business is to continue, a new leader will have to be selected when the owner is no longer capable of carrying on. In nonfamily businesses, this choice is the result of an extensive process, involving intense competition among a wide number of candidates. In a family business, the field of acceptable successors usually consists of the children of the owner. If none are interested in or capable of assuming this role, the business is normally sold or liquidated.

Despite their favored status, children in family businesses are often driven to excel because of the commitment and pride that they bring to their jobs. Joan, who works in the building supply company founded by her father, drove through a blinding snowstorm at night to deliver some equipment that had been promised to a customer. When asked about it, she said: "We made a commitment, and that's our name on the door."

You may have many concerns about working in your family business such as:

- How can I ever follow Dad's act? Will I fail in full view of everyone?
- Will I be able to retain my independence as a person?
- Will I be able to live up to Dad's expectations? Can we both adapt to an employer-employee relationship?
- How will I get along with my siblings in the business?
- How can I gain the respect of the employees?

Children in a family business have a unique opportunity to build a career that provides challenging and interesting work, economic security, and a ready-made vehicle to exercise their entrepreneurial skills. Because of the emotional complexities, however, life in a family business can also seem like a prolonged root canal. The chances of success are higher when the child and the owner approach the challenge in an organized way.

BEFORE ENTERING THE BUSINESS

Evaluate the Trade-Offs

Working in a family business involves many trade-offs. The benefits are obvious: The business is established. It offers job security and probably an attractive income. Family members enjoy a unique status, rather than being a cog in the wheel of a giant enterprise, and may someday own the business.

However, there's a price to be paid for these advantages, and if you enter the business for the wrong reasons, it could be a decision that you'll always regret. Do you share Dad's enthusiasm and have an interest and an aptitude for the business? Or do you view it as a haven, where you won't have to prepare a résumé and compete on equal terms with your peers? Most family businesses require long hours and hard work. Are you prepared to make this commitment?

Think beyond the immediate future. If working in the family business doesn't excite you, and if it's not where you would *really* like to spend the rest of your business life, consider other alternatives while there is time. With the passage of the years it gets more difficult.

If, however, you share Dad's dream and are willing to make the commitment to build on his accomplishments, your career can be enriching and rewarding. As with anything else worth achieving in life, it's not an easy task.

Establish Dialogue with Dad Early

Plan your career with Dad, taking nothing for granted. Ask about his aspirations for the business and his timetable for the future. This may be even more important for daughters as many fathers, accustomed to a different era, don't think of them as potential successors, particularly if the nature of the business, such as the construction industry, is typically thought of as a man's business.

If you're uncertain about your direction, try to elicit his support for you to try other alternatives. It's better to have this discussion before you have invested several years of your life and before the time and effort to train you have been expended. If you're not sure that the business is right for you, consider entering on a trial basis. Before you enter the business, discuss the possibility that it won't work out and that your business career may take place elsewhere. If you don't discuss this in advance, you may find that Dad will consider your decision to leave as one that abandons him and his dream after he has invested in your training. This kind of discussion may be distasteful before you enter the business, in the same way that people getting married avoid prenuptial agreements because they imply a lack of commitment; however, it's better that it be discussed before there is a problem.

Get Experience Elsewhere First

There are many reasons why it's preferable to get work experience elsewhere before joining the business:

• *You'll learn how other businesses work.* Almost certainly, this will benefit you throughout your business life. It may be of particular value if you work for a bigger, more professionally managed business than your family's and if you stay long enough to earn at least one promotion. It's helpful, but not necessary, for it to be in the same industry. Edgar Bronfman, Jr., showed no interest in joining the family's business empire (which includes Seagram's, Du Pont, and natural gas production), choosing to be a movie producer. After his father persuaded him to join the company, with the provision that he "could leave it if he hated it," he joined the business. Four years later, he was named as his father's successor.[1]

A son's experience as an underwriter with an insurance company made it possible to provide customers with better coverage at lower cost when he joined the family insurance agency.

A daughter's experience as a buyer for a large department store enabled her to introduce some much badly needed sophistication in merchandising methods when she entered her family's retail store chain.

• *It enhances your sense of independence.* When you succeed on your own, away from the family cocoon, it helps to build your self-esteem and gain the confidence that comes from achieving your own merit. This can be particularly valuable if you should choose to leave the family business, in which case, you won't be burdened by fear of the outside world. You'll have the comfort of knowing that you can compete in an environment where the required qualifications go beyond having the right last name.

• *It enhances credibility with employees.* As a child, you may have gone to the shop with your father. In this context, you may have been viewed affectionately as Jr. Boss or some similar term. When you enter the business as a career, it's different, and there may be mixed emotions among employees of long-standing when they see you achieve status beyond what they could ever attain. Your credibility will be enhanced when you enter the business with experience, having made your beginner's mistakes elsewhere.

• *It helps eliminate the "grass is greener" syndrome.* Sometimes a child enters the family business, only to leave after a few years with the expectation that a career in another business would be better. You are undoubtedly aware of all of the shortcomings of your business. Experience elsewhere will teach you that every business has them; they just come in different shapes and sizes.

WORKING IN THE BUSINESS

Plan Your Business Education

For the first several years, your principal objective should be to learn as much as you can about the business. Develop an organized plan with Dad that involves your own areas of responsibility with full accountability. Ask for line positions, where you can learn in the trenches, rather than staff jobs. Avoid the role of Dad's shadow; the "watch me" approach is not an effective way for you to develop your own abilities as a leader.

Try to rotate through every phase of the business. This will not only give you insight into the "nuts and bolts" of the business but will help you to determine which job is of most interest to you. Maybe you'll be fascinated by production. Or you may find sales to be of most interest. Most importantly, try to spend your time on meaningful learning experiences, if possible, and not on menial or repetitive jobs. The size of the business is a determining factor. For example, a child entering a family manufacturing business doesn't necessarily gain from being a machine operator. But in a machine shop, it's an integral part of the business.

Take responsibility for your business education. Ask questions Use the magic words, "Will you help me?" Most people are willing to help, and will respond favorably to requests for guidance. Find a mentor, other than your parent, who will take you under his wing, and become your teacher and friend. Your mentor may be Dad, but preferably it will be a key manager of long-standing who takes an interest in you. This will provide a relationship unencumbered by the emotional aspects of your family relationship.

Join your industry's trade organizations, and read their publications. Read books about your industry as well as the leading works on business management.

In addition to learning specific tasks, take a broader view of the business. What is its mission? Its strengths and weaknesses? Where is it headed in the next three to five years? What strategies are in place to achieve its goals? If your business has a strategic plan, you'll find many of these answers there. If not, you'll have to dig to get the answers.

Earning the Respect of Employees

It's to the employees' advantage for you to succeed because you represent the continuity of the business on which their job security depends. Their acceptance, however, is not automatic and must be earned. Edsel Ford, great-grandson of the founder of Ford Motor Company, works 11-hour days to prove his merit and is conscious of the need for humility. "My father stressed it," he says. "Don't be so quick with an answer. Learn to listen. I try awful hard not to walk around with the Ford logo tattooed on my back."[2]

You must prove that you're anxious to learn, and willing to work hard, without seeking special privileges. Don't make the mistake of thinking that Dad's authority extends to you. And don't become the company snitch. If you run to Dad every time you see something wrong, you'll lose your credibility.

Acceptance as a leader does not come with your title. Perry joined the family's chain of dry cleaning stores five years ago, soon after his father's death, and is now vice president. Perry leaves early at the end of the workday and is content to run one of the stores without involvement in overall management, which is handled by Walt, a key employee. Although Perry may eventually inherit the business and become president, the employees will still look to Walt for leadership.

Your Spouse's Role

If you are married, your spouse can be a valuable sounding board as well as a source of support. He, or she, in a desire to be supportive, can also be a destructive factor.

There are countless instances where family members might have been able to work out their differences if their spouses hadn't gotten involved and elevated business disputes into major family warfare. In one extreme case, a wife took a tape measure to the shop because she was determined that her husband should not have a smaller office than his brother. In our experience, it's usually healthier if spouses who don't work in the business don't get involved with business matters.

Maintain a Business Attitude at the Shop

Everyone knows you're the boss's kid. Your goal should be to establish your own identity and succeed on your own merits. Encourage a strictly business relationship with Dad at the shop. Unless it would be too uncomfortable for you both, try to call your father what everyone else calls him, rather than "Dad." Encourage him to call you by the same name as your peers and not by any cute nicknames. Discourage special favors, such as extended vacations or lunches at the club.

Don't Be Afraid to Ask Why

A visitor to the royal palace in czarist Russia was intrigued to see guards maintaining a round-the-clock patrol around a large tree. Inquiry revealed that the czarina had planted a sapling when she was a young girl and her father had ordered it to be guarded so nobody would trample it. Everyone had assumed there was still a reason for the guard and nobody had thought to question it, so it continued for years after the need had ended.

You are coming into the business with a fresh viewpoint, and one of your most important contributions may be to question its operational procedures. You will probably find that the organizational structure of the business and its systems and procedures came about through patchwork and evolution, rather than by thoughtful design.

At first, it may come as a surprise to you that, although yours may be a substantial business, it may lack structure and organization. The accounting system may be inadequate. There may be no job descriptions. If someone messes up, they hear about it, but there are no constructive performance evaluations.

Everyone's time may be consumed by daily operations, and little or no time is spent planning for the future. It may seem to you that the business is successful in spite of itself.

This may be contrary to your education and training, and your impulse may be to start a crusade to introduce more modern methods. You may perceive a need for professionalization and feel that intuition alone is no longer sufficient to manage the business.

Go carefully, and remember that you're a new kid on the block. Whatever its shortcomings, the business works. People are comfortable with the familiar, and there is bound to be resistance to the know-it-all kid who's going to change it. Learn how the existing methods work and how they evolved before you try to change them. There may be underlying reasons that are not obvious.

Expect Dad, as well as the employees, to oppose change. He probably views structure as bureaucratic and is averse to it. His idea of formal planning may not go beyond tomorrow morning, and he is probably inclined to remain with comfortable procedures that have proven to be successful. You have a selling job to do with both key employees and Dad. Take it a step at a time, and build your own credibility first. Be patient, and don't give up if your ideas don't meet with immediate acceptance. Your objectivity, unencumbered by "the old days," may play an important role in helping to position the company for its next stage of growth.

Learn from Your Mistakes

Morton Seaman, a second-generation member of Seaman's Furniture (one of the country's largest furniture retailers), was thrust into the business when his father, who had founded the business, died of a heart attack at age 48. "Unfortunately, when I came into the business, there was nobody to teach it to me," he said. "The disadvantages were that I made plenty of mistakes, but the advantages were that I learned how to make my own decisions and be creative."[3] Unless you never undertake new challenges, you will make mistakes. While you're in a learning mode, it's wise not to take risks that could involve major consequences if you are wrong. Sometimes, with hindsight, you'll wonder how you could have made such a dumb decision.

Paula, who was CEO of a family textile manufacturing company, had warned her son Larry about extending credit to a certain customer. While she was away, Larry didn't want to reject a large order and overrode her warning. When the customer entered bankruptcy soon afterward, Larry said: "I don't know how I'm going to face my mother on this one." But face her he should, and soon.

We all make mistakes. Most bosses understand this; however, a mistake should be a learning experience, and don't expect much sympathy if you make the same mistake more than once. If you should blow one, admit it, and face the music at the earliest time. If you don't own up, it can hurt your credibility, and the longer you delay it, the more difficult it becomes.

Meet the Key Players

Develop relationships with the key managers in the firm. They will be important to your learning process and important to the future management of the business if you become successor. Ask Dad if you can accompany him when he meets with the company banker. Bankers are concerned about the continuity of their customers, so this will not only be a learning experience for you but reassuring to the banker. Ask if you can sit in on selected meetings with the company lawyer, CPA, and insurance agent even if you don't have anything to contribute.

Prepare Yourself for Succession

If it is to continue as a family enterprise, every family business must face the challenge of management succession. Your challenge is to learn every facet of the business and to demonstrate the ability and commitment that will earn you the respect of the employees and, most importantly, Dad's confidence. Ideally, this will result in your assuming gradually increasing responsibility so that you will be able to take over when the time comes.

If another family member is selected as the next CEO even though you wanted the job, provide him with your full support or seek other opportunities outside the business.

Avoid Destructive Sibling Rivalry

Try to establish an agreement with your siblings recognizing that the business is the "golden goose" that must be protected. Agree to subordinate your own personal agendas and jealousies and to discuss your differences constructively and openly even if you don't agree.

If one of your siblings feels that there is an inequity, be sensitive to it, and try to understand. Don't keep score and count the peas on your sibling's plate.

Jim and his sister Carla both work in their family's food distribution business and both have aspirations of becoming boss when their CEO/mother retires. Jim is married and, while a hard worker, reserves time for a normal family life. For Carla, who is single, the business is her passion and she can be found there almost all the time, including weekends. This has all of the ingredients for a "I work harder than you" scenario. Fortunately, they talk about it, and they both agree that Jim should not have to give up his family life to compete for the top job.

There's not always such a happy ending. Pete (46) and Charley (44) inherited equal interests in a profitable box manufacturing business from their father. In their growing-up years, Pete was a star football player and honor student. At home, Pete was the "fair-haired boy." Charley had to follow in his brother's footsteps and, never quite measuring up, was exceedingly resentful of his brother. This carried over into the business where Pete was in charge of production and Charley in charge of sales. When their father was alive, their quarreling was squashed by his firm hand; however, he died without naming either of them as his successor.

Pete was clearly the more capable manager of the two, and he gradually started to fill the void left by his father's death. Charley became jealous. Not having any positive ideas of his own, he asserted his authority by blocking his brother's decisions. The result was paralysis in leadership, demoralization of employees, and decline in the business.

After attempts at resolution failed, the conflict was resolved by Pete buying out Charley's interest. Pete went on to build the business successfully while Charley invested the proceeds of the buy-out in a series of losing ventures.

Later, with the benefit of hindsight, Charley charged his brother with depriving him of his birthright, and there was a blow-up. The brothers did not speak until their mother's funeral some years later. Standing at the grave site, Charley turned to his brother and said, "I wish that were you in the casket, you son of a bitch."

It's said that 99 percent of families with multiple children will admit to sibling rivalry, and the other 1 percent lie about it. As discussed in Chapter 3, the key is whether you manage it or allow it to manage you

YOUR RELATIONSHIP WITH THE BOSS

Your relationship with your father is critical. If you enjoy being with him and if your motivations and expectations blend with his, you can have an enjoyable and productive business life together. Doug entered his father's real estate brokerage business at age 35 after a previous career as a stockbroker, and it worked out better than either of them had hoped. Doug said, "I enjoy working with my father. I've got a lot to learn; he's a wonderful teacher, and I hope he stays around for a long time If we tried this 10 years ago, it wouldn't have worked " As

Laurence J. Peter put it, "By the time a man realizes that his father was usually right, he has a son who thinks that he's usually wrong."

If there is excessive conflict between you and your father and if you don't share common views of the future, your business life can be one of agony rather than fulfillment. Consider the age differences. You probably will enter the business in your mid-20s when he is likely to be in his early 50s with a probable life expectancy of another 25 years. If he is not inclined to retire, you could find yourself in your 50s and still unable to be the decision maker. If you're in general agreement on policy, this won't be a problem, but if your philosophies are different, you can be in an unwinnable contest.

Although you are an adult and value your independence, it may seem as if you are a small child "trapped in the family business" and dependent on your father for your economic sustenance. Bill's father is an autocratic boss who doesn't allow his son any authority and opposes every idea that Bill advances. Their daily life involves frequent heated arguments, often in front of employees. The obvious cure would be for Bill to leave the business; however, his family has become accustomed to a lifestyle that includes a big home (with a big mortgage), private school for the kids, and enjoyable vacations. How can he ask his family to give up all of this when his only qualification for a new job is boss's son?

What are Bill's alternatives?

1 He can stop fighting and reconcile himself to being Dad's helper, playing out the string until his father dies, or the business is sold
2 He can continue to fight it out until someone weakens or Dad dies
3. He can leave the business and start a new career elsewhere, perhaps at the bottom, with his family getting used to a drastically reduced lifestyle.

In any event, the animosity and resentment may never abate

Understanding Dad

It's important that you understand Dad's management style, his values, and his fears This requires maturity

Dad was born in a different generation. He's probably "street smart" and didn't enjoy your educational advantages. (According to the L&H/AMA family business survey, more than half of business owners do not have college degrees.) If he's the typical entrepreneur, he's apt to be somewhat secretive, has a need to be in control, and tends to manage by intuition.

The business may have grown, and long since passed the survival stage, where one slip-up may have meant the end. However, he remembers the old days and may still operate the business as though its survival were still at stake. He may be autocratic, with a need to be in control of every aspect of the business and to be involved with every decision, no matter how small.

Your perspective is probably quite different. You may see the need for more organized management methods. The organizational structure of the business may have been outgrown a long time ago. Maybe Dad will welcome and support your recommendations, or perhaps he'll take the position that "if it ain't broke, don't fix it." After all, the business may be doing well, and he may see little reason to change methods that have been effective over the years. He may see proposed changes as limiting his ability to be in control, and may oppose a more structured organization, because he may perceive it as limiting his creativeness and flexibility.

His Aversion to Risk

You have entered an established business and you may see many opportunities for growth. With your career in front of you, and a fire in your belly, you probably want to build the business to its maximum potential. If incurring debt is required, so what? It's a normal part of doing business.

Dad may have a different view. He's at a later stage of his life and has invested considerable "sweat equity" in the business. Having incurred great risks in the early years, he's now probably more concerned with conserving the business and protecting his financial security than with taking new risks, no matter how much long-term sense it makes. As one owner said, "At my age, I don't even buy green bananas."

His Concerns about Retirement

From your viewpoint, it's relatively simple. Dad has paid his dues, has earned the respect that goes with his accomplishments, and is entitled to take life easy in retirement while you pick up the burden he has shouldered for so many years.

Dad's perspective may be quite different. In many ways, the business is his baby, and he's about as ready to part with it as a parent would part with a child. He enjoys ultimate authority in his domain, and he is a *very important person.* His self-esteem may be directly associated with this position, and he may fear that if he retired he would lose his status. For many years, the business has probably been his consuming interest, and he may have few outside activities.

He worries about retirement. What would he do with his time? Would his usefulness as a person disappear? Would he lose his position as the patriarch of the family? Would retirement hasten his death? Would he be financially secure? Can anyone but him manage the business properly?

Your Role in the Retirement Process

Perhaps your situation is idyllic. You and Dad agree on major policies and management philosophy, and he's looking forward to retirement with a sense of relief. The business that he has worked so hard to build will be preserved, and your ability to carry the torch will provide him with financial security during his retirement years. He'll be free to pursue hobbies or other interests that he never had time for before, and he will have provided for the security of his employees.

For most, however, it's not that easy. Dad may hang on, feeling that he is indispensable. You may feel that the business has outgrown him and that he stands in the way of progress. If he weren't in the way, perhaps you could get on with building it.

The conflict may be intense, and if you're in this position, you may be faced with some difficult and unpalatable alternatives. You may have to reconcile yourself to the fact that Dad will never leave the business willingly. Will you be in the position of hoping for the death of the father you love? Can you endure another 10 or 20 years in these circumstances? You may choose to leave the business although you have devoted many years to it, are excited by the opportunities it offers, and have achieved a high level of status and economic security. Starting over again somewhere else is a difficult choice and is obviously a last resort when the strain of the impasse becomes unbearable.

Tom (47) was a professor at a university in the Midwest when his father induced him to join the bus company that he owned in California. "I'm in my 70s," his father had said, "and I need you." Responding to the call, Tom quit his job and moved his family. His wife and children loved their new environment as well as the enhanced lifestyle that his increased income provided. Now in anguish, Tom is frustrated by his father's intransigence in regard to company policy and unwillingness to discuss retirement. As Tom put it, "Although our business is highly profitable, my father is a skinflint who will not pay our employees properly. Our older employees are exploited, and the employee turnover is terrible. Also, he won't spend the money that is necessary to modernize our fleet. We argue about it all the time, and he tells me that my liberal ideas belong in college, not in the business world. This is a good business with enormous opportunity if only Dad would retire and take his antiquated ideas with him." And then he wistfully added, "But he'll probably live forever."

Here are some suggestions:

• Recognize that succession may be an emotionally difficult, and possibly traumatic, experience for Dad. Encourage him to talk about it. Try to understand, and be sympathetic to his concerns. It's the first step in knowing how to deal with them.
• If he has financial concerns, address them directly, and try to work out a satisfactory arrangement.
• Remember that the business is not your birthright. It's Dad business, and he's not going to step down until he's ready. He may be concerned that his usefulness will end with his retirement. Help him to carve out a new role as chairman of the board, and make it clear that, after he retires, you will continue to need his guidance and support. Openly acknowledge the importance of his accomplishments.
• Your principal relationship with Dad may have been in the business. Try to expand your family relationship. Maybe you can understand

Dad better if you know him better. Cultivate an interest in his hobbies or outside interests. Consider short vacation trips together.

• If he will agree to it, help to develop a succession plan that will be a covenant between you. It should include a timetable for your assumption of his responsibilities and establish his retirement date. At best, this should be done several years in advance of his retirement so that you both can adjust gradually, and it should be known to employees as well as to important business contacts outside of the business.

• If conflict has escalated to a point where you cannot talk about succession on a rational basis, it may be helpful to engage a family business consultant or a behavior therapist. If Dad won't agree to participate, you may gain new insight by seeking help yourself.

• Encourage Dad to establish an independent board of directors. The objectivity of an independent board can be important to the elimination of the emotional elements of the succession process.

SUMMARY

Before Entering the Business

• Make sure that, if you enter the business, it's because you're really interested in it and not because it's easier or because your parents expect it.

• Get outside job experience first. It will help to enhance your sense of independence and self-esteem, and will probably provide valuable experience if you should join the family business.

If You Work in the Family Business

• Help to establish a planned training process that provides you with exposure to all facets of the business.

• Be willing to work hard and to provide an extra dimension of commitment.

• Don't take advantage of being "the boss's kid." Earn the respect of employees by your behavior and attitude.

• You only have a limited number of years to get the benefit of Dad's wisdom and experience. Take advantage of them, and be a willing pupil.

• If your siblings are also employed in the business, don't contribute to rivalry among yourselves. Jealousy can be destructive.

When It Comes to Succession

• Try to understand Dad's concerns. Talk about them openly, if you can, and work together for their resolution. It may seem a long way off, but someday you may be standing in his shoes.
• Work with Dad to establish a succession plan with a mutually agreeable timetable.
• Even in the best circumstances, retirement is probably a difficult time for Dad. Understand it, and help him to feel useful while according him the respect that he has earned and deserves.

Your challenge will be to make the most of your opportunity, and, in your own way, with the help of others, to build a better and more successful business to hopefully hand on to the next generation

NOTES

1. Alix M. Freedman, "He Has Style Galore, But Can the Boss's Son Run a Liquor Empire?" *The Wall Street Journal*, December 3, 1987, pp. 1–2.
2. Stewart Toy, "The New Nepotism: Why Dynasties Are Making a Comeback," *Business Week*, April 4, 1988, p. 106.
3. Burr Leonard, "Heir Raising," *Forbes*, September 7, 1987, p. 74.

CHAPTER 10

■

DISMOUNTING FROM
THE TIGER

A man who has money may be anxious, depressed, frustrated and
unhappy, but one thing he's not—and that's broke.

Brendan Francis

It's good to have money. It keeps the kids in touch.

Bumper Sticker

*An owner's successful retirement is generally contingent on his financial se-
curity, which may be achieved through tax-advantaged investments. Sometimes, however, the best solution is to sell the business.*

Owning a family business can be compared to riding a tiger. The ride
can be exciting, but how do you get off? For some owners, it's not a
difficult leap. If you have enough invested outside of the business to
guarantee a secure retirement and you've planned for management succession, you may want to bequeath your shares in the business to the
next generation. Ways to best accomplish this will be discussed in
Chapter 11.

Successful succession, however, may not be in the cards in your
situation. Perhaps the kids don't get along, and tension in your family
may be exacerbated if you attempt to keep the business in the family.
Maybe you've had enough of the business and would like to pursue
other alternatives. The answer may be to sell the business.

One owner, after refereeing the latest in a long series of squabbles
among his children, said, "Sell the business? Hell, I wish I could sell
the family!"

In this chapter we'll explore ways to provide for your financial security during retirement, as well as how to sell the business, if that is your objective. Income taxes play a prominent role in both areas, and while we confine our focus to federal taxes, state tax implications should also be considered. Tax laws are complex and are constantly changing and you should consult your tax advisor before implementing any suggested courses of action.

BUILDING FINANCIAL SECURITY

The L&H entrepreneurial survey asked owners to describe their personal financial plans from both investment and tax viewpoints. Only 19 percent of the respondents said that their plans were excellent and 48 percent said that their plans were good. The remaining 33 percent responses were fair, poor, and don't know. Our experience indicates that even these results are probably overstated because many owners are so immersed in the day-to-day operations of their businesses that they neglect their own financial needs.

You may have owned the business for a long time and may be accustomed to a substantial salary, a company car, health care, and other benefits. Unless you die with your boots on, however, you will probably find that your financial picture in retirement is quite different. If you continue to own the business, the amount of income that you can draw from it is limited by the company's capacity to pay both your salary and that of your successor/CEO and by rules limiting tax deductibility.

With today's increased life expectancy, a person's life may be divided into three phases: education (20 to 25 years), work (25 to 40 years), and leisure (15 to 20 years). Your leisure (or retirement) years can either be a time to "smell the roses" and enjoy the rewards of your labor, or it can be an unhappy time of life, particularly if you have financial anxieties.

If your business constitutes your primary asset, as it does for many owners, will your income in retirement be dependent on the ability of the next generation to manage it successfully? While this is no problem to some owners, many have been forced to abort their retirements and return to the fray because the kids couldn't manage the business properly

Having adequate income outside of the business can provide you with the financial peace of mind so important to a successful retirement. You won't have to depend on the success of the business to support your lifestyle. You can leave the business to your heirs, if you're so disposed, without burdening them with the costs of purchase. And, as explained in Chapter 11, it may also allow you flexibility in estate planning that can help prevent future conflict in the family. And, as will be explained later, the sale of a business generally triggers income taxes that would be permanently avoided if the business is held until death.

"That's all well and good," you say, "but there's a limit on how much salary I can draw. Then Uncle Sam wants his share, and with the cost of living and education, how can I ever save enough out of my salary to build substantial assets outside of the business?" It isn't easy, but if you start soon enough, you may be able to create an asset base far beyond what might seem possible.

How Much Income Do You Need in Retirement?

Once you retire, your needs change. You may no longer enjoy all of the "perks" that you did when you ran the company, but you also don't have many of the expenses associated with being active in business, and you're no longer in the position of saving for the future. . . . The future is now.

The needs of retirees differ depending on their lifestyles and income levels. For example, it is estimated that once you exceed the $30,000 a year income level, you'll need approximately 70 percent of your preretirement income to maintain your way of life. Thus a person earning $50,000 a year would need $35,000 in retirement and a person earning $100,000 would need $70,000, without considering inflation.

At lower levels, social security may provide the greatest part of the retirement income package, with income from investments, savings, and corporate retirement plans increasing in importance as your retirement needs escalate.

Compound Interest and Inflation

During their work lives, owners should plan ahead for retirement, determining the amount of income they'll need. This is best addressed early because the options generally decrease with the passage of time. Benjamin Franklin said, "Money is of a prolific, generating nature. Money can beget money, and its offspring can beget more." For example, if you invest $100 a month at 5 percent interest, your total in 30 years would be $83,713. If it were invested at 10 percent, it would appear that it would grow twice as much. In fact, the amount accumulated would be $217,131. The results are dramatically decreased, however, if a substantial amount of each year's income is paid in taxes. Much of this chapter is dedicated to ways that you can compound your return by putting pretax investments to work for you.

Ask anyone who retired on a fixed income within the last 10 to 20 years, and you'll realize the importance of inflation in retirement planning. For example, if inflation is at an annual rate of 5 percent and you are 10 years from retirement, you'll need 160 percent of your present income when you retire to retain the same buying power. At an 8 percent annual inflation rate, it's 220 percent.

A Personal Financial Planner Can Help

There is a bewildering array of investment alternatives, many of them highly sophisticated, and most owners, while knowledgeable about their own businesses, are amateurs when it comes to managing their own finances. We've seen hard-nosed owners, who would negotiate intensely with a supplier over a minor increase in product cost, commit significant personal funds to spurious investment deals with only casual examination.

Unless you are willing to acquire the expertise and willing to spend the time necessary to plan your financial future properly, consider hiring a financial planner who can help you plot your financial future with due consideration of your age, risk tolerance, and financial goals. Financial planners either charge on a fee basis or are compensated from commission on products they sell to you, such as life insurance or investments. The ranks of financial planners include competent professionals; however, they also include opportunists who are more interested in their own welfare than yours. Take the time to make this important decision carefully. Ask your lawyer and accountant for recommendations, interview more than one advisor, and verify his track record with other clients.

Social Security

Social security benefits can play an important part in your retirement plans. Benefits are based on your average yearly contributions, and a spouse is entitled to one half of the worker's benefits even if the spouse was never a contributor. For example, a worker who paid in the maximum contribution and retired at age 65 could receive approximately $900 a month at this writing. Thus he and his spouse, aged 65, would be entitled to an annual benefit of approximately $16,000 a year. If she was a contributor on her own account the benefit could be higher.

These amounts are decreased if retirement commences between 62 and 65 and increased if benefits start later than at age 65. Remember, however, that there are limitations on how much income you can earn while collecting social security. Cost-of-living adjustments are added periodically to retirement benefits, and disability and health care benefits are also included in the social security package. Also if your income is over a certain amount, part of the social security benefits are taxable.

For more information and to be sure that your payments have been properly credited, write to the Social Security Administration, P.O. Box 57, Baltimore, Maryland, or call 1–800–234–5772.

Tax-Advantaged Plans

There are almost no tax shelters that allow you to avoid personal income taxes altogether; however, there are several ways to defer such taxes into the future. These allow you to invest funds that otherwise would have been paid in income taxes, with such funds accumulating tax-free until withdrawn in the future when they are subject to taxation. These plans include the following:

Individual Retirement Accounts (IRA)
In the past an individual was allowed an income tax deduction for contributions to an IRA; however, the rules now allow deductions only to individuals who aren't active participants in an employer-maintained

retirement plan. Subject to certain rules, the annual deduction is limited to $2,000 for an individual plus $250 for an unemployed spouse.

If you're covered by a qualified retirement plan you may still be able to contribute up to $2,000 a year to your IRA. Although you don't get a deduction for the contribution, the income is not taxed until it is eventually withdrawn.

Qualified Plans

These allow the employer to make tax-deductible contributions to a plan on behalf of an employee with no tax effect to the employee until the funds are withdrawn in the future. They include *profit sharing plans*, which base contributions on a percentage of corporate profits, and *pension plans*, which base contributions on an actuarially determined retirement benefit or a percentage of compensation. Because substantial amounts can often be contributed to these plans they often constitute a principal source of retirement income for corporate employees, which, of course, includes the owner. There are, however, strict rules governing the amounts that may be contributed on behalf of employees and stockholders.

Section 401 (K) Plans

In essence, these allow an employer to contribute a portion of an employee's annual compensation to a fund, with the employer getting a current tax deduction. The employee is not taxed on either the compensation or the annual income until the funds are withdrawn. At present, the maximum annual contribution is $7,627, with future limitations subject to a cost of living index.

Nonqualified Retirement Plans

Bert owns a heating oil company, and although he could easily document that a fair salary is $80,000 a year, he only draws $60,000 a year. With a nonqualified plan, he can arrange to receive the difference after he retires, either in installments or in a lump sum, with payments tax-deductible to the company and taxable to him. While qualified plans are prohibited from discriminating against employees, nonqualified plans have no such restrictions. However, transactions between an owner and a company that he controls are subject to question by the Internal Revenue Service (IRS). If you enter into such a plan, be sure to carefully document the facts and be prepared to defend them.

As nonqualified plans aren't required to be funded in advance, the company's financial ability to meet its obligation when it becomes due can be a concern to the owner. In one prominent ruling, a rabbi, seeking to protect against a possible change of heart by his employer, required that the funds for his deferred compensation plan be placed in a trust. There's no assurance that the IRS will accept this arrangement, but the "rabbi's trust" concept may be worth looking into if you're insecure about the business's capacity to meet its obligation after you retire.

The two principal forms of nonqualified plans are described here.

Supplemental Executive Retirement Plan (SERP)
This provides additional retirement benefits beyond those allowed in qualified plans, possibly including early retirement subsidies, postretirement cost-of-living increases, and salary continuation plans for the participant's spouse in the event of death.

Deferred Compensation
In essence, this arrangement allows the deferral into the future of compensation that would otherwise be due currently. Properly planned, it allows owners to receive deferred compensation after retirement even though they render no services. It may also allow income to be paid to a named beneficiary after the owner's death.

Life Insurance

In Chapter 11, we'll discuss the place of life insurance in estate planning; however, life insurance can also help to provide retirement income. There's a lot of fine print and IRS rules that must be complied with, but a competent life insurance agent can help you evaluate whether cash-value life insurance should have a place in your investment plans. Some examples follow:

• Over the years, you pay the premiums on a whole life insurance policy, and cash values accumulate. At retirement, you don't need all of the protection you needed in the earlier years, and you may be able to convert the cash value that has been building up tax-free to an annuity for the remainder of your and your spouse's lives.

• A lump sum of cash is invested into a single-premium life insurance policy and grows tax-free. In the future, you may withdraw the entire amount, convert to an annuity or put the policy on a reduced, fully paid-up status. This may provide a safe, higher return than could have been realized by other forms of investment.

An S Corporation Can Be Advantageous

Most conventional corporations are C corporations, which involve double taxation of income, once at the corporate level and again at the stockholder level when dividends are paid or the corporation is liquidated.

If you have no more than 35 stockholders and comply with various other rules, it's possible for your business to be taxed as an S corporation, allowing the income from the business to flow through to the stockholders without being taxed at the corporate level. Not only does this prevent double taxation, but after a certain level, personal tax rates are now lower than corporate tax rates.

S corporation treatment often has unique application to family businesses. For example:

• A C corporation is not allowed a tax deduction for compensation paid to stockholder-employees in excess of that considered to be "reasonable" by the IRS. In an S corporation, the total income of the company passes through to the stockholders without question, generally eliminating the need of owners to justify their salaries.

• An S corporation can allow flexibility in meeting family needs. For example, John, who owns a successful tire distributorship, would like to provide financial help to his daughter, who is divorced with three small children. A C corporation could not pay her a tax-deductible salary as she renders no services to the business. If, however, she owned stock in a S corporation she could receive a proportion of the company's earnings without double taxation.

• When a business is started it may incur losses for a period of time. Under certain circumstances, an owner can deduct these losses from income derived from outside sources

- The owner's retirement may be financed by his share of the income of the business without affecting his social security benefits.

If you are eligible but haven't already made the S corporation election, consult your tax advisor to see if it makes sense for you.

SELLING THE BUSINESS

What if there are no heirs who are willing and able to carry on the business? What if they're willing, but the owner doubts their ability to carry on the business? What if the owner lacks sufficient funds independent of the business to provide for a comfortable retirement, or what if he just wants to "cash out." Selling the business may be the best solution. If you want to get the best price, however, sell when things are going well and you can deal from strength.

A Tough, Emotional Decision

Some entrepreneurs start businesses, build them up, and then sell them, only to start over again. For most owners of businesses, however, it's not that easy. After years of sacrifice and hard work, they're emotionally involved, and parting with their businesses, which have been the center of their lives, is often a gut-wrenching experience, almost like parting with a child.

Sometimes it's not even the owner's intent to sell. Ed started a waste management company several years ago and, after several lean years, built it into a thriving company. His daughter Ellen joined the company and rapidly proved that she had the ability to run the business when Ed was ready to step down. While in his mid-50s and far from ready to retire, something happened that changed both Ed's and Ellen's lives drastically.

Representatives of a large public company came to see Ed and offered to buy the business at a price that was far beyond Ed's wildest dreams. Accumulation of wealth had never been his principal concern but the big numbers validated the saying that everything has its price Ed's conversation with the proposed buyer went as follows

ED:

> That's a very generous offer, but I enjoy my business and have no intention of selling it. Besides, I want to leave it to my daughter.

BUYER:

> That's perfectly understandable. We're desperate for top managers, and we need you both for key roles, running even larger operations. You'll have all the support you want and unlimited resources. We're prepared to back it up with lucrative employment contracts for you both.

ED:

> I just don't think I'm ready to sell.

BUYER:

> OK, but remember that we're only offering you this price because we want an operation in your area. If you decline, we'll probably buy one of your competitors, and you'll never see this kind of opportunity again.

Remembering when times were tough and seeing an opportunity to provide financial security for his family, Ed finally sold the company. After the sale, however, rather than being given challenging new responsibilities, he quickly became submerged in a flood of paper, far removed from the decision makers. Ellen was assigned routine administrative chores.

Within six months, he couldn't take it any longer, and a termination of both employment agreements was negotiated. Prematurely forced into retirement and prohibited by a noncompetition agreement from working in the one field that he knew, Ed found that playing golf every day and watching the stock market were poor substitutes for the satisfaction of running his own business. Although Ellen had the resources to buy another business, she never achieved her dream of running the family company.

It doesn't always turn out this way. Sometimes the owner fits into the new organization, and he lives happily ever after. In our experience, however, the bureaucratic cultures of many big businesses are so different from those of smaller family businesses that most owners find the transition to be difficult, if not impossible.

One owner, after selling her cosmetics business to a giant company, said, "It took me 20 years to build that business, and they're screwing it up by the numbers, disregarding everything I tell them. It would mean nothing to them if they wrote off their investment, but it kills me to see what they're doing. I wish my name weren't on the door."

If you plan to stay on with the acquiring company, don't place too much reliability on the sweet talk during the courtship or on the employment contract. Many buyers view such contracts as merely an addition to the purchase price. As one officer in an acquiring company put it, "We treat the owners of acquired companies like mushrooms. You bury their heads in the ground and cover them with horse manure." Maybe you can sell your company and enjoy a satisfying work experience after the sale, but don't count on it.

Tax Effect: Selling versus Keeping

Under present tax laws, any gain realized on the sale of your business is taxed at ordinary income tax rates. If, however, you own the business until you die, your income tax basis is "stepped up" to the fair market value as of the date of your death, and income tax on the appreciation in value is *permanently avoided*. The tax may be substantial, involving up to one third of the gain. This is particularly applicable to family businesses that were started with small investments and have appreciated in value.

Finding a Buyer

If yours is a growing and profitable business, you may have already been wooed by larger companies and brokers, and it may be relatively easy to start negotiations discreetly. For others, finding the right buyer is a sensitive and difficult task. If the world knows that your business is "on the block," it might affect your relationship with customers, suppliers, and employees. There's no sure way of preventing the word from getting out, but here are some approaches:

• Work through a broker or merger/acquisition firm that is committed to confidentiality. If you take this approach, be sure to check them out carefully. While there are many ethical people in this field, some of them would sell you out in a minute to make a commission.
• Your accountant and lawyer, both of whom are used to dealing with

confidentiality, may be authorized to make discreet inquiries for an "undisclosed client."
• If yours is a smaller business, consider a "blind" advertisement in the newspaper with the identity of the business disguised.
• Conduct negotiations at a place other than your shop, possibly your lawyer's or accountant's office.

Valuing Your Business

There are no absolute ways to value a business. One executive said, "I use the SWAG method (scientific wild-assed guess)." Another said, "I figure it every which way, and whichever is the highest is my way."[1]

According to Paul B. Baron, an authority on the subject, here are the factors that a sophisticated buyer considers when establishing the purchase price of a profitable company:

• The underlying assets of the company.
• The earnings. (How much and how secure.)
• Discount rate. (What is the rate of return that the investor is looking for? The greater the risk, the higher the discount rate.)
• The growth rate and the growth period.
• Some comparable sales (if possible).
• Supply and demand of companies for sale.
• Tax position of the buyer and the seller.
• What the "opportunity costs" are. That is, what could I get from an alternative investment?[2]

Do Your Homework

Make it easy for the buyer to get the answers to these questions in the most favorable light. Recast your financial statements so that they will reflect the realities from the buyer's perspective. For example, real estate and fixed assets should be reflected at market value, and inventory should be stated realistically. If yours is a substantial business, it probably pays to hire a professional appraiser who is experienced in valuing businesses of your size.

Recast your income statement to eliminate family salaries, perquisites, and deferred benefit costs that won't constitute continuing expenses to the buyer. Be prepared to furnish the buyer with at least three years of historical financial statements (preferably audited), and prepare three years of projected financial statements, *as recast*, so the buyer will have as clear a picture of the future as possible. If they are to be credible, your projections should be reasonable rather than "pie in the sky." When projecting growth rates, consider three scenarios— worst case, probable, and best case.

Computing the Value

It's amazing how many companies are sold at book value (the amount of stockholders' equity in the financial statements). This method often has little relationship, however, to the real value of the business. For example, the financial statements show fixed assets at cost less depreciation rather than at real values and inventory reserves may have been established with taxes rather than with a sale in mind. There may also be many "off balance sheet" assets such as favorable leases or contracts and customer goodwill.

There are no absolute formulas for computing the value of a business, and the negotiated price is often a hybrid of many factors. For example:

• Public companies are generally valued on a price times earnings basis. For instance, if the stock market places a value of 10 times after-tax earnings on public companies in your industry, it may make sense to base your asking price on the same basis, with a "kicker" if your balance sheet is exceptionally strong.
• One of the principal factors to most buyers is the period of time in which their investment will be recovered from after-tax earnings. Figure it out for yourself first so that you can at least understand their perspectives. In all likelihood, they'll want to recoup their investment in five years or less.
• If your projections indicate substantial growth, you probably want to get paid "on the come" for escalated earnings after the sale. The buyer, however, may say, "I'll believe it when I see it." One possibility for dealing with this situation is an "earn-out," with part of the purchase price to be paid in the future based on results. Remember, however, that you no longer can control the operation or the accounting that de-

termines the outcome. If you go this route, be careful to establish rigid criteria for control, preferably using sales, rather than income, as the criterion. Even then, it'll come down to a matter of trust, as buyers can generally play games with the books if they're so inclined.

• Consider a leveraged buy-out (LBO) with the bulk of the purchase price obtained by borrowing against assets, cash flow, or some combination of the two. This may justify a higher purchase price because the buyer's out-of-pocket investment is minimized and interest cost on the debt is generally tax-deductible. However if you help with the financing by taking back a note for part of the purchase price, carefully evaluate the risks involved. Once you sell the company, you won't have any influence over its management.

The Negotiation

According to investment authority John Spooner, the steps in a deal are "conception, confusion, panic, punish the innocent, and reward the nonparticipants."[3] Hopefully this won't apply to you. While the business is "your baby" and you obviously want to show its prettiest face, don't make any statements that you can't back up. It can hurt your credibility and possibly result in litigation. Conversely, if you see any signs of bad faith by the buyer, run for the nearest exit. No matter how rosy the deal, if the buyer is lacking in integrity, you'll almost certainly end up with trouble, regardless of the legal documents. Litigation involves substantial time, expense, and grief, even if you win.

You've probably established a higher price than you'd be willing to settle for, and the buyer probably started with a lower price than he'd be willing to pay; it's negotiating time. According to master negotiator Herb Cohen, there are three crucial elements in every negotiation:

Information—The other side seems to know more about you and your needs than you know about them and their needs.

Time—The other side doesn't seem to be under the same kind of organizational pressure, time constraints, and restrictive deadlines you feel you're under.

Power—The other side always seems to have more power and authority than you think you have. . . . All power is based on perception. If you think you've got it, then you've got it. If you don't think you have it, even if you have it, then you don't have it.[4]

Negotiations often become heated, with owners becoming defensive when the deficiencies of their "baby" are pointed out. We've seen many deals broken because conflict of personalities obscured the merits of the situation and where animosities incurred during the negotiation injured the owner's chances of staying on with the acquiring company. In any negotiation, take pains to argue the issues only, and don't let it become personal even if you're provoked. If you really want to sell your business, don't say "go to hell" too fast to unreasonable offers. The buyer may be just trying to start the negotiations at the lowest possible level. You can always cut off negotiations if they don't get realistic.

According to negotiation authorities Roger Fisher and William Ury, any method of negotiation may be fairly judged by three criteria: It should produce a wise agreement if agreement is possible. It should be efficient. And it should improve or at least not damage the relationship between the parties.[5]

The agreed price generally depends on a combination of elements, including:

1. *The terms.* One negotiator said, "You can name any price that you want, just let me negotiate the terms." Will it be a cash deal or a long-term payout? Will the price be fixed or contingent? The numbers may be the same as in a cash deal, but risk can be an element, and the value of a dollar in the future is less than its present value.
2. *The need to buy/sell.* Whichever side has less need for the deal generally has a superior bargaining position. The ability to walk away is a strong bargaining chip.
3. *The right buyer.* A business may be more valuable to some buyers than others. If possible, try to find a buyer who has a unique need for the business.
4. *Negotiating ability.* Better negotiators usually end up making better deals. It's often better to have someone other than the decision maker negotiate the deal so that you "get two bites at the apple."[6]

Tax Implications Are Critical

Tax implications can have a profound effect on the deal, and your tax advisor should be consulted early in the deal.

This may be particularly applicable if the business is to be kept in the family. One owner said, "Wouldn't it make the kids 'hungrier' if I sold the business to them rather than leaving it to them in my estate?" Yes, it might, but if you sell it during your lifetime, you'll have to pay federal income tax on the gain while if they inherit it the tax, which may be as high as one third of the value of the business, will be permanently avoided.

There have been constant rumblings over the years that the stepped-up estate basis rules should be eliminated, but at this writing, they are alive and well. Such a rule change, if it was to happen, could result in a severe blow, if not a death knell, for many family businesses because many would lack the liquidity to pay income taxes on the appreciation of the value of the stock in addition to estate taxes.

Selling Stock versus Assets
Under present tax law, if a C corporation sells an asset, the resulting gain is taxed at corporate rates. When the corporation is liquidated, as is usually the case when a business is sold, another tax is imposed (there are special rules for S corporations).

Sellers can avoid double taxation by selling their stock in the company, rather than assets; however, buyers prefer to buy assets because the onus of double taxation passes on to them if they should buy stock. Buyers also prefer to buy assets because they don't have to be concerned about undisclosed liabilities.

The amounts involved can be substantial and may be an important part of the negotiations. In almost every circumstance, you should try to sell your stock in the company, rather than assets, if you can.

Selling to Your Children

Outright Sale
There are times that selling the business to your children, rather than bequeathing it, makes sense despite the income tax effect. Alan's son Greg left a secure job to join the family lamp manufacturing company,

with the understanding that his father would retire at a predetermined time. Greg's performance, however, has caused Alan to doubt Greg's ability to manage the company, and he's reluctant to leave it in his son's hands. This has caused escalating tension, with the son accusing his father of reneging and the father repeating a daily litany of the son's screw-ups.

They resolved the situation with a family business version of a leveraged buy-out. Greg obtained a bank loan, secured by the company's assets, sufficient to buy his father's interest in the business. Although Alan had to pay income taxes, which would have been avoided had he owned the company until he died, his financial peace of mind was not dependent on his son's ability to manage the business, and Greg had the opportunity to either succeed or fail on his own merits. *If you sell the business to your children, be careful not to burden the business with more debt than it can service.*

Installment Sale/Private Annuity
If the heirs are unable to obtain the funds to acquire the business outright, they may be able to buy it in installments. Payment for the stock can take place over time, with the seller being taxed as payments are received; however, the owner, being still at risk, may not be as willing to give up control as in an outright sale, particularly if he has guaranteed a bank loan. Also, the unpaid balance of the purchase price would be included in the owner's estate at death.

Another approach is through a private annuity, which is similar to an installment sale, only instead of a fixed obligation, the time frame for payment is based on the life expectancy of the seller, with no further obligations after his death.

Both of these approaches may trigger income taxes that would be avoided if the owner held the stock until death, and they may be subject to "anti-freeze" provisions discussed in Chapter 11. If you proceed in this direction, make sure that you have competent tax advice

Selling to an Employee Stock Ownership Plan (ESOP)

Many owners are astounded to learn that they may be able to realize far more from selling their businesses to employees than from selling to outsiders.

The employee stock ownership plan (ESOP) concept was founded by lawyer Louis Kelso on the belief that the future of capitalism depends on a more even distribution of ownership. With this objective, and to stimulate American productivity, Congress instituted extensive tax incentives in 1974, with additional legislation added over the years, to encourage employee ownership of business. While there are critics who view ESOPs as a "tax dodge," studies indicate that "properly structured employee ownership leads to increased sales growth, increased employment growth, and increased productivity."[7]

In any event, there's a rapidly escalating trend in this direction, and it's estimated that there are now more than 10,000 ESOPs in the United States, covering more than 12 million employees.[8] Many large public companies have adopted ESOPs, motivated in part because centralized control of the company's stock may help defend against hostile takeovers. Prominent companies with ESOPs include Anheuser-Busch, Avis, Lockheed, Procter & Gamble, Polaroid, and ITT.

The late James E. Casey, founder of United Parcel Service (UPS), decreed that the "company must be owned by its managers and managed by its owners." Now, almost all the stock in the company is owned by its employees, and many who began as clerks and truck drivers retire as millionaires. One director said, "When we have our meetings, we directors troop downstairs to the cafeteria, stand in line, and pay our $2.17 for a tuna sandwich. The only difference is we sit at a reserved table so we can talk."[9]

Since instituting its ESOP, Avis has increased its share of the highly competitive car rental business, on-time arrivals of airport buses have risen, and service-related complaints, which were rising, have decreased. However, chairman Joe Vittoria says, "just creating an ESOP isn't going to make you a better company. It's how you maintain a dialogue, listen to their input, and use it."[10]

Don't think that ESOPs are just for big, public companies. According to a government-sponsored study, approximately half of all ESOPs were used to buy the shares of retiring owners of closely held businesses.[11]

Selling to an ESOP, in whole or in part, can be a win-win situation, allowing you to reward your employees for their contributions to the success of the business, providing a meaningful incentive for them to continue it, and resulting in a considerably higher price than if you sold to outsiders.

Some employers terminate or scale-back their contributions to qualified retirement plans once an ESOP is in place. This allows them to save on annual contributions to the plan and avoid the consequences of recent onerous legislation governing such plans. For better or worse, this ties the employees' retirement income to the performance of the company.

A leveraged buy-out by an ESOP typically works as follows:

• An ESOP is established for the benefit of employees.
• The ESOP borrows money from a third-party lender, with the loan guaranteed by the company. As the tax incentives presently provide that lenders are only taxed on 50 percent of the income that they receive on ESOP loans, they generally charge less interest than their usual rates, often at less than the prime rate. Alternatively, the loan may be made to the company with the proceeds loaned to the ESOP.
• The ESOP uses the proceeds of the loan to buy all or part of the stock in the company from the owner of the business.
• The company contributes enough cash each year to the ESOP to pay the interest and principal of the loan. Subject to certain rules, this is tax-deductible to the company, indirectly allowing a tax deduction to the company for both the interest and for the principal of the loan.
• The employees' equity in the ESOP starts at zero in this scenario and gradually grows as the loan is amortized and the value of the company increases. Each employee is allocated a share of the equity in the ESOP, based on preestablished criteria but limited to $30,000 a year (plus cost of living increases) on behalf of any one employee. When an employee leaves the company or retires, his shares are normally sold back to the company at the then market value. Private companies are *required* to purchase the employees' stock when they leave.
• If the company pays dividends, it's allowed a tax deduction for payments to the ESOP, if the funds are used to pay loans in connection with the buy-out.

This all adds up to increased borrowing capacity, which may translate into the ability of an ESOP to pay a higher price for the business than an outsider who doesn't enjoy the same tax advantages.

There is an additional, very powerful incentive to the owner/seller if 30 percent or more of the company's stock is owned by the ESOP. Subject to certain rules and limitations, the owner/seller can defer taxable gain on the sale by reinvesting the proceeds of the sale into qualified securities of other domestic corporations that operate active businesses (e.g., GM or IBM). Furthermore, tax on the gain can be avoided permanently if the investment is held throughout the seller's lifetime.

The estate tax consequences are also beneficial. If the owner still owns company stock when he dies, his estate can sell the stock to the ESOP and subject to certain limitations, receive an estate tax deduction for up to 50 percent of the taxable estate. (This benefit expires December 31, 1991).

Louis Carr, third-generation president of the family picture frame business, experimented over the years with a variety of employee incentives. After extensive study, in 1977, he replaced part of the company's profit sharing plan with an ESOP. As his retirement drew near, and with no interest by his children in taking over, he pondered his alternatives. Wanting the business to continue as an independent company and feeling that the employees deserved to be rewarded for their contribution, he sold the rest of his stock to the ESOP in 1981 and the employees became the sole owners. Two years later, the value of the profit sharing plan and the ESOP was $5.5 million, with the ownership of the stock distributed as follows: top management, 22 percent; foremen, 21 percent; and shop-floor workers, 51 percent. The remainder was unallocated.[12]

Here are some other points:

• The ownership of shares in the company doesn't necessarily give the employees the right to manage the company. The shares of the ESOP are voted by a trustee who is generally appointed by management.

• The rules require that the company stock in the ESOP be appraised every year, establishing a market value for the stock. The costs of establishing an ESOP and the annual administrative costs tend to limit their uses to substantial businesses that can utilize the tax benefits of ESOPs effectively.

• The debt incurred in an LBO must be serviced and it can constitute a strain on the financial resources of the company. *Consider the ability of the company to weather economic downturns and be careful about overleveraging the company.*

• There must be a sufficiently large and deserving employee base to justify the purchase of a substantial interest in the plan. Despite the many benefits, don't consider an ESOP unless you really want to share ownership with your employees.

The rules governing ESOPs are complex, and subject to constant change, so make sure that you engage skilled professionals if you want to establish an ESOP. For more information contact the ESOP Association, 1100 17th Street N.W., Suite 310, Washington, D.C. 20036, and ask for its introductory booklet *How the ESOP Really Works* ($10) and for a copy of *ESOP Directory* which lists both ESOP companies and specialists in the field. Also see Joseph R. Blasi's book, *Employee Ownership-Revolution or Ripoff* (Ballinger, 1988), and *Employee Stock Ownership Plans* by Robert W. Smiley, Jr., and Ronald J. Gilbert Larchmont (Prentice-Hall, 1989).

BUY-SELL AGREEMENTS

Family business tensions are often caused by too many participants with different viewpoints, and in other chapters, we've advocated limiting the number of players. This often pleases everyone, as family members who aren't active in the business are usually happier to have income-producing assets rather than a minority-interest in a company that probably doesn't pay dividends.

Inheritance is the most common reason for the proliferation of stockholders. For example, two partners start a business. If the stock is bequeathed to their respective families when they die, in the next generation, there's apt to be 5 or 6 stockholders and in the following generation 12 or 15—that is, if the business lasts that long, which is unlikely.

An effective way to limit the number of owners is to establish a buy-sell agreement that provides, in effect, for the surviving stockholder to buy the shares of another stockholder who is first to die.

The best time to deal with this issue is when the participants are healthy and nobody knows who will be first to die. It's usually in the survivor's best interests to obtain total ownership of the business while the family of the deceased is usually better off with cash.

For example, Nick and Marty own the ABC Company that they both agree is worth $400,000. They each enter into an agreement with ABC Company that in the event of their death, their stock will be sold back to the company for $200,000. ABC Company takes out life insurance policies in the amount of $200,000 on each of their lives with the company as beneficiary. Nick dies first, and ABC Company uses the proceeds of the life insurance policy to buy Nick's stock from his estate. Nick's estate ends up with cash, and Marty ends up owning the company outright without the necessity of liquidating assets to buy Nick's interest. As will be explained in Chapter 11, the unlimited marital deduction can make the entire sum available for Nick's widow, undiluted by federal estate taxes at the time of his death.

If the agreement isn't funded by life insurance, it can provide for a long-term payout; however, the obligation may put undue strain on the business, which may jeopardize its ability to make the payments to the family of the deceased. While life insurance may result in a windfall for the survivor, it protects the family of the deceased and allows the business to be unencumbered by excessive debt.

Another way to accomplish a similar result is through a cross-purchase agreement between the stockholders, rather than with the company; however, the approach used by Nick and Marty is the most common.

According to one survey, most buy-sells of privately owned companies use a formula plan based on book value to establish the value of the company. (See "Computing the Value" for the use of book value in measuring the worth of a business.) Some owners use outside appraisers and consider elements such as capitalized earnings and percentage of gross billings.[13] *If your agreement is for a fixed-dollar amount, rather than by formula, make sure that you review it at least every year to avoid inequities.*

There can be unforeseen results of buy-sell agreements. If Nick's children had an interest in joining the business, they would no longer have the position that goes with being co-owners. It's hard to question the fairness, however, as neither Nick or Marty knew who would be first to die when they entered into the agreement.

Whatever the side effects, buy-sell agreements are generally effective in helping all of the parties to achieve their individual objectives and in avoiding the conflict that comes when multiple families become involved.

Corporate Stock Buy-Back Plan

Let's assume that Nick and Marty didn't enter into an agreement before Nick died or that there wasn't enough life insurance to buy all of his stock in ABC Company. His widow would probably find that non-dividend paying stock in the company didn't help pay her bills, so she might enter into a corporate buy-back plan with the company.

If ABC Company had the financial capacity, it could simply buy her shares at a negotiated price. More likely, however, a long-term buy-back agreement would be executed that would provide her with a steady stream of funds. One approach would be for a sale at the current value, with interest and principal being paid over the term of the note. Another way would be to peg the payments to a formula tied to profits over the term of the buy-back.

In another situation, where no partners were involved, the owner bequeathed his shares in the business equally to his two children, Jerry and Millicent, although Millicent was active in the business and Jerry was a school teacher. The dialogue went this way:

JERRY:

Dad thought he was leaving me a valuable asset when he left me the stock in the company, but my shares are of little value to me. I'd like to sell the company.

MILLICENT:

You know that Dad wanted the business to continue, and I don't want to sell it. I'll buy you out.

JERRY:

How do I know that after you buy me out you won't turn around and sell it for far more than the price that we agreed on?

The dilemma was solved: They agreed on a corporate buy-back, but if Millicent sold her shares at a higher price within 10 years, there was a "look back" provision that increased the amount of the purchase price.

Stockholder Buy-Back Plan

If there is a large number of stockholders, the company can act as an informal broker, helping to establish values and arranging for stockholders to buy and sell among themselves rather than to the company.

Going Public

If yours is a substantial company *and* if conditions in the stock market are favorable, going public is a way to raise additional capital for the business and for the owner to "cash out" while still retaining control and partial ownership of the business. There are principally two kinds of stock offerings. In the first, the company itself sells shares to the public and in a secondary offering, the shareholders sell their shares.

Advantages of going public include:

- Additional capital to finance the growth of the business.
- Conversion of the owners' stock from paper into cash, allowing them to diversify their risks and probably increasing their discretionary income.
- The status and prestige of being a public company.
- The establishment of a ready market for stock owned by family members.
- Stock in the company can be used to make acquisitions.

Disadvantages include:

- Accountability to public shareholders is often unpalatable to owners who are accustomed to making all of the decisions without having to explain their actions. This is often the principal negative, and it can result in management placing emphasis on quarterly results rather than on the best long-term interests of the business.
- Complete disclosure to the Securities and Exchange Commission (SEC) is required, and financial and other important information about the company can no longer be kept confidential.
- Greater formalities in the administration of the company. Having an outside board of directors generally ceases to be discretionary. Extensive filings must be made with the SEC on an ongoing basis and there are additional annual costs.
- Salaries and perquisites to family members take on a different color when the company is public. In addition to complying

with IRS requirements, the interests of outside stockholders must be considered.

There's no right or wrong for every situation. Many family businesses find that going public is highly advantageous. In others, the wail is heard, "What did I get into?"

SUMMARY

Building Financial Security

• Financial security is important to a successful retirement for the owner. This may mean building up enough investments outside of the business, getting retirement income from the business, or selling it.

• Many owners neglect their own finances and are well-advised to hire a professional financial planner to help. It's important to start early to get the benefit of compound interest and to protect against the ravages of inflation. Social security benefits can be an important part of your retirement program.

• Tax-advantaged retirement plans provide for a deferral of taxes, allowing the investment and buildup of funds that would have otherwise been paid in income taxes. These include individual retirement plans, pension and profit sharing plans, and section 401 (k) plans. Nonqualified plans provide for deferred compensation to the future without a current tax benefit to the business.

• In addition to providing protection, life insurance can provide a tax-free buildup of funds to help fund retirement needs. An S corporation election eliminates the double taxation of corporate income.

Selling the Business

• The sale of a family business is often an emotional decision for the owner. While some owners can be happy as an employee of the new owner, most find that the cultures are incompatible. Tax implications are critical and can have a significant impact on the final price.

• Finding the right buyer is important, but the search must be made discreetly to avoid upsetting important business relationships. Negotiations are important and are often best handled by someone other than the owner. They should be planned for and not treated casually.

• Important personal objectives may be attained and the sale price maximized by either selling the business to the children or to an employee stock ownership plan (ESOP).

Buy-Sell Agreements

• The conflicting objectives of family members and the complications that result from multiple-family ownership may be resolved by the use of buy-sell agreements that provide for buy-outs of some of the shareholder interests.

Going Public

• The owners of larger enterprises may achieve personal liquidity and raise additional capital for the company by going public. Responsibilities to other shareholders, however, involve many trade-offs.

NOTES

1. Paul B. Baron, *When You Buy or Sell a Company* (Meriden, Conn.: Center for Business Information, 1980).
2. Ibid., pp. 5–17.
3. John Spooner, "Smart People, Smart Money," *Atlantic Monthly*, 1979.
4. Herb Cohen, *You Can Negotiate Anything* (Secaucus, N.J.: Lyle Stuart, 1980).
5. Roger Fisher and William Ury, *Getting to Yes* (Boston: Houghton Mifflin, 1981).
6. Cohen, *You Can Negotiate Anything*; and Fisher and Ury, *Getting to Yes*.
7. John Weiser, Frances Brody, and Michael Quarrey, "Family Businesses and Employee Ownership," *Family Business Review*, Spring 1988.
8. Christopher Farrell and John Hoerr, "ESOPs: Are They Good for You?" *Business Week*, May 15, 1989.
9. Kenneth Labich, "Big Changes at Big Brown," *Fortune*, January 18, 1988.
10. David Kirkpatrick, "How the Workers Run Avis Better," *Fortune*, December 5, 1988.
11. E. Chelimsky et al., *Employee Stock Ownership Plans: Benefits and Costs of ESOP Tax Incentives*, GAO/PEND-87-8 (Washington, D.C.: U.S. General Accounting Office, 1986).
12. M. Quarry, J. Blasi, and C. Rosen, *Taking Stock: Employee Ownership at Work* (Cambridge, Mass.: Ballinger, 1986).
13. Stanley B. Block, "Buy-Sell Agreements for Privately Held Corporations." *Journal of Accountancy*, September 1985.

CHAPTER 11

NOBODY GETS OUT OF HERE ALIVE

> You can get much farther with a kind word and a gun than you
> can with a kind word alone.
>
> *Al Capone*

*If the business is to survive beyond the lifetime of the owners, careful planning
is needed to transfer the ownership of stock into the right hands in the next
generation, without incurring crippling estate taxes.*

More has been written about management succession than any other
family business issue; however, it's only part of the equation in the
transfer of power to the next generation. In a business, the ultimate
power is represented by ownership of the stock, and whoever controls
the stock directs the destiny of the company.

For example, one owner said proudly, "I've really planned for
management succession. Of my three children in the business, I've selected my youngest son to be the next CEO. It'll take 10 years to train
him, but I know he'll do a great job." And then he added, "But he
won't get a swelled head because I'm leaving my stock in the company
to the three of them equally." Of course, the owner didn't take into
consideration that on the day following his death the successor's siblings, owning two thirds of the stock in the company, could vote him
out, cancelling all of their father's careful planning.

In Chapter 10, ways were discussed for the owner to dispose of
his interest in the business during his lifetime. Here, we'll explore
ways that the business can most effectively be gifted or bequeathed to
the owner's heirs.

The L&H entrepreneurial survey indicated that only 80 percent of
owners of companies with annual sales volume from $5 million to $50

million have reviewed their estate plans within the past five years; 8 percent reviewed the plan more than five years ago, and 12 percent either didn't have an estate plan or didn't know. If this survey included respondents with sales under $5 million, there's little question that the number of owners with current estate plans would have gone down dramatically.

Even among the 80 percent who responded positively, the quality of planning is suspect. Many owners believe their estate plans are in good shape, when all they have are woefully inadequate simple wills leaving their entire estates to their spouses. These "sweetheart wills" may be appropriate in some instances; however, they often validate H. L. Mencken's comment, "There is always an easy solution to every human problem—neat, plausible and wrong."

Ineffectual estate planning can lead to war in the family and excessive estate taxes, both of which may be avoidable. An entrepreneur says, "I executed a simple will 20 years ago when the business was just starting and the kids were infants, and I probably should update it." Then he adds, "I did add a codicil when I divorced and remarried five years ago." Since then, he's acquired several businesses, his children have grown up, and the estate tax laws have changed drastically, but he still hasn't found time to plan his estate. If the Internal Revenue Service (IRS) knew about it, they'd be licking their chops. If his children knew about the devastating implications, they'd wonder how such a responsible man could be so irresponsible.

Mark Twain's comment that death and taxes are inevitable is only partly true. Estate taxes, which can have a devastating impact on your family and business, are the easiest type of taxes to minimize or avoid with proper planning. Despite their potentially crippling effect, many owners have no idea of the extent of the taxes that will be due on their estates. Are you among them?

While this discussion deals with federal estate taxes, many states have estate and inheritance tax laws that should be considered in your planning. As these differ substantially among states you may want to consider state tax law when choosing a retirement domicile.

Here are basic questions that every owner should consider:

1. How can I protect my spouse financially?
2. How can I be fair to my heirs?
3. Does fairness necessarily demand equality?
3. Who should own the stock in my business in the next generation? The controlling interest?
4. How can I arrange my affairs so that my heirs are not burdened with excessive estate taxes?

Estate tax laws have changed considerably in recent years, and family circumstances constantly change. Unless you've reviewed your estate plan with a competent professional advisor within the past two years, it's probably obsolete and the consequences may be devastating to your families. Many owners neglect this important responsibility for the following reasons:

• *Unwillingness to face mortality.* If you're not going to die, estate planning becomes moot. Some feel the same way as comedian Woody Allen who said, "Some people try to achieve immortality through their children, and others through their work. I prefer to achieve it by not dying."

Let's face it—nobody gets out alive, and if you fail to plan for the eventuality, crucial decisions affecting your business and family are apt to be made by lawyers, the state, and the tax authorities. If you're comfortable with this or if you don't care what happens after you depart from this world, you won't find the rest of this chapter to be of much interest.

• *Procrastination.* Many owners of family businesses are so preoccupied with day-to-day problems that they just don't take the time that's required to plan their estates carefully. After all, death is believed to be a long way off, and they have more immediate problems. In view of the possibly catastrophic effect of neglect, we believe that owners should plan according to the "Mack truck possibility."

What would happen to your family and your business if you're hit by a Mack truck tomorrow on the way to work and your appointment with the grim reaper becomes accelerated? Almost without question your demise would be a great loss to both your family and business; however, this is beyond your control. What about the elements that are within your control? Would your stock in the company end up in the right hands? Would estate taxes cripple the ability of your heirs to continue the business?

A will can be modified or revoked at any time, so if you protect your business and family under the Mack truck possibility, you can always change your will as future circumstances dictate.

• *Lack of awareness.* Many owners are unaware that the IRS is their silent business partner. Rest assured, however, that when you die, your heirs will hear from them if your estate is large enough. Under present laws, the top rate for most estates is 55 percent of the value of your assets. (And that's real value, not book value.) If your business is typical, it's assets consist mostly of equipment, inventory, and receivables. Where are the funds going to come from? Will your children be burdened with debt? Will your heirs be forced to liquidate the business that you worked so hard to build in order to pay the estate taxes?

• *Lack of easy answers.* Most owners are astute problem solvers, and they're accustomed to dealing with situations where the results are predictable. Estate planning doesn't fit into this mold, however, and there are often no "right" answers to questions such as: Who should own and control the business? Would wealth cause my children to cease living productive lives? Will my spouse be a target for fortune hunters?

A judge sentenced an aging, repeat felon to a long prison sentence. "Judge," the felon pleaded, "I'm not as young as I used to be. I just can't do that long a stretch." To which the judge responded, "Just do the best you can." In estate planning, that's all you can do. You cannot look into the future and provide for every eventuality.

How to Make Your Widow Hate You

Here are some proven methods to make your widow hate you. One way is to die without a will, in which case the court will appoint an administrator and your estate will almost certainly be tangled in confusion, unnecessary expense, and probably excessive estate taxes. One survey found that when the decedent (the dead guy) died intestate (without a will), over half of the families ended up in conflict.

Another guaranteed way is to avoid making the difficult decisions that this area often demands (such as control of the business in the next generation), and to dump them on your spouse who not only must deal with your death but may have to act as referee among warring children.

YOUR ESTATE PLANNING PHILOSOPHY

Before you can develop an appropriate estate plan, it's necessary to establish a planning philosophy. Think it through, and put your objectives in writing so that they can be conveyed to your professional advisors. In a family business, there are many considerations.

What Is Fair?

Johann Kaspar Lavater died in 1801, but he probably was talking about family business when he said, "Say not you know another entirely, till you have divided an inheritance with him."

No matter how hard owners try to be fair to all of their heirs, fairness lies in the eyes of the beholder, and conflict over inheritances is common, particularly when a business is involved. The principal cause of unhappiness is probably the assumption that fairness, by definition, means equal. When applied to a business the concept of equality can be destructive, as it fails to recognize the differing interests of children who are active in the business and those who are inactive.

A research study involving heirs concludes, "Because there are so many possible interpretations of what is fair or what is equal and because people often seek fairness or equality, a dispute may not be resolved easily. Each disputant is impelled by the feeling that important principles, endorsed by society at large, are being violated if the opponents triumph. In addition to the lengthy struggle in seeking fairness, there are likely to be cleavages, cliques, or new boundaries that develop among family members. In particular, disputes over inheritance may be one of the major reasons for adult siblings to break off relationships with each other."[1]

Heirs often equate their inheritance with their parent's love and are deeply hurt by perceived inequities. It's worse when it appears that the owner had a confidant, or favorite child, who was privy to his plans while the other heirs were left out. Your best chance of helping your family to avoid this turmoil is to share your thinking with your heirs. They're more apt to accept perceived inequities if they understand your rationale. It isn't always possible to satisfy everyone, but if you can talk about it, at least you may be able to prevent the bitterness that often results from misunderstandings.

Active and Passive Heirs

The conflict of interests between active and inactive heirs is a principal cause of many family blow-ups. Active members tend to reinvest profits to build the business while passive members usually want dividends. Active members may feel that their compensation and benefits are low in view of the demands of the business while passive members may feel that the active members are grossly overpaid.

Woody founded a successful high-technology business 25 years ago, and he and his wife Beth had three children. Tom was active in the business and had been carefully groomed over the years to succeed his father as CEO. Will, a biochemist, was never interested in joining the business. Sarah married a college professor and they have a hard time making ends meet.

When both parents died within a short time of each other, their wills provided that each of their children were to receive equal shares of the business. Tom drew the same substantial salary as when his father was alive, drove a luxury car, and enjoyed the benefits of the company's pension plan. He continued his father's policy of reinvesting the company's earnings to finance growth, rather than paying dividends. The trouble started when it became obvious to Will and Sarah that while their stock in the company had considerable value on paper, it didn't help improve their lifestyles. The dialogue went as follows:

WILL:

We've got these marvelous stock certificates, Tom, but when are we going to see some dividends? If we invested what that stock is worth it would probably pay over $40,000 a year.

TOM:

I'd like to do it, Will, but to remain competitive, we must reinvest our earnings in new equipment just as Dad did.

SARAH:

It seems that there's enough for your big salary and the expense-paid vacation that you and your wife took.

TOM:

That wasn't a vacation. It was an important convention, and I don't get paid half enough for the sleepness nights and the 12-hour days while your husband takes it easy in academia.

You get the picture. Deservedly or not, the active members in the trenches often find themselves second-guessed by inactive members who want a greater piece of the pie. Compounded by sibling rivalry, the potential for strife is so great that owners who would preserve family harmony should consider the following options:

• If possible, bequeath the shares in the business to the active members with other assets going to the inactive members. However, the business may constitute most of the value in your estate and this option may not be available. Here are some alternatives:

• If you can afford the premiums, provide cash for the inactive members through life insurance to balance off the value of stock bequeathed to the active members.

• Bequeath the company stock to both active and inactive members, but provide for buy-sell agreements (as discussed in Chapter 10) requiring that the inactive members tender their stock to the active members or to the company. If you establish the tender price or formula it's less apt to be a cause of contention than if the children are left to fight it out by themselves.

• If you own the real estate on which your business is situated, consider leaving it to inactive members and the stock in the business to the active members. As this could result in a hostile landlord/tenant relationship among siblings, consider establishing the lease terms while you're still around.

• If it's impractical to bequeath all of the stock in the business to the active members, at least leave them with voting control. Methods of accomplishing this follow.

Sometimes it's too early to tell which family members will be active in the business. For example in one family, two daughters (aged 28 and 31) haven't yet decided whether or not to enter the company. A son who has been in the business for two years is still unproven. In these circumstances, it probably makes sense to provide for a voting trust until the roles are crystallized, rather than bequeathing the voting stock to the son. (For more on voting trusts, see "Control of the Business" which follows.)

Some inactive heirs are delighted to receive cash instead of stock in the company. Others, however, feel deprived of their share of what they perceive to be a family heritage and resent that it may preclude their option to enter the business at a later time. They may als be concerned that their children will be denied an opportunity to enter the business. This proves once again that there may be no absolute right answers in the complex world of family business.

Control of the Business

Ownership of stock in the company involves two basic rights: the right to the equity in the company, and the right to vote. Whoever controls the voting rights has the power to name the board of directors, which, in turn, appoints the officers. In many situations this is simple. The owner is the sole or controlling stockholder, chairman of the board of directors, and CEO. When there are multiple owners in the next generation, however, it gets more complicated and, as pointed out elsewhere, the proliferation of stockholders is a principal reason for the high mortality rates of family businesses.

Whoever owns more than 50 percent of the company stock generally controls the company. For example, if an owner were to leave his stock equally to three children, only one of which was active in the business, that child would need a coalition with at least one other sibling to control the business. If the child was unable to accomplish it, the inactive siblings would control the company and could force him out if they so chose.

If it's not practical to provide for control of the business through a majority of stock ownership, here are two ways in which it can be accomplished regardless of who owns the stock.

Voting Trusts

This is an agreement among stockholders whereby they relinquish their voting rights to the trustee without giving up any of their equitable ownership of company stock. It may be initiated during the owner's lifetime or come into existence upon his death.

When there are a large number of shareholders, frequently the case in third- or fourth-generation companies, voting trusts can be particularly applicable. For example, the Ford family, which owns 40 percent of the voting control of the automobile giant, has a voting trust that allows the family to be represented in a unified manner.

A voting trust can also help provide orderly management of the business if the owner should suffer a premature death, or it may be used to allocate control of the business among heirs.

Inasmuch as the trustee has the power to control the business, the choice of trustees is important. Ideally, it should be someone with business acumen and experience who enjoys the trust and confidence of the family. You may wish to select co-trustees including your spouse. While corporate fiduciaries, such as banks, are commonly used when investments are involved, trust officers may not be qualified to make business decisions, nor may they wish to assume the responsibility of being trustees of a going business.

If the successor/CEO is named as trustee, it's a good idea to prevent abuse of authority by establishing clear rules on compensation and other benefits for company officers. This should provide adequate incentives to those with the responsibility for running the company while protecting the interests of those without voting rights.

Create Two Classes of Stock

It's possible to divide the company's stock into two classes, with only one class having voting rights. In this way, you can bequeath the voting stock to those heirs whom you wish to control the business, and leave nonvoting stock to the others. If yours is an S corporation, with income and losses being passed through directly to stockholders, there is a restriction against two classes of stock. At this writing, however, the restriction does not apply when the only difference applies to voting rights.

The Estate Freeze

The estate freeze was a common estate planning strategy until it was severely restricted in 1987. Usually there was a recapitalization into two classes of stock: preferred stock, which generally reflected the current value of the business, and common stock, which appreciates with the future growth of the business. By gifting the common stock to their children, owners could freeze the value in their estates at present levels, thus avoiding future estate taxes on the appreciation in value.

The elimination of the freeze dramatically increased the estate tax bite on many family businesses and there is considerable public pressure for the repeal of the change, which was enacted without congressional hearings or debate.

Sharing in Future Growth

Two brothers who owned a successful chain of hardware stores had 10 children between them, of which only one was involved in the business. He was competent and a hard worker, and it was obvious that he had the leadership skills to succeed his father and uncle in managing the business in the next generation.

When the estate plan was discussed and he learned that the common stock in the company was to be divided equally among the 10 children, he said, "Even if voting control is not an issue, I'll be busting my tail while the others are living the good life. That's OK, but I'll be making my siblings and cousins wealthy while I only share in 10 percent of the growth. The salary isn't worth it."

Not all managers feel this way and many are satisfied if the compensation package is satisfactory. If the intent is to allocate the future growth of the business to active members, it can be done by providing for a recapitalization of the company at death with dividend-paying preferred stock going to inactive members and common stock to active members.

While having two classes of stock such as this precludes S corporation income tax treatment that was previously discussed, it may provide the means to satisfy all of the heirs. The inactive members get current income and have a preferred position in the event of liquidation, and the common shareholders assume more risk and get the fruits of future growth.

Protecting against Hostile Shareholders

While some owners are under the impression that minority stockholders have no rights, those that have experienced disruption caused by litigious minority stockholders can attest otherwise. Minority shareholders can demand that the company pay dividends, question the propriety of the CEO's salary and benefits, and become all-around nuisances. In some jurisdictions, they can even sue for the appointment of a receiver or seek the liquidation of the company.

There is no sure way to protect the company from attacks by hostile shareholders; however, there are preventive measures that should be considered.

One owner gave a few shares to a then deserving employee. However, the relationship deteriorated and the employee left the company. Later, when a unanimous vote of shareholders was needed, the employee refused to agree and an important business initiative was lost. For example, the S corporation election previously discussed requires the approval of all shareholders.

It is common for ownership of corporate stock in family businesses to be restricted to bloodline family members with a requirement that the stock must first be offered back to the company before it may be transferred or sold. While this doesn't guarantee harmony, at least it limits the number of shareholders.

This provision may be particularly relevant in case of divorce. Some owners, in order to prevent the problems that can arise when company stock is a central issue in a divorce, require family members to tender their stock back to the company if they become involved in divorce proceedings, which could involve unpalatable public disclosures that may be injurious to the business.

After Arthur divorced and remarried, he amended his will to provide that his business be bequeathed to his three children who had been important to its success. However, when he died suddenly, his widow claimed her right under state law to one half of the estate. His will was overturned and she became a part owner of the business with disastrous effect to both the business and his children. A prenuptial agreement between Arthur and his new wife may have prevented this by providing for an agreed disposition of his assets in the event of either death or divorce.

Prenuptial agreements contemplating the possibility of divorce often present emotional barriers, particularly among first marriages, as such agreements may be seen as implying less than full commitment to the marriage. However, some owners, in order to protect the business from becoming a bone in a divorce dogfight, require family members to tender their stock back to the company if they marry without a prenuptial agreement. This is more apt to be accepted if it's part of a broad family policy, rather than applying only to specific family members.

Another way to protect against stock falling into the hands of hostile stockholders is to keep its ownership in an irrevocable trust. If you make this choice, be careful in choosing trustees and consider that this may preclude an election to be taxed as an S corporation.

Will You Spoil the Children?

Many owners, particularly those who have come up the hard way, are concerned that if their children come into wealth it would spoil them and provide a disincentive to live productive lives. Investment genius Warren Buffett, the billionaire chairman of Berkshire Hathaway who is planning to leave the bulk of his estate to charity, said, "My kids are going to carve out their own place in this world, and they know I'm for them whatever they want to do." He believes that setting up his heirs with a "lifetime supply of food stamps just because they came out of the right womb" can be "harmful" for them and is "an antisocial act." Minnesota travel and real estate magnate Curtis L. Carlson said, "There's nothing people like me worry about more—how the hell do we keep our money from destroying our kids?"[2]

Most owners in business don't have problems of this magnitude but still worry about making it too easy for their children. Sybil Ferguson, cofounder with her husband of Diet Center Inc. of Rexburg, Idaho, wonders "whether they'll ever know the thrill of achievement we had . . . in watching our dreams come true."[3]

Some parents reach out "the long arm from the grave" and bypass their children, whom they know, and set up trusts for grandchildren not yet born. Others allow their children to inherit substantial sums at their 21st birthday when they are far from ready to handle it.

In our experience, values are learned while the child is growing up, and children with high levels of self-esteem aren't going to suddenly become indolent if they come into an inheritance. By the time your offspring are in their 30s, they're probably about as mature as they're going to be. Many owners plan for children to come into their inheritances and installments, starting in their middle or late 20s and concluding before their 40s. If there is concern that control of an inheritance may not be in the beneficiary's best interests, it may be placed in a trust with reasonable restrictions.

Chicago psychoanalyst Roy Grinker, Jr., says that all too often parents pay too little attention to the kid's upbringing. His advice is "Rather than give rich parents money advice, I would give them child-rearing advice. Pay attention to your kids, spend some time with your kids, love your kids."[4]

CREATING THE ESTATE PLAN

Once you've established your philosophy it should be implemented in your estate plan. While the following discussion focuses only on the federal estate tax implications, many states have estate and inheritance tax laws that should be considered. If you're planning to move to another state when you retire it's a good idea to familiarize yourself with that state's inheritance laws; they vary considerably.

The Estate Planning Team

With complex and rapidly changing tax laws, this is a highly specialized area, and it's imperative that you surround yourself with a competent planning team. Don't assume that your professional advisors are up-to-date or skilled in this area just because they're knowledgeable about income taxes, and don't be concerned about hurting their feelings by insisting that a specialist be brought in. We've seen many disasters caused by professionals who felt that they must be all things to all people, and by wills drawn up from standard books on the subject or copied from other wills.

Your estate planning team should include your CPA and lawyer, augmented by an estate planning specialist if neither of them qualifies. A qualified life insurance agent can also be an important member of the team, as well as the trust officer if you intend to use a corporate fiduciary. You should appoint one member of the team to the lead position with responsibility for coordination. Remember, they are there to implement *your* philosophies and to help you achieve *your* objectives.

Don't let taxes drive your plan. Tell them what you want to achieve and challenge them to develop a plan that will result in the lowest tax.

Your Will

A will is a statement of your intentions for your estate, and *everyone* should have one. If you should die intestate, the state, rather than your intent, dictates the outcome. Don't assume that your spouse will automatically inherit your estate; some state laws indicate that a spouse is entitled to one third; others stipulate one half, depending on the number of children. Also, the state, rather than you, will choose the administrator.

It is also important that your spouse have her own will to prevent unintentional results even if she now has little or no assets. Stipulations in your will, such as for protection of your children, don't carry over to your spouse's will and your intentions could be negated if you predecease your spouse or if you both die simultaneously. Unless otherwise stated, a will is revocable, and you can change it at any time.

Choosing Fiduciaries

In your will, you'll name an *executor* who has the fiduciary responsibility to collect the assets, pay liabilities, file estate and income tax returns, and distribute the assets as directed by your will. The executor's job ends once these tasks are completed. One testator put it this way: "I want that mine brother Adolph be my executor and I want it that the judge should please make Adolph put up plenty bond and watch him like hell. Adolph is a good business man but only a dumpkoff would trust him with a busted Pfenning"—from the Will of Herman Oberweiss.[5]

If a trust is established, a trustee must be appointed as fiduciary to administer it in accordance with your directions for the term stipulated in the trust.

A fiduciary may be an individual or a corporation (generally a bank or trust company), and the same fiduciary can act as executor and trustee. While fiduciaries are obligated to follow the general directions of your will or trust, the role often requires judgment. Choosing a fiduciary is often a difficult task, and it involves trade-offs.

The Individual Fiduciary

An individual fiduciary, while not necessarily an expert in estate matters, should be a responsible, mature person whose judgment you trust and whom the family respects. Advice on technical matters can be obtained from professional advisors. The person's age and health are also important. While an executorship role may be fulfilled in a reasonably short time, the term of a trust can extend beyond the fiduciary's lifetime so contingent fiduciaries should be selected with care.

In smaller estates, an individual fiduciary is generally appropriate; however, be careful about selecting a family member who is also a beneficiary as other family members could question his objectivity.

Corporate Fiduciaries

While corporate fiduciaries provide experience and technical skills, they tend to be impersonal, lacking the caring approach that you would expect from an individual who is a friend of the family. If long-term trusts are involved, corporate fiduciaries offer the major advantage of continuity because their stewardship is not limited to the lifetime of one individual. If you're concerned about their investment capabilities, ask for their track record with similar trusts. If you're still not satisfied, you can stipulate that investments are to be handled by another institution.

All fiduciaries don't charge the same fees and unless you choose with care, your heirs may be indefinitely burdened with excessive costs. It's possible to provide your heirs with the right to change fiduciaries in the trust instrument.

In order to obtain the benefits of continuity that institutions offer, without sacrificing the caring approach most apt to be found in individuals, many owners appoint co-fiduciaries.

Trusts

A trust is essentially a device where you give property to another person or institution, to administer for the benefit of a third party or group. They consist of *living* (inter-vivos) trusts, which take effect during your lifetime, and *testamentary* trusts, which are created by your will and which become effective at your death.

One of the advantages of a living trust is that it enables your estate to avoid the expense, publicity, and inconvenience of probate. It may be revocable, in which case it is disregarded for income tax purposes during the settlor's life, or it may be irrevocable, in which case it is a taxable entity.

How Estates Are Taxed

Estate and gift taxes are separate and distinct from income taxes. At this writing, there is a federal "unified" estate and gift tax, based on total cumulative transfers both during lifetime and at death. The rates reach 37 percent on a taxable estate of $600,000 and increase to 55 percent on estates over $3 million. There is a credit of $192,800, which is the equivalent of an exemption allowing every individual to pass on wealth of up to $600,000 to their heirs or anyone else free of federal estate and gift taxes. Properly used, this credit allows you and your spouse to transfer up to $1.2 million of property estate tax-free, even if the property is only owned by one of you if the one owning the property dies first. *This doesn't happen automatically; it must be planned.*

Valuation of the Business

Both for annual gifting and estate tax purposes, it's necessary to compute the value of the stock of the company. If the company is publicly traded or is sold to an unrelated party near the time of the owner's death, it's a matter of record. Most family businesses, however, don't fit this profile, and there is no set formula that can establish what a willing buyer will pay a willing seller when a private company is involved.

If a substantial gift or estate is involved, it's generally advisable to retain an experienced appraiser because valuation often becomes a contest, with the IRS claiming a high value and the taxpayer arguing for a low value.

Valuation criteria used by the IRS include: the nature of the business and its history, the economic outlook in general and in the industry, the book value of the stock and the financial condition of the business, the earning and dividend-paying capacity of the company, good will and other intangible value, previous sales of stock, and market value of publicly traded stocks in the same industry. Private companies are usually valued at a substantial discount from publicly traded companies because their stock is not readily marketable.

The value of property is usually the fair market value of the property at its highest and best use on the date of the owner's death. However, if certain conditions are met, the executor may elect to value real estate used in farming or other business operations on the basis of its value in the farm or business rather than at its highest and best use.

Life Insurance

In other parts of this book we have pointed out that many of the conflicts that afflict family businesses can best be resolved by the buyout of some family member stockholders. In addition, the transition to the next generation may trigger potentially crippling estate taxes. The liquidity to meet these possibly large cash requirements is often found in life insurance, which can provide the necessary funds to:

- Fund buy-sell agreements between partners or family members.
- Pay estate taxes and administration costs.
- Provide cash legacies to inactive heirs so that ownership of the business can be bequeathed to heirs who are active in the business.
- Enhance the financial security of surviving spouse.
- Provide funds to help offset the loss of one of the business's major assets, the owner, through so-called "key man" insurance.

Don't be lulled into a sense of false security because the marital deduction may eliminate estate taxes when you die. This doesn't consider the possibility of your spouse predeceasing you or that the estate tax that will be triggered, possibly at higher rates, on both estates when your spouse dies. Life insurance companies offer "survivorship," or "second to die" policies that provide the necessary funds when they are apt to be most needed—when the survivor dies. Because only one policy is needed, the premium cost is generally significantly less than what two people would pay to purchase the same amount of individual whole life coverage.

Some owners have a low level of trust in life insurance agents, not all of which is unjustified. Comedian Woody Allen characterized it with his comment, "The ultimate torture is being locked in a room of insurance salesmen." While some life insurance agents have earned their negative reputations, there are many competent professional life underwriters who perform valuable services and who subordinate their own financial rewards to the best interests of their clients. When an agent is a "Chartered Life Underwriter" (CLU), it means he is a member of a professional society whose members have passed tough examinations and maintain continuing professional education standards.

Don't make this important selection purely on the basis of a casual relationship. Ask your peers, lawyer, and CPA for their advice and take the time to interview more than one agent. A competent professional agent will get competitive bids from multiple life insurance companies, will help you to obtain the right coverage, and will not sell you more insurance than you need.

Ownership of a life insurance policy includes certain rights, such as the right to the cash value and the ability to name the beneficiary. *Be aware that if you own the policy, the proceeds will be taxed in your estate.* If, however, you assign these rights and survive for at least three years, the proceeds may be paid to your heirs *tax-free*. Ask your advisors about using an irrevocable life insurance trust that may allow life insurance proceeds to bypass both your and your spouse's estates.

Lifetime Gifts

In addition to the exemption provided at death, a taxpayer is allowed to make annual tax-free gifts of up to $10,000 per year per recipient, with the amount raised to $20,000 if the spouse joins in the gift. Such gifts escape taxation in your estate.

For example, if you wished to make a gift to three children, five grandchildren, and a parent who needed support (a total of nine recipients) you could gift up to $180,000 a year tax-free. (If you wished to exceed this it may make sense to make a taxable gift, or utilize your unified credit.) Gifts, however, are irrevocable, and you should be careful about gifting so much of your assets that you become dependent on others for your financial security.

Instead of gifting cash in an annual gifting program to children, consider gifting property with the greatest potential for appreciation, such as real estate or stock in the family business. In this way, not only will the current value be excluded from your estate but also the future appreciation. Think twice, however, about gifting control of the company. Founder L. S. Shoen of U-Haul Rental Systems gave over 90 percent of the company's stock to his children. He was then kicked off the board of directors and resigned from the company.[6]

Marital Deduction

In general, there is an *unlimited* marital deduction for assets that you gift or bequeath to your spouse. Thus, federal estate taxes at the time of your death may be avoided entirely by leaving your estate outright to your spouse. However, the marital deduction is only a postponement, as the piper generally has to be paid when the spouse dies.

For example

Value of estate	$2,000,000
Bequeath to spouse	2,000,000
Subject to tax	0

However, assuming the same values when the spouse dies, the computation would be:

Value of estate	$2,000,000
Exemption	600,000
Subject to tax	1,400,000
Estate tax	512,800

In these circumstances, if you had not previously used your $600,000 exemption via gifts, it would have been lost. A common way to provide for a spouse's security, without losing this valuable exemption, is through the use of a trust, sometimes called a credit trust.

Following the same example, assume that the owner establishes a credit trust and bequeaths $600,000 to it for the benefit of his wife and/or children. (The spouse can have the right to distributions from this trust subject to certain limitations.) There still would be no estate tax at the time of his death, as there would be a marital reduction of $1.4 million for the assets bequeathed to his spouse and $600,000 for his exemption. Assuming the spouse died shortly afterward and the same numbers applied, the picture would be as follows:

Value of estate	$1,400,000
Less: Exemption	600,000
Subject to tax	800,000
Federal estate tax	267,800

This is a simple example of how planning could save $245,000. There are many other considerations in formulating strategy. For example, the spouse could decrease the eventual tax on her estate even further by making annual tax-free gifts of stock in the company or other assets.

The QTIP Trust

Many owners want to provide for the financial security of their spouses but are concerned about their spouse's ability to manage substantial investments and their vulnerability to fortune-hunters in a subsequent marriage.

A qualified terminable interest (QTIP) trust allows property to qualify for the marital deduction while preventing the surviving spouse from exercising any control over the ultimate distribution of the property. In order to qualify, all of the income from the QTIP property must be paid to the spouse during her life and the principal must be used for the sole benefit of the surviving spouse during her life. This ensures that the property will eventually be distributed according to the owner's wishes.

Gifts to Charity

Contributions to recognized charities during your lifetime generally allow you to save on income taxes, while bequests to charities in your will are deductible from your estate. Properly structured, there are ways to realize both income and estate tax savings with the same gift.

If it's your intention to leave property to a charity at your death, but would like the benefit of the income during your lifetime, you could set up an irrevocable *charitable remainder trust*. Assume that you are 50 years old and own property worth $100,000, with an annual yield of

$8,500, and that you intend to gift the property to a charity in your will.

You could gift the property to the charity now with the provision that you get the income during your lifetime and that the charity will get the property when you die. In this example, you would get a current income tax deduction of $21,072 in addition to the exclusion of the value of the property from your estate. There are variations of this approach and certain rules that must be followed, so be sure to consult your tax advisor.[7]

Grantor Retained Income Trust (GRIT)

One of today's most effective estate planning strategies is called a GRIT, which allows you to transfer assets into an irrevocable trust for the benefit of your heirs. Both the current value and appreciation are excluded from your estate and there may be little or no tax cost to you.

Here's how it works. You transfer property to the trust for the future benefit of heirs, retaining an exclusive right to the income during the term of the trust, which can't exceed 10 years. When the trust terminates the property goes to your heirs, however, if you should die during the term of the trust the GRIT is disregarded and the property is taxed in your estate.

There are gift tax considerations when you transfer property to the trust; however, they are discounted to present value, based on IRS actuarial tables.

While it makes sense to gift assets with appreciation potential, be sure that you get expert advice if you plan to gift stock in the family business as it's still unclear whether the "anti-freeze" rules apply. If so, the value of your heirs' interest could be subject to a gift tax when the trust matures.

Generation-Skipping

In order to avoid the estate tax bite at each generation, a common strategy in the past was for wealthy parents to bypass their children and make substantial bequests directly to grandchildren. There are now harsh new rules that impose substantial taxes on such gifts and they are imposed in addition to gift or estate taxes. There are some exemptions, but if generation-skipping is part of your estate plan be sure to consult your tax advisor.

Paying the Estate Tax

Estate taxes may become due within nine months of your death and your estate plan should carefully consider how such taxes and administration costs will be paid. Here are some options:

• An irrevocable life insurance trust, established by the owner for the benefit of his family, can use life insurance proceeds to buy the owner's stock from his estate. The insurance proceeds are tax-free to the beneficiaries of the trust, and the estate gets the necessary funds.

• If more than 35 percent of the estate consists of an interest in a closely held business, estate taxes may be paid over 14 years, subject to certain rules. Interest is charged at an annual rate of 4 percent on the first $1 million in value of the business with a formula applicable to the balance. In recent years the rate has fluctuated between 9 and 11 percent. Payment of principal is not required to commence for five years.

• The business may redeem all or a portion of the owner's stock in the company for cash, possibly with the proceeds of life insurance on the decedent's life. It's important that the tax rules be followed to prevent this from being treated as a dividend.

• Funds could be provided as a result of a buy-sell agreement as described in Chapter 10.

SUMMARY

The Purpose of Estate Planning

• Proper estate planning is necessary to provide for an orderly transition of assets to the next generation. In a family business, the principle objectives are usually to provide for the financial security of the spouse of the decedent, provide for ownership of the business to end up in the right hands in the next generation, and to prevent estate taxes from crippling the business.

Estate Planning Philosophy

• A philosophy should be developed defining how the shares in the business are to be owned in the next generation. This may require

AN ESTATE PLANNING CHECKLIST

My Philosophy

- Have I defined a concept of "fairness" to my heirs?
- Does this concept demand equality in every respect?
- Should heirs who are active in the business be treated differently from those who are inactive?
- What effect will my response to the previous question have on future family relationships and on the operation of the business?
- How should active and inactive family members share in future growth of the business?
- How can I protect the business against hostile stockholders?
- Who will control the business in the next generation?
- Should family members be required to execute premarital agreements relating to their ownership of stock in the company?
- Will an inheritance remove the incentive of my children to live productive lives?

My Estate Plan

- Do my spouse and I have properly prepared wills?
- Have they been reviewed within the past two years?
- Do I have an estate planning team that is both professionally competent and interested in my welfare?
- Have I given sufficient thought to the selection of individual or corporate fiduciaries who are committed to my family's best interests?
- Should I consider joint fiduciaries?
- Do I know the extent of potential federal and state taxes on my estate?
- Should I leave property to my wife and children outright or in trust?
- Have I discussed my estate plan with my family?
- Have I arranged my affairs so that others would have full knowledge of all relevant aspects if I should die unexpectedly?

My Estate Planning Strategies

- Have I evaluated the cost/benefits of life insurance?
- Consistent with my objectives, have I utilized the benefits of lifetime tax-free gifts to heirs?

- Have I realistically valued my business for estate tax purposes?
- Does my estate planning strategy make proper use of my unified credit and the marital deduction for gifts or bequests to my spouse?
- Should I consider a QTIP trust to protect my spouse and family?
- If I intend to make bequests to charity in my estate, should I consider making the gifts now for maximum benefits?
- Does a GRIT make sense in my circumstances?
- If I plan generation-skipping bequests do I understand the rules?

My Estate's Tax Liability

- Have I provided enough liquidity to pay estate taxes and administration costs?
- Does my estate qualify for payment of taxes over 15 years?
- If payment of taxes will result from a redemption of my shares by the business will it pose an excessive burden?

differing treatment of heirs who are active in the business and those who are passive, and the bequeathing of control of the business to selected heirs. The possibility of shares falling into hostile hands and the effect of wealth on children may also be considerations.

The Estate Plan

- A team of competent estate planning professronals ıs an ıntegral part of the process. An executor must be named, and, in many cases, a trustee. Choices should be made with care

Estate Taxes

- Estate taxes, which can reach 55 percent of the value of most estates, can be minimized through proper planning. This includes the use of tax-free lifetime gifts, the marital deduction, the use of the unified credit, and other planning technıques

Paying the Taxes

- Estate taxes may either be paid soón after death or, when a family business is involved, over an extended period In any event, the liability can threaten the continuity of the business. Many owners provide for this through life insurance.

NOTES

1. Sandra L. Titus, Paul C. Rosenblatt, and Roxanne M. Anderson, "Family Conflict over Inheritance of Property," *The Family Coordinator*, July 1979, pp. 337–46.
2. Richard I. Kirkland, "Should You Leave It All to the Children?" *Fortune*, September 29, 1986, pp. 19–26.
3. Ellen Wojahn, "Share the Wealth, Spoil the Child?" *Inc.*, August 1989, p. 76.
4. Ibid.
5. Alexander A. Bove, Jr., "The Choice of an Executor Depends on Many Factors," *The Boston Globe*, June 29, 1989, p. 58.
6. David Pauly, "U-Haul Hits the 'Skids,'" *Newsweek*, September 14, 1987, p. 55.
7. Troy Segal, "Good Donations, Great Deductions," *Business Week*, July 24, 1989, p. 85.

EPILOGUE

FAMILY BUSINESS IN THE YEAR 2000

> If we do not learn from history, we shall be compelled to relive it.
> True. But if we do not change the future, we shall be compelled to
> endure it. And that could be worse.
>
> *Alvin Toffler*

If the last 50,000 years of human existence were divided into lifetimes of approximately 62 years each, there would have been approximately 800 lifetimes. Of these, 650 would have been spent in caves.

Only in the last six lifetimes has it been possible to communicate by the printed word. Only in the last four has it been possible to measure time with any precision. Only in the last two were electric motors in usage. And the overwhelming majority of material goods that we use in everyday life today was developed in the present, the 800th lifetime.[1]

If you're one of the many who founded your business in the post–World War II era, you have witnessed explosive progress in transportation, technology and communication, which has had a significant effect on the business environment.

Some examples are:

- In the computer industry, tasks that once required a roomful of equipment are now performed by inexpensive, small machines that are faster and better.
- Federal Express, the "fax," office copying machines, and cellular telephones came into being.

- Air transportation went from propeller aircraft to supersonic and space travel.
- Foreign competition eroded the United States' position as the dominant force in international trade, and the world moved toward a global economy.
- Leveraged buy-outs of big businesses became commonplace, and a new term, "junk bonds," entered our lexicon. Many businesses were forced to restructure and operate more efficiently in order to compete, or even survive.
- A major transition commenced as America moved from an industrial to a service-based economy.
- Women entered the work force in large numbers and are starting their own businesses at an unprecedented clip.
- The labor union movement declined and the beginning of a potent new vehicle for employee ownership, the Employee Stock Ownership Plan (ESOP), was born.
- The business environment evolved from the "big is beautiful" era to the present focus on being "lean, mean, and flexible." Most of the growth of the 1980s was fueled by the private sector, many of them family businesses.

While these developments represent enormous advances in the business world, the increased pace, the "freedom" given us by technological advancement, and the need for mothers and fathers to balance home and business careers have taken their toll on family life.

According to a survey by pollster Louis Harris, the amount of leisure time enjoyed by the average American has shrunk 37 percent since 1973 and the average workweek, including commuting, has jumped from under 41 hours to nearly 47 hours.[2]

Children grow up with less parental involvement and the generation gap appears to be widening. Drug and alcohol abuse have become national crises. With divorce rates at an all time high, single-parent families are commonplace as well as extended families resulting from multiple marriages.

The traditional patriarch or matriarch who was the ultimate authority figure has, for the most part, disappeared; in many cases, leaving a leadership void and confusion as to the role of the parent.

With the rapidly changing business environment and the increasing stress on family life, what does the future hold in store for family businesses?

OUR PREDICTIONS FOR THE NEXT DECADE

One economist said that to be safe in making predictions you should either specify the event or the time frame, but never both. Nevertheless, if Nostradamus will step aside, here are our fearless, out-on-a-limb, predictions for family business in the year 2000.

• If you are the owner of the business and survive, you will be approximately 10 years older as the decade closes. You may have already retired, or will be that much closer to a critical transition in management. How you use the next 10 years may be critical to the outcome.

• Your heirs in the business will be 10 years older and will have a different perspective than they do now. For example, at 30 they may be quite content to be in your shadow, learning the business. At 40 they'll probably want to run it. It's now time to be planning ahead for this eventuality.

• The needs of your customers will be affected by the forces of change and the future of your business will depend on your ability to anticipate and meet these needs. Competition will be intense and the success of your business will depend on your ability to differentiate yourself from competitors through quality products and service.

• Technological advances will continue at a dizzying clip. Whatever the size of your business, you will be affected and you'll either take advantage of the benefits or be left behind.

• The internationalization of business will accelerate even more. The European community will be established in 1992. Asia will continue on its impressive roll, and freer trade with Canada, already our largest trading partner, will increase opportunities with that country. Social changes now under way in the USSR and mainland China may lead to these countries becoming important trading partners.

Small and medium-sized American businesses that take advantage of foreign trade opportunities will enjoy a competitive advantage.

• Women now constitute 45 percent of all employees and 70 percent of all married women with children under age 18 are working outside their homes. They will be an increasingly important factor in the workplace and pressure for equality in job opportunity will escalate.
• Shortages in the work force loom for smaller businesses that traditionally hire young workers. Although the U.S. population is expected to grow from 228 million in 1980 to 268 million in 2000,[3] the 16 to 34 age group, or fully half the labor force, will *lose* more than 4 million members.[4]

In order to compete for quality employees, businesses will be forced to provide child-care facilities, allow flexible hours, offer competitive healthcare benefits, and encourage telecommuting that allows employees to work at home through the use of modern technology.

Minorities and members of older age groups will occupy a greater role as native white men are projected to constitute only 15 percent of the entries to the labor force in the next decade.[5]

• Start-ups will become more difficult because of the high cost of doing business and the lack of availability of capital for situations that don't offer big payoffs. As a result, more young entrepreneurs will seek their futures in their family's business rather than striking out on their own.
• The high costs and faster pace will decrease the margin for error. Fewer businesses will be able to coast on their past accomplishments, survive with sloppy methods, and manage on gut feel.

There isn't time enough and most businesses don't have the resources in this fast-moving environment to learn from their mistakes. It is said that the trouble with using experience as a teacher is that the final exam often comes before the lesson. Only well-managed businesses will survive.

THE SUCCESSFUL FAMILY BUSINESS IN THE YEAR 2000

Many family businesses, powered solely by the drive and ingenuity of their founders, enjoy brief ascendencies before they disappear into oblivion. In others, family conflict will be so intense that their days are numbered, regardless of any advice that we may offer.

We believe, however, that the vast majority of established family businesses have the capacity to succeed, and that rather than being a source of conflict, the business can be a unifying influence, with family members working together in a joint endeavor.

The focus on family business has accelerated in recent years. Many universities now offer programs on the topic, media coverage has intensified, and research studies have helped members of family businesses gain a greater understanding of both the challenges and the pitfalls. This emphasis will escalate in the 1990s.

Here are common denominators that we believe will be shared by most successful family businesses in the years ahead:

1. Family members will reconcile the differing values and demands of family and business life and maintain appropriate boundaries. The sanctity of family life and the future of the business depends on their ability to maintain this balance.

2. The business will be "professionalized" to provide organization and discipline. For many, this will originate with a strategic business plan that answers these questions: Where are we? Where do we want to go? How do we get there?

3. Management will attract, motivate, and retain high-quality employees who will be allowed to help determine how their jobs should be done and will be recognized for their achievements. Family members will treat them with respect and not as "outsiders," or second-class citizens.

4. Communication will be open, frequent, and two-way, both in the family and in the business. Management standards in the business and ground rules governing family involvement will be clearly delineated, and both family members and employees will be encouraged to provide input.

5. A working, independent, board of directors will help guide the company by providing objective support to the CEO. Only outside advisors who are both competent and dedicated to the best interests of the family and the business will be retained.

6. Planning for management succession will commence early and it will involve a mutual commitment by the owner/CEO and the successor.

7. Owner/CEO's will recognize when the necessary ingredients to continue the business under family management are lacking. Rather than forcing the issue and continuing the business under family management, they will sell the company, divide it, or install professional managers.

8. Owners will plan their estates carefully in order to leave ownership and control to the right heirs while avoiding excessive estate taxes.

9. Families will establish means to resolve disagreements constructively, rather than allowing them to destroy both the family and the business. Outside assistance will be sought when needed.

10. In the hyper-competitive business world, only market-driven companies will achieve real success. The culture of the company will be focused on meeting customers' needs.

While every business is subject to market conditions over which there is no control, we believe that most family businesses will greatly enhance their chances of success if they follow these precepts.

Former president John F. Kennedy said, "When written in Chinese, the word 'crisis' is composed of two characters—one represents danger and the other represents opportunity." We believe that this is particularly true of family businesses which bode to be an even more important part of the American business fabric in the year 2000 than they are today.

It is our hope that more family businesses than ever before, armed with more awareness of the pitfalls, will be able to skirt the dangers and realize the extensive benefits that can be theirs.

NOTES

1. Alvin Toffler, *Future Shock* (New York: Random House, 1970), p. 15.
2. Nancy Gibbs, "How America Has Run Out of Time," *Time*, April 24, 1989, p. 58.
3. "You Could Look It Up." *Time*, May 22, 1989. Taken from Statistical Abstract of the United States, 1989.
4. John Case, "The Real Age Wave," *Inc.*, July 1989, p. 23. Taken from

Workforce 2000: Work and Workers for the Twenty-first Century (Indianapolis: Hudson Institute, 1987).
5. Ibid. Taken from Amanda Bennett, "Firms Become a Social Agent of Change," *The Wall Street Journal*, Centennial Edition, 1989, p. A22.

INDEX